HERBERT KÜHN

The Rock Pictures
of Europe

TRANSLATED FROM THE GERMAN BY

Alan Houghton Brodrick

OCTOBER HOUSE INC.
NEW YORK

First published 1952 in German under the title
DIE FELSBILDER EUROPAS

First published in English 1956 by Sidgwick and Jackson

This edition published 1967 by
October House Inc.
134 East 22nd Street
New York, N.Y. 10010
Copyright © 1966 by Sidgwick and Jackson Ltd
All rights reserved
Library of Congress catalogue card no. 67-10784
Printed in Great Britain

Contents

Line Drawings in the Text

The Plates

(following page 102)

xi

xiii

Translator's Introduction

SINCE Professor Kühn's *Die Felsbilder Europas*—of which this book is a translation—is intended for the general reader, I have not introduced technical terms which would demand explanatory notes. For instance, the archæologist differentiates between a 'gallery-grave' and a 'passage-grave', but they are sufficiently alike for us to ignore the difference in a work that is primarily an illuminating essay on the origins and development of art. I have, however, added a few notes when the text seemed to call for them. I have also tightened up the text here and there, but I have, of course, made no attempt to modify the author's presentation of his views concerning the succession of art-phases throughout the ages, views, indeed, that some prehistorians and archæologists tend to regard as rather too simplified. There can be no doubt, however, that *The Rock Pictures of Europe* is a stimulating, and indeed fascinating, account of our forbears' most ancient art.

A. H. B.

Introduction

WHAT men in past ages thought and felt, what they believed and wished, that they engraved upon rocks which have retained the pictures to this day. Before Man had devised writing to lend permanence to the fleeting word, it was the picture upon the rocks that transposed experiences and dreams from the present to an endless future. Man's hope is ever to halt what is transitory and to make it endure long beyond the passing day. Our own writing, our photographs, our pictures are attempts to halt time and to secure what is vanishing.

In a similar way prehistoric men recorded their wishes and their ideas. Our remote ancestors carved their desires upon the stones which appeared to have eternal life. And such pictures speak to us now, after many millennia. He who knows how to read aright these most venerable drawings may discover much about the emotions and the mind of whole generations of mankind.

Man's aims have varied. What was most longed for lay at one time in one sphere, at another time in a different sphere. Man's spirit hovers between two poles, the Here and the There, the momentary and the everlasting. This vacillation expresses itself in the art of the most ancient pictures. If we survey the whole panorama of prehistoric art we must notice, on the one hand, highly realistic pictures and, on the other, pictures which are extremely stylized. That is to say, in many of the pictures the artist has been concerned with reality as he saw it. I should call such art, therefore, sensorial, since it owes all to the senses, to what the eye has seized and has then reproduced.

Other pictures, again, are imaginative. They are composed of symbols, or signs. Like a script they hint only at objects which compose the world of our senses.

These, then, are the two poles between which all the

phenomena of pictorial art, of representational art, move. And these two extremes can not only be observed in the most ancient art but also in later epochs. We have only to remember the naturalistic art of the first and second centuries of our era—and the rigidity of the Byzantine mosaics. Nearer to us we have the colour, the light and the atmosphere of the 19th-century Impressionists and then the flat and geometrical designs of the 20th-century Expressionists and Cubists.

At no period in Man's story, however, are the contrasts in style so marked as in prehistoric times, and these contrasts, indeed, constitute one of the great charms of the rock-pictures if we regard them from the point of view of art history. There are pictures full of life and light, with depth, with fascinating contours and with lines executed quite in the modern Impressionistic manner. And there are pictures all angles, stylized, flat, geometrical, in a word, representations remarkably like those the modern Expressionists give us.

The questions that rise to our lips, questions about the reasons for change, about what induced the different styles and then determined their fading away, can be answered, at least in part, from analogies to the art of historical periods.

If, as did, for instance, Wöllflin, we follow up the evolution of a style, say, only in the early Renaissance and the Baroque, we may easily be drawn to form conclusions that throw light only upon a comparatively short period and not upon the whole panorama of art throughout the ages. If we follow the stylistic changes we must take very long periods of time into consideration. Prehistoric art allows us to review the evolution of styles over a very long period. Moreover, prehistoric art must be considered not only as a decisive factor in the history of Man's artistic achievement; it also throws much light upon the evolution of religion.

We depend, indeed, for our knowledge concerning the early forms of religion entirely upon the pictures on the rocks. They are the expression of men's dialogue with the eternal values. These paintings and engravings are addressed to the divinities and they mark places of sacrifice, the places where cult ceremonies were performed.

In fact we may call some of these most ancient paintings the reredos of prehistory.

Indeed, in many places where our remote ancestors engraved their pictures, sacrifice is still offered up. Not a few painted caverns have become Christian churches. Lourdes, the greatest place of pilgrimage in France, is built around a cult-cavern dating back to Ice Age times. I myself have found traces of sacrifice in the Zenaga Mountains of North Africa. There by the 'Written Rocks' covered with prehistoric pictures, a few days before my visit, nomads from the desert had offered up their oblation at the place of the god, a place where, for millennia, ceremonies have been performed.

Moreover, the art of the Rocks, though far away in time, is bound to us, nevertheless, by a thousand threads. For instance, Pope Calixtus III forbade the Spaniards to carry out rites in caves that had pictures of horses in them.[1] We cannot now determine exactly to what cave the Pope was referring but it must obviously have been a prehistoric cavern on whose walls representations of horses still existed.

In 1598 Lope de Vega wrote a play in which he refers to rock-pictures at a place called Las Batuecas in the province of Salamanca.[2] In his verse Lope de Vega warns us of the power and the might of the demons that frequent these rock-pictures. By the poet's time legend had become attached to the paintings which were regarded as *figuras de demonios* or 'figures of devils'. It was also believed that the souls of slain Visigoths haunted the rocks, the souls of those who had fought with the Moslem but which could not attain to eternal rest. It is worth remarking that it was this reference in the play of Lope de Vega that led to a search for prehistoric pictures in the neighbourhood of Las Batuecas, a search that was successful in 1909.

When, in 1923, I was in the small town of Alcobácer and enquired for a guide who would conduct me to the rock-paintings in the Valltorta ravine, most of the inhabitants

[1] Calixtus III, the first of the two Borgia Popes and uncle of Alexander VI, came from Valencia and was for long Bishop of his native town. He died in 1458.
[2] Las Batuecas is a most isolated place in the poverty-stricken Jurdes region whose inhabitants are in Spain proverbial for their simple wits. (Translator's Note.)

refused to consider accompanying me. Demons lived in the ravine, ghosts and spirits hovered between the rocks and their pictures.

Two years later, at Minateda, near Hellín, the local inhabitants could not be induced to help me with my copying of the paintings. They were afraid to touch them, for there was a power innate in them which might wreak some dire evil.

So to this day prehistoric pictures are, if not sacred, at least instinct with maleficent might. Since they retain some numinous or religious character such pictures must not be damaged or destroyed.

On the shores of Lake Onega in Russia there are rock-engravings which have crosses superposed upon them, crosses carved by Christian monks who thus sought to exorcize the spirits and to abolish their demoniac power.

On visits to the prehistoric pictures of Africa, Spain, France and Scandinavia I have always found men who would not approach the Written Rocks. The religious awe they inspire has lasted to this day and maybe will endure for a long time more.

We have mentioned that the prehistoric pictures are full of information about the earlier stages of religion. They are, indeed, pictures of very ancient religious beliefs, of most venerable hunting-magic. There are representations of beasts that have been shot at, in which arrows are shown, arrows, or spears and boomerangs. Before these pictures danced men whose footprints, in some cases, are still to be seen in the hardened clay of a cavern's floor. Magic rites. And then, later, we have engravings of cult-ceremonies, of sacred vehicles, ships, of divine horses, pictures that reveal the Northern Gods to us, the deities with the Lance and the Hammer.

In northern Europe, indeed, where writing appears comparatively very late, we have nothing but such engravings to tell us about the gods. Here we may see Thor with his Hammer, his Goats and his Wheel, just as he is described two thousand years later in the Icelandic Edda. Here we may recognize Odin (or maybe his prototype Tyr) with the Lance, the Horse and the Ring—as he is referred to in the

Edda. On the Scandinavian rocks we have also the figures of still older gods whose faint images are hardly hinted at in the Edda: the deity, probably called Ull, with bow and arrow; and another divinity with a sword. In fact these rock-carvings are so rich in content that they offer an inexhaustible field for research.

Another point I should like to stress is this: besides their value for the history of art and of religion, the prehistoric pictures tell us much about the history of material culture. From the paintings and drawings we can see how Man, ages ago, managed to organize his existence.

There are phases of culture in which men are the hunters and women the food-gatherers. This phase is mirrored in an art that is devoted to representations of animals. Beasts occupy the foreground of men's preoccupations. The chase goes on throughout the ages. The men who practise an agriculture still hunt and in the prehistoric paintings animals still play a great part. But gradually, as pastoralism develops, we get pictures in which men are shown holding animals by halters. On the Swedish rock-pictures again we can see rows of cows standing close together, and we get representations of ploughs. On the Italian rock-engravings the ploughs occur in great numbers.

If the prehistoric pictures give us information about economic conditions, then from these paintings and engravings we may also learn about phases of culture. Running all through prehistoric art are pictures of weapons. First of all harpoons, then bows and arrows, then boomerangs. Real specimens of the weapons represented have been found in the strata of cave-fillings; thus the pictures can be dated from the types of the weapons. Harpoons, arrows and boomerangs were known in the Ice Age, the Upper Palæolithic, while the typical weapon of the New Stone Age or Neolithic is the 'polished' (or, more rightly, ground) hatchet.[1]

Stone hatchets are often represented upon the Swedish rock-engravings, while the Italian frequently offer images of triangular daggers with bronze handles. Paintings or

[1] A representation of a neolithic hatchet at Ksar Ahmar in North Africa has played a significant part in the dating of the site.

engravings of bronze weapons are especially valuable for dating purposes.

There is at the Peña Tú, not very far from Oviedo in Spanish Galicia, an engraving of a bronze dagger with five rivet-holes. Exactly this type of weapon is frequently dug up in well-dated strata, so that we have, thus, a means of dating the Peña Tú picture. On the Swedish rock-engravings there are many representations both of daggers and swords. Since, from excavated material, the stylistic sequence in the evolution of prehistoric dagger- and sword-forms is well known, we can match each representation on the rocks with a real object and thus date the rock-pictures with considerable accuracy.

With the dating we can get, very often, a good idea of economic conditions. On the Swedish rocks we find a great many pictures of ships. Now, razor-blades engraved with representations of ships have been excavated and these ships correspond rather closely in form and shape to those upon the rocks. As we can date the razor-blades so we can also assign a date to the pictures.

Lastly, the rock-pictures are of great importance for the history of human settlement. The pictures fall into a number of groups, each of which is characterized by its own style— and this style varies from region to region. Probably, then, we have here evidence of the existence of different tribes which engraved their hopes and desires upon the Written Stones.

Thus, sharply differentiated from the palæolithic Franco-Cantabrian art, we have the Levantine Spanish art and it has, for long, been a problem whether or not we have here evidence for the existence of two human groups living in the Iberian Peninsula contemporaneously, or whether the Franco-Cantabrian art and the Levantine art followed on one after the other.

The Swedish rock-pictures resemble those of Russia, yet there are differences which may possibly be due to the representation of similar ideas by two different groups of human beings. In the neolithic and Bronze Age rock-pictures of Spain there can be distinguished several groups whose styles and designs correspond, generally speaking, to the ornamentation upon various groups of pottery vessels. Therefore, we may conclude that in prehistoric Spain there were several different tribes, related in culture, but whose development was varied.

The rock-pictures thus throw light upon many different branches of Man's activity; they afford us a view of the spiritual and material culture of our remote ancestors, and they may be more clearly interpreted than pottery vessels or ancient stone and metal weapons.

Indeed, without these marvellous monuments of a most ancient art we should know little about the life of our predecessors on this continent of Europe.

THE ROCK PICTURES
OF EUROPE

Pictures of the Ice Age to 10,000 B.C.[1]

THE Late Palæolithic, or Ice Age, paintings and engravings upon rock-surfaces constitute the most ancient art of Europe and that is to say, as far as we can see, of the whole earth. Since the revelation of prehistoric painting in 1901 we have been in a position no longer simply to theorize about ancient art and thought, but we have firm ground on which to stand. Of the old hypotheses put forward to account for the phenomenon of human artistic creation none is satisfactory. The urge was attributed to a need for adornment, to a desire to imitate, to a feeling of empathy or just to the play-motive.

But we recognize now that the origin of art lies in religion —if we take, of course, that word in the widest sense of the term. During the last century the religious origin of art was hardly even thought of. In the course of the study that has been devoted, for decades now, to prehistoric art, it is clear that not only does Ice Age art partake of a religious character but that all the paintings and engravings upon the rocks have a religious significance and one just as marked as that displayed by the art of medieval Europe.

Of course, religious forms change, but there seems to be a fundamental human need for some sort of religion, and also for an art which can render permanent the content of religious experience.

What is holy must be set aside, the numinous must be removed from what belongs to everyday life. It is this distinction, this cleavage, that constitutes the essence of religion. It is a certain concept of something that is different, that is 'sacred' and not a clear-cut idea of a god, which is the criterion for judging what is 'religion' and what is not. Nevertheless it does seem as though there may have been some idea of a divinity in late palæolithic times.

[1] The author puts in his text '60,000 to 10,000 B.C.'. I shall explain in a later footnote why it has been thought best to suppress this figure of 60,000. (Translator's Note.)

3

If we accept this definition of the word and concept 'religion', then the places of the rock-pictures are holy places. If our word 'temple' is derived from the same root as that of the Greek word *temnō*, to 'cut', to 'cut off', to 'separate', that is to say, to "remove from the profane and the secular", then we may look upon every rock-picture site as a 'temple', a place dedicated and distinguished from the mass of all apparently similar places.

Thus, among the very many caves in the Pyrenean region few are painted. Among the innumerable ravines that gash the hillsides of Levantine Spain only some are decorated with pictures. There are countless rock-surfaces that the Scandinavian glaciers once polished, but relatively few of these smoothed stones bear engravings.

I have often explored the surroundings of rock-picture sites and have sought paintings or engravings in neighbouring caves or rock-shelters or ravines, but my trouble has been almost always in vain. It is a most remarkable thing that, for generation after generation, men painted their pictures on the same spots. The reason for such limitation of the pictures to certain sites must surely have lain as much in the sacredness of the site as in the religious character of what was there drawn and delineated.

It is perhaps easiest for us today to appreciate the religious character of the Ice Age, or Upper Palæolithic, paintings since these are nearly all in caverns. A cave, in itself, awakens in us feelings that it is a place set apart. Grottoes and caverns are dark and mysterious. We need artificial light in them. We feel no movement of air. In their remotest depths there is hardly any variation of temperature at all. There is something essentially uncanny about caves. Men have always avoided them as abodes of evil spirits—and of wild beasts.

It is no mere coincidence that the word *Höhle* (that is, 'cave' in German) is derived from the same root as *Hölle* (that is 'hell').[1]

Modern psycho-analysts would see in the cave an image

---

[1] Both are derived from the Old High German Word *hel* (that is, 'concealed' or 'hidden'), which also appears in the modern German word *verhelen* (that is, to 'conceal').

of the womb, so that caverns would be symbols of the 'concealed' phase in human life. In any case, it is often hard for us to repress a shudder when, after long and painful creeping through narrow passages, we straighten up to walk through huge, dim halls in which the dull plopping of drops of water is the only sound that disturbs the uncanny and overpowering stillness. One has no idea as to where passages may lead. One never knows what may await one. Indeed, there is always the feeling that something unexpected will happen—that maybe even some beast will loom up out of the murk.

We may be sure that men of the Ice Age experienced the same sensations as we do. If we often get the impression that we are treading where no man has ever passed before, how much more poignantly must our remote ancestors have been impressed by what really was untrodden ground. Those men lived at the same time as the formidable cave-bear and each time that they penetrated into a cavern there was the chance that within might be lurking a cave-bear. Then it would be a struggle to the death between the beast and the man.

Such thoughts occurred very forcibly to me when, years ago, I was guided by the discoverer, Count Bégouen, for the greater part of an hour through an almost inaccessible cavern. First we had to glide through a subterranean river on a little skiff and then to creep and wriggle and worm our way through passages very nearly impassable. When we could walk upright we could make out, in the gloom of a side-passage, the skeleton of a cave-bear and as we shambled on our feet struck the articulated skeleton of a snake.

The last hall we reached was that where are the now celebrated sculptures of bisons. Around the sculptures the clayey flooring of the cavern has, in the course of millennia, dried to a stone-like hardness and it still retains the impressions of the footprints of prehistoric men.

The cave was no longer visited at the end of the Magdalenian period, that is the end of the Ice Age, and even during the latter epochs of that age the furthermost passages were no longer trodden by the foot of Man.

Stalagmites and stalactites completely blocked the

passages when Count Bégouen and his sons discovered the cavern. They had, indeed, to hack their way through.

In that last hall of the sculptured bisons there was, sticking in the wall, a flint-knife such as served, doubtless, for the carving of the figures.

The imprints of feet around the sculpture-group indicate clearly that here dancing took place. Curiously enough, only the heel-marks are impressed upon the ground. Maybe the dancers mimicked the bisons' gait as they danced a bison-dance to ensure fecundity, the increase of herds and good luck in the chase. The sculpture-group certainly relates to fertility-magic since the male bison is shown as about to mount the female. Magic for birth. Magic for death. So much must be apparent to a visitor who today penetrates into this sanctuary thousands of years after the men who there danced their cult dance.[1]

I WIZARD SHOWN IN A CULT DANCE Les Trois-Frères

[1] It is perhaps worth while stressing that this sanctuary in the Tuc d'Audoubert cavern served probably as much for initiation ceremonies as for magic directed at immediate luck in the hunt. (Translator's Note.)

6

2 WIZARD PLAYING A FLUTE AND REPRESENTATIONS OF ANIMALS Les Trois-Frères

And this impression of magic for birth and for death does not grip us in only one of the prehistoric caves. In the neighbouring cavern of Les Trois-Frères, the visitor must crawl on all fours along a low, narrow passage for some 45 yards, a corridor so restricted that one cannot raise one's head but must wriggle forward on one's belly like a snake. But after this burrow one comes upon vast halls and in the last of these, the most spacious and the most beautiful, there are engraved upon the walls over five hundred pictures of beasts.

Above them all is the picture of the magician himself (Fig. 1), the portrait of the man who may, indeed, have executed some of the engravings. With his large, dark eyes he gazes at the visitor. It is impressive, it is even alarming to look steadily into those eyes which for millennia have stared down from a height into vacant space. This shaman wears upon his head the mask of a stag with its antlers. Bear's paws cover his hands and a horse's tail hangs from his waist. One leg is raised as in a dance.

No, there cannot be much doubt about it. These prehistoric caves are cult-places comparable in their essence with the rock-cut temples of Ellora or Ajanta in India and of Lung-men, Yün-Kang or Tun-huang in China. Magic and wizardry had their holy places in the Ice Age, places where beasts were enchanted and by supernatural means brought under the power of men.

In this same cave of Les Trois-Frères there are other pictures of shamans or magicians (Fig. 2). One of them

7

wears upon his shoulders a bear's fell and is playing a flute. So we may gather that music, of some sort, was used in the ceremonies of palæolithic cults. Also in this cavern is the engraving of a naked man disguised in a bison's mask (Fig. 3). He also is shown dancing. The bent upper part of the body, the flexed knees, the outstretched arms, the leg held high all remind us of some of the cult-dances performed to this day by African, Amerindian and Asiatic tribes. I have seen dances of this sort at Taos near Santa Fé, in New Mexico and performed by Tibetan folk near Darjeeling.

Pictures of masked dancers are not uncommon in Ice Age caverns and there are such figures at Altamira (Figs. 4–5), Le Font-de-Gaume, Les Combarelles, Marsoulas, Hornos de la Peña, Los Casares (Figs. 6–8), Cabrerets, Le Portel, Tuc d'Audoubert, Lascaux (Fig. 10). And this list only comprises some of the pictures to be seen upon the walls of caverns. There are many more similar figures drawn or engraved upon stone, horn and bone (Fig. 9). If we take into account these latter we have some fifty-five representations of masked dancers from fifteen different palæolithic sites—a considerable number.

From such drawings and paintings we can get a fairly good idea of what Ice Age magicians looked like. They danced naked but they wore animal-masks (mostly those of lion, stag or bison) and also, generally, beasts' paws and a tail. The clothing or adornment may have varied according to the sort of beast it was sought to enchant. I have witnessed buffalo and eagle dances among the Amerindians. At first

3 WIZARD WEARING AN ANIMAL-MASK
AND APPARENTLY DANCING
Les Trois-Frères

8

the dancers strutted and fluttered like eagles and then, later, the men imitated the heavy, shambling gait of the buffalo. These were hunting dances too. Magic for the chase.

Frobenius reports that once he observed a Bushman perform a ceremony before he went hunting. In the sand he drew the figure of an ostrich. Then he took bow and arrow and shot at the neck of the ostrich drawing. That evening he brought back a slaughtered ostrich to camp.

Customs, comparable with those of Ice Age men, live on to this day among peoples who exist in approximately the same economic conditions as did palæolithic populations in Europe.

We may take it that the Ice Age pictures were drawn and painted for essentially the same reasons that induced Frobenius's Bushman to delineate the figure of an ostrich. The palæolithic pictures were magic pictures and that is one of the reasons why they are so true to life. The more accurately a beast was portrayed, the better the proportions of the picture, the more vivid the impression produced, so the more successful in his spells the shaman was likely to be. And the pictures were for the initiated only.

Thus the Bushman Frobenius tells us about had gone out

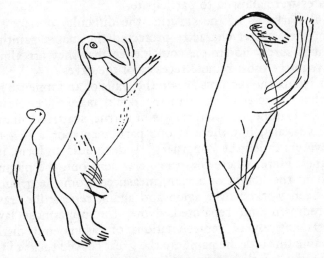

4 & 5 WIZARDS IN ANIMALS' SKINS Altamira

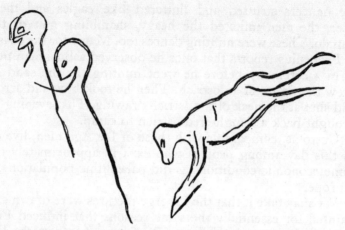

6 & 7 THEANTHROPIC FIGURES, PROBABLY WIZARDS Los Casares

from the camp to an isolated height where he drew his picture before sunrise. When he had used his drawing, he effaced it.

So, we may imagine, the men of the Ice Age sought out the uncanny recesses of the caves. No unauthorized person must see the pictures. Communing with the sacred things was secret. So, much later on, in the Greek mysteries only initiates were allowed to participate.

The darkness of the caverns, the difficulty of access to them, their secret character protected the magic paintings and it is surely no simple coincidence that they are almost always in the most remote recesses of the caves.

At Niaux the pictures are on the walls of an immense hall on whose spacious floor dancing could take place. At the Font-de-Gaume, the pictures are, it is true, scattered all over the cave-walls, but there is one particular spot which the discoverers called the 'sanctuary'. Indeed, it is, in form, like a chapel. Here, where the passage widens out, the pictures (at about the height of a man, measured from the ground) have been worked over again and again, repeatedly drawn and redrawn and repainted. Now, the uppermost layer consists entirely of representations of bisons, but distinguishable through the paint are the great curved tusks of the mammoths which had been limned upon these walls when

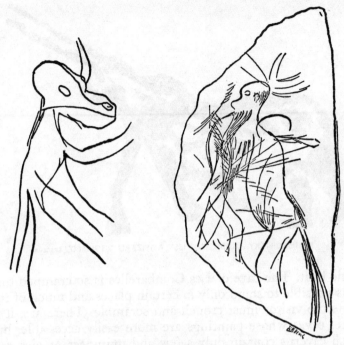

8 WIZARD DISGUISED AS AN ANIMAL Los Casares
9 WIZARD WEARING ANIMAL DISGUISE Grotte des Espélugues

mammoths still lived in the valley of the Vézère, where the
cavern lies. It is still possible to make out the mammoths'
feet and their round eyes so different from those of bisons.
Generations of men painted pictures in this cave and they
used again and again the surfaces which had been utilized
before.

At Altamira the paintings are upon the ceiling of the last
great hall. The entrance used today, and opening into this
hall, is not the original one and was discovered accidentally
by a hunter: it has since been enlarged. The old entrance
lay somewhere else and, in ancient times, in order to reach
the pictures, the men of the Ice Age had to crawl upon
hands and knees and make their way through strait ways
and narrow passages.

The Montespan cave must be reached by swimming.
Those who would explore the Tuc d'Audoubert must use a

10 IMAGINARY ANIMAL, POSSIBLY A WIZARD DISGUISED Lascaux

little boat. The cave of Les Combarelles is so cramped that it is possible to stand only in certain places and much of the time the visitor must crouch and scramble. There are, it is true, caves whose paintings are more easily accessible, but such caverns contain only a few and unimportant pictures. The large caves, with the significant paintings and engravings, indicate that care was taken to make the magic things hard to reach, and even almost inaccessible.

Many of the prehistoric pictures show beasts struck by weapons. Arrows are to be seen at Niaux as well as at Peña de Candamo, Tuc d'Audoubert, El Castillo, La Pasiega, Le Portel, Santimamiñe, Buxu, Les Trois-Frères (Fig. 11), Los Casares and Lascaux. P-shaped boomerangs are found on the pictures at Les Trois-Frères (Fig. 12), Pindal (Fig. 13), El Castillo and Niaux.

Curiously enough many of the paintings and engravings actually have been shot at. At Montespan (Fig. 34), there is the engraving of a horse being driven towards a snare. The animal's body is riddled with scores of holes. In the same cavern, the sculptured figure of a bear shows no less than forty-two holes. At Les Trois-Frères (Fig. 11) similar marks are to be observed upon the figure of a bear with sagging head and from whose snout blood gushes forth.

The main significance of the Ice Age pictures is, therefore, clear enough, although they are so ancient. From the
beginning it would appear that art and religion have been
closely linked, while music, too, from very remote times,
served the ceremonies of our far-off ancestors' cults. This
combined character, at once, religious, artistic, musical,
dramatic, was retained by the rock-pictures until the latest
that we know. So, if the pictures seem strange to us and
alien, we may remember that they were holy things, in and
by which Man expressed his longings.

Magic is one of the most ancient adjuncts of religion. In
fact, magic is an essential part of religion. Without magic
most of men's faiths—even those we call the highest—
could hardly be conceived. We have but to reflect upon how
great a part magic played in the lives of the Babylonians and
the Assyrians, the Greeks and the Romans. In medieval
Christianity magic was an integral part of religious experience. Magic of witches. Magic of exorcisms. Magic of
sacred pictures. And much of this magic survives until
today.

The storm that broke in A.D. 726[1] swept up from the

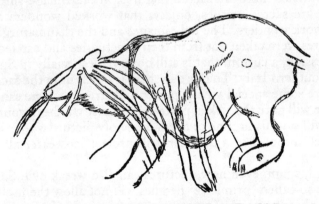

11 CAVE BEAR PIERCED WITH ARROWS Les Trois-Frères

[1] It was in A.D. 726 that the Emperor Leo, the Isaurian, issued his rescript in
"favour of overthrowing the holy and venerable images", as Theophanes later
wrote. In 740, under Leo's son, the Emperor Constantine V, a more active
iconoclast, the persecution of the image-worshippers began in real earnest. It was
not until A.D. 842 that the holy images (and then solely as pictures) were restored
in Byzantium. (Translator's Note.)

12 HORSE HIT BY BOOMERANGS Les Trois-Frères

custom of ascribing to a saint's image a like power to that thought to have been possessed by the saint himself. Generally speaking, the Church has striven against this identification of the image and the person represented, but, on the whole, the efforts have not been very successful. Miraculous powers are still ascribed to images and paintings. In churches there are sacred pictures, in pilgrimage-shrines there are sacred statues, objects that worked wonders and still work wonders. The holy images and the thaumaturgical pictures were taken out from their sanctuaries and carried in procession, a custom that is still observed especially in Spain and southern Italy. To this day there is inherent in the sacred picture some special virtue, power and strength. One saint's image will cure the sick, a portrait of Christ will heal wounds and will save us in time of need. The holy picture worn as an amulet, a medal or a talisman will protect its wearer all his life long.

And, again, even now, pictures can also wreak evil. Some of the so-called 'primitive peoples will not allow themselves to be photographed. The possessor of a man's picture holds a secret power over the man himself. With a picture many sorts of magic can be wrought.

Boethius[1] tells us that when King Duffus was sick and wasting slowly away, two women were discovered who had

[1] A.D. 480–524.

14

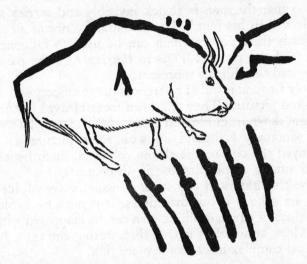

13 BISON, ENGRAVED AND PARTLY PAINTED IN RED, WITH ARROW AND BOOMERANGS
Pindal

prepared a waxen image of the sovereign. One of the two
turned the figure over a spit while the other woman sang her
enchantments. Fortunately the witches were apprehended
and punished, so the king's life was saved. It was, during the
Middle Ages, an ever recurrent accusation against 'withces'
that they had prepared an image of a man and had stuck it
through with needles or had buried it in the earth so that the
victim of their malpractices might die. The evidence given
at witches' trials reveals any number of such 'crimes' which
have by no means even yet quite died out. I know of two
judicial reports made by examining magistrates, reports in
which accounts are given of people who accused themselves
of having stuck needles through the photograph of a faithless
lover. When the victim died shortly afterwards, the per-
petrators of the 'magic' felt so guilty that they had to confess
their misdemeanours to the police.

In Paracelsus[1] there is a passage which reads: "Some
wizards make images in the form of a man whom they have
in mind. Then they drive a nail into the sole of the image's

[1] I.e. Theophrastus Bombast von Hohenheim (1490–1541), the famous German
physician. (Translator's Note.)

15

foot so that the man is struck invisibly and carries an invisible nail in his foot." The essential feature of all sacred images is their power which can be used to influence the subject of the picture. Thus in the Ice Age the paintings influenced the animals represented.

Holy Legend is full of references to the efficacy and might of sacred pictures. They fall down from Heaven or they are brought down from Heaven by angels. The fate of a town or of a sanctuary is bound up with some picture. If it be destroyed the city or the shrine collapses. Such beliefs are found among all peoples and in all countries.[1]

The thoughts and the spiritual experiences of Ice Age Man are echoed in our own times. It is most probable that the beliefs of late palæolithic men can be compared with our own ideas, although it is true that, during the ages, Man's spiritual complex has become more rich.

So much for the religious content of prehistoric art. It is, however, also now possible to appreciate the æsthetic content of the ancient pictures, to arrange them in a series chronologically, and thus to learn much about the history of the development of the Ice Age pictures.

If we look at the whole mass of such paintings and engravings we see that there are three main phases (although it is true that these influence each other) which can be clearly distinguished. In the first, and oldest, group the pictures consist only of outlines. This can be assigned to the Aurignacian[2] period. The second group is what may be called 'pictorial'. The contours have lost something of their significance. Means have been found to convey an appearance of depth in space, of plasticity. New problems are also tackled such as those of light and shade, of perspective and of texture. This art-style begins in the early Magdalenian and reaches its highest development in the mid-Magdalenian.[3] The third phase is that of the later Magdalenian (that

---

[1] Reference to such things is common in classical and medieval literature. Such modern writings as Vollmöller's *Miracle* and Oscar Wilde's *Picture of Dorian Gray* are modern examples of analogous stories.

[2] So called from the Aurignac site in the French Haute-Garonne.

[3] So called from the La Madeleine site in the French Dordogne department and not far from Les Eyzies-de-Tayac.

is to say, the end of the Ice Age) and shows a return to linear conventions and to the accentuation of outline.

This movement from linear to 'pictorial' and then again to linear may be paralleled to a certain extent in the phases of ancient Greek art, that is to say, from the accentuated linear forms of the Archaic, through the Classical to the Hellenistic and even farther on to a new stylization in late Antiquity. Or, again, we may think of the movement from the art of the early Renaissance to the Baroque and then to the accentuation of the linear that is characteristic of the 'Romantic' periods.

It looks as though Wöllflin may have been right when he postulated a rule in art development, and it is of great interest to observe that prehistoric art also seems to obey such a rule. If, therefore, we would trace the style-sequences of prehistoric art we must find some way of dating the pictures. Are the datings assigned to them arbitrary or do we stand on some sure ground?

First of all we may say that the relative dating can be established without a doubt and, after all, the relative dating is the most important thing in this problem of dates.

All the indications we possess point to the ice having rolled back by about 10,000 B.C.[1] The Aurignacian culture-period, according to the 'radiation curve', should be dated at from 60,000 to 40,000 B.C. The subsequent Solutrean would have lasted from 40,000 to 30,000 and the Magdalenian from 30,000 to 10,000. In any case, the culture-periods in question must have lasted long, for during them a number of natural upheavals, on a huge scale, took place. For instance, glaciers which had covered Scandinavia and northern Germany—almost to the site of Berlin at their

---

[1] The author states here that "absolute dating is arrived at by the help of the 'radiation curves' associated with the work of Milankovich and by the aid of the varve calculations of de Geer", but during the last few years it has been possible to determine, up to an age of about 41,000 years, the antiquity of any object of organic origin. The technique used is that of the carbon-14 or radio-carbon count. For all living things absorb carbon-14 while they are alive and after death give up the carbon-14 at a regular rate in any circumstances whatsoever. The tests which were at first conducted solely in Dr. Libby's laboratory at Chicago are now (for Libby has moved over to the Atomic Energy Commission) being effected at several different laboratories in the United States. (Translator's Note.)

highest peak—slowly melted. Such phenomena demand long periods of time.[1]

In a number of caverns it is possible to assign a date to the pictures because these first came to light when the cave-fillings (consisting of strata laid down during the Ice Age) were removed. Obviously the pictures thus revealed must be more ancient than the layers of earth and débris that covered them. There are several instances of such 'auto-dating'. In 1904 Ampoulange discovered the La Grèze (Plate II) cave pictures after he had removed a layer of early Magdalenian filling and then an underlying stratum of Solutrean.[2] Ampoulange was not looking for paintings or engravings, he was searching for prehistoric tools and implements. He had long been at work in the cave before he suddenly became aware that the outline figure of a bison was coming to light. It was obvious that the picture could have been executed only before the Magdalenian and Solutrean layers of cave-fillings had been laid down, that is to say, at some time during the Aurignacian culture-phase. So, this drawing was at once recognized as typical of Aurignacian art. It shows a firmly sketched outline, an accentuation of contours and a pictorial treatment of the rock surface. There is, however, no attempt at perspective. The legs on the farther side are not shown and the horns are depicted as though seen from head-on.

There was a similar case at Pair-non-Pair (Fig. 14). In this cavern in the Gironde department of south-western

---

[1] Since the culture-phases of the Upper Palæolithic were named after sites in France and since it is in France (and northern Spain) that the sequence of palæolithic cultures is most clearly to be seen, some comments are called for on these passages of the author's text. First of all, very high dates for the phases of the Upper Palæolithic are no longer generally held. We know now from radio-carbon tests that what is usually called 'Upper Perigordian 5' flourished about 25,000 years or so ago. And this 'Perigordian' phase is what used to be called 'Upper Aurignacian'. It does not look, then, as though the beginning of the Aurignacian could be set anything like so long ago as 60,000 years. (Translator's Note.)

[2] The sequence of cultures (as shown in western Europe) is as follows: (a) Mousterian (associated with Neanderthaloid *non-sapiens* types of men), followed by (b) Aurignacian (*sapiens* type of Man), then (c) Perigordian (subdivided into five or six phases), and (d) Solutrean, and (e) Magdalenian (subdivided into at least six phases some of which may have been local). The Magdalenian is the last culture-phase of the Upper Palæolithic and is followed by the Mesolithic. (Translator's Note.)

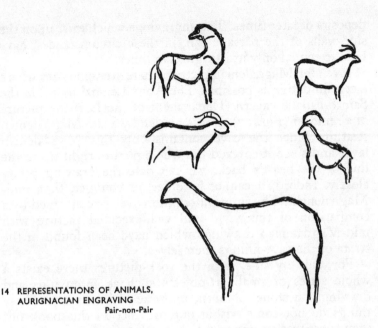

14 REPRESENTATIONS OF ANIMALS,
AURIGNACIAN ENGRAVING
Pair-non-Pair

France, Daleau, who had been excavating from 1882, had revealed four superposed layers of the Aurignacian-culture period. Each layer was separated from another by a sterile stratum.[1] It was not until August 1896, when he had dug down through the cave-fillings to a depth of nearly nine feet, that he found revealed upon the cave-walls the outline figures of animals. There were, altogether, twelve engravings and their dating to the Aurignacian is certain. These Pair-non-Pair drawings are, like those of La Grèze, only outlines, but they are firmly delineated and the proportions of the animals are skilfully reproduced. The style, indeed, corresponds closely to that of many finds of mid-Aurignacian date.

A third instance is that of the Gargas Cave (Fig. 15) in the French department of the Hautes-Pyrénées. Here, towards the end of the Aurignacian, a huge block of stone came to obstruct the entrance to the cavern. The boulder lay upon an Aurignacian stratum and was itself covered by

[1] That is to say a stratum in which no traces of man's handiwork have been discovered. (Translator's Note.)

deposits of later times. The engravings which exist upon the side-walls of the passage can, in these circumstances, have been executed only in Aurignacian times.

Even for Magdalenian pictures there are some sites where a certain dating is possible. The Abbé Lemozi found in the Sainte-Eulalie cavern (Department of the Lot) the picture of a reindeer (Fig. 17). It was hidden by a late Magdalenian stratum. Since the cave contains only this Magdalenian layer and since it covered the whole picture right up to the line of the beast's back, we can date the drawing pretty closely. Indeed, it cannot be older, or younger, than mid-Magdalenian. The supposition, moreover, is confirmed by a comparison of this vivid and well-executed picture with mid-Magdalenian drawings which have been found in the strata of the cave-fillings themselves.

For, side by side, with the rock-pictures there exists a whole series of small art-objects such as engravings and drawings on stone, or horn, on bone and on ivory. These things do not come within our province in this book but they constitute an important part of Ice Age art.

These small objects are of many different sorts. Thus hundreds of 'staves' have been found. They are made of reindeer or stag bone and appear to be cult-objects. They all bear holes bored through them and the use of these things has often been debated: the name they bear in archæological terminology is *bâtons de commandement*—a not very significant term. More probably they are wizards' wands, symbolical cult-sticks used in ceremonies such as those of initiation. The sticks cannot have served any practical purpose and, moreover, the holes never show any sign of use or wear. These staves are decorated with drawings of animals, with ornamental and sexual symbols.

15 REPRESENTATIONS OF ANIMALS, AURIGNACIAN STYLE Gargas

The 'lamps' used to illuminate the caves were concave stones in which fat and a wick were placed. These 'lamps' are also decorated with figures of beasts. We have, again, propulsors (for hurling javelins or spears) that are ornamented, while the pendants the women wore about their necks are also decorated.

So, by a careful analysis of the contents of the cave-strata, it is fairly easy to date, with some accuracy, the rock-pictures on the cavern-walls. If, therefore, direct evidence is lacking at any given site, dating may be effected by comparison with the style of objects whose age is known.

At Altamira, for instance, were recovered heads of hinds engraved on pieces of bone (Fig. 18). The stratum was early Magdalenian. Similar heads, treated in an identical style, occur on the Altamira cave-walls. An almost exactly identical engraving of a hind's head was found in El Castillo cavern in northern Spain, while here, again, there is, so to speak, an 'enlargement' of the drawing on the walls (Fig. 19).

Clearly, then, before he tackled the large paintings, or engravings, on the cave-walls, the artist made sketches on bits of bone.

There is another instance of this practice at Font-de-Gaume. The Font-de-Gaume grotto, indeed, is an important landmark in the story of prehistoric art's revelation. The Font-de-Gaume was discovered in 1901, while in 1910 Breuil published his important monograph on the great polychrome paintings in the cavern. The year 1910, indeed,

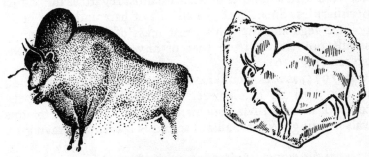

16 WALL PAINTING Font-de-Gaume
ENGRAVING ON STONE Abri de la Genière

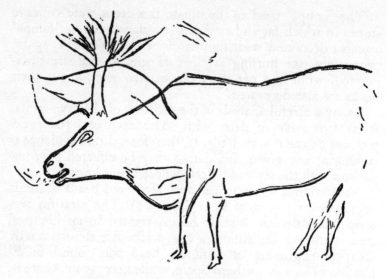

17 REINDEER IN MAGDALENIAN STYLE Sainte Eulalie

may be regarded as that of the recognition of prehistoric art
as a reality.

Among other paintings in this cave is one representing a
bison with withers so huge that they bunch up into a sort of
bag of fat behind his head. Such a hump does, in fact,
develop in old males and is characteristic of the bison
family. It may be that the hunter-artist, or the hunter-
wizard, had one particular animal in mind when he was
performing his enchantments. The creature, indeed, is
depicted with a number of what we must regard as individual
peculiarities. Small head, small tuft of hair under the head,
pointed legs and then this great mass of fat. The painting
stands out clearly from that of any other animal in the
cavern (Fig. 16).

In 1925, as luck would have it, Gaillard, while prospecting
in the Abri de la Genière, near Serrières-sur-Ain,[1] discovered, in a mid-Magdalenian stratum, the sketch for this
wall-painting. What Gaillard found is a small engraving on

[1] In the Ain department and at least two hundred and fifty miles from Les
Eyzies-de-Tayac, that is to say the Font-de-Gaume cavern. (Translator's Note.)

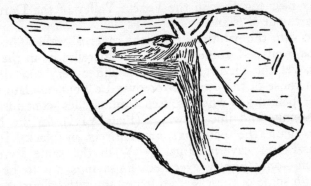

18 HIND, ENGRAVING ON BONE Altamira (Excavation)

a limestone sliver about 2½ inches by 3 inches, but this picture shows exactly the same beast as the large painting at the Font-de-Gaume—similar small head, pointed tuft, short, thin legs and great boss upon the withers. When the wall-painting was discovered Breuil at once dated it to the mid-Magdalenian, and he dated it on stylistic grounds. The La Genière discovery fully confirmed his attribution.

A whole series of stones has been recovered on which are mazes of drawings, inextricable masses of intermingled lines. With great patience individual figures can be made out and it is probable that some, at least, of these stones were sketching-blocks upon which the palæolithic artists practised their craft.[1] The slabs seem to have been used again and again. The surface was covered with red pigment and, when the stone was covered, then more paint would be put on and the sketching-block used over and over again.

We may suppose that painting lessons were given in schools conducted by wizard-artists or artist-wizards, and most of the caves have, each one, a dominating style. The style of the Laugerie Basse cavern (Fig. 21) (from which only small art-objects have been recovered) is not the style of the Limeuil cave (Fig. 20), although the two sites are

[1] Some of these stones, however, were, no doubt, cult-objects of a 'lucky' or sacred character, as, for example, the now celebrated engraved stone found at La Colombière by Dr. Hallam Movius of Harvard in 1950.

fairly near together in the Vézère Valley of the Dordogne department of France.

So with the paintings upon the caverns' walls. The caves of Le Font-de-Gaume and Les Combarelles lie in the same hills, yet the pictures of the one differ very considerably from those of the other. Moreover Le Font-de-Gaume has large paintings, whereas Les Combarelles contains only engravings and line drawings (Plate VIII). In the Niaux cave again the paintings are entirely in black[1] In the Trois-Frères cavern (Figs. 1–3)—in the same Pyrenean region—only lightly executed engravings are to be seen though some of these were touched up with colour. Yet the pictures date from the same epoch—mid-Magdalenian.[2] Not so very far from the Altamira cave, that contains both the largest and the most beautiful of the palæolithic polychrome paintings, is La Pasiega cavern, near Puente Viesgo.[3] In style and in technique the pictures at the two sites are completely different, though both sets of paintings belong to the Magdalenian.

However, the fact that in remote times men were able to create pictures of such a high æsthetic value presupposes the existence of what we may call art-schools where the lessons

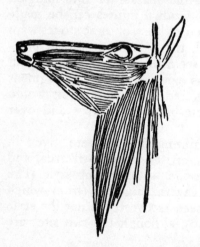

19 HIND, WALL ENGRAVING El Castillo

[1] Niaux is near Tarascon-sur-Ariège.
[2] But the mid-Magdalenian phase must have lasted long.
[3] Province of Santander, Spain. (Translator's Notes.)

24

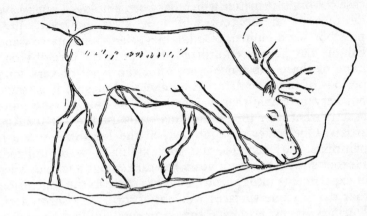

20 REINDEER BROWSING Limeuil

of technique and tradition were handed down from generation to generation.

The painter is a wizard and the wizard is a painter. He was the artist who drew, who engraved on bone, who made pictures. The nearer the image was to the things represented, then the greater would be the chance of good luck in the chase. And the wizard would have his pupils who would work under his direction and guidance.

The palæolithic painters possessed a palette of considerable range and richness. Only greens and blues are absent; evidently in Ice Age times men did not know how to utilize substances that yield such pigments. For black, manganese earths were employed or iron oxide or charcoal. For white, white marl. For browns, red and yellow ochres. Nothing is known, with certainty, about the origin of purple, mauve or violet that is not rare, especially at Altamira and Lascaux. Maybe this hue was obtained by a mixture of pigments since the technique of the preparation of colours was well developed.

There has been discovered a whole collection of rubbing bowls in which the pigments were reduced to powder. Since if one's finger is dabbed on some of the paintings they seem greasy to the touch, it appears probable that the powder was mixed with fats. However, what chemical analysis has been conducted hitherto has not led to conclusive results. In any case the organic matter which has been employed must have disappeared in the course of ages. It is, however, quite possible that albumen, blood, honey, suet, bone marrow and fish-oil may have been utilized. Except in the case of blood none of these substances can, after the lapse of very long periods of time, be detected by chemical means. It is, thus, not very probable that we shall ever be able to determine exactly what were the binding materials used by the Ice Age artists. Obermaier thought that, in the Levantine Spanish paintings, fat, blood-serum and albumen were utilized. Herberts, who in recent years has carried out a whole series of experiments into this problem, has come to the conclusion that damp stone surfaces will not absorb fatty substances. During his experiments the pigments applied to damp surfaces coagulated into lumps and lost their consistence. Herberts was most successful in his experiments with blood. The colour held both on dry stone and on wet, especially when a little water was added to the mixture. In fact, Herberts concluded that not fat but water was used as a medium and that the pictures are therefore a sort of fresco.

In considering the problem of the preservation of the prehistoric pictures we must also take into account that the calcium in the rocks combines—in dry conditions—with the carbonic acid of the atmosphere and thus forms a coating of calcite, as hard as enamel, that fixes the particles of the

21 BISON, ENGRAVING ON STONE, MAGDALENIAN Laugerie Basse

pigments. Thus, indeed, we could have something like the conditions of fresco painting where what are natural circumstances in the prehistoric caves are produced artificially through the application of mortar. On dry rock-surfaces, then, the fixing of the colours has been effected by the formation of a calcite crust, while in those places where the rock-surfaces are damp a process of natural preservation is still going on.

Though these explanations are convincing enough in themselves, they do not tell us why, in some places, the colour feels greasy to the touch, and it is difficult to escape the conclusion that, to some extent, fat was utilized. Still, whichever way we look at it, the preservation of the pictures through so many millennia is astounding, especially when we reflect that Leonardo da Vinci's *Last Supper* in Milan, though only a few centuries old, has been very grievously damaged by the atmosphere. We have, then, a very utilitarian and practical reason for wanting to find out how pigments were prepared in Ice Age times. For could we but discover this then we should, perhaps, be able to prepare our own modern paintings that would last thousands of years.

However, this much is certain: in palæolithic times the pigments were applied mixed with some medium, although crayons of dry colour also appear to have been used. At Altamira such crayons, neatly sharpened and laid upon a sort of stone bench and, moreover, arranged in their colour-sequence, have been found and look, for all the world, like the crayons used by modern artists. Probably these crayons were employed to accentuate the colour laid on wet.

Colours were applied partly by hand and partly by brush. Many of the delicate lines and gradations of shading could only have been effected by a wet brush. Probably prepared birds' feathers were used. One of the feathers of the snipe is to this day called in German *die Malerfeder*—or the 'painter's feather': it has an excessively fine tip and has been used by artists from time immemorial. Many of the thin lines of the rock paintings (and some are not more than a millimetre wide) could only have been drawn by a very fine brush. But the varied thickness of the painting strokes also

27

indicates that the Ice Age artists usually drew, first of all, the outline and then filled in the body of the picture. After having done this, they effaced the contour-lines.

There are, however, examples, such as the paintings at Niaux, which lead us to suppose that the artist was such a master of his technique, was, in fact, so sure of himself and was so excellent a draughtsman, that, utilizing brushes of varied thicknesses, he laid the wet pigment directly upon the rock-walls. In one case—that of the wolf's figure at Font-de-Gaume—the background was first of all tinted a dark red and then the representation of the wolf was painted in black pigment onto the surface. Spraying also was practised, especially at Lascaux. Presumably the pigment was blown through a hollow bone on to a previously prepared wall. In any case that a spraying technique was employed is obvious from the outlines of the pictures themselves.

The Ice Age artist appears to have paid great attention to the condition of the natural surface. Curiously enough, flat, smooth rocks seem to have attracted him very little. On the other hand, in the protuberances, in the irregularities of surfaces, he would see shapes and figures that he could complete with a few touches of colour.

Thus, for instance, at the Covalanas cave (in the Province of Santander, Spain) the earliest artist saw a beast's back in a ridge of rock; to this he painted belly, legs, head and horns until he brought a fine aurochs to life. In the Comarque cavern in the Dordogne, there are no less than three separate places where the rock-shapes have been transformed into the likeness of beasts. There are comparable instances in the caves of Nancy, Niaux, Mas d'Azil, Le Portel, Tuc d'Audoubert, Pindal, Hornos de la Peña and La Pasiega, while the famed bison ceiling at Altamira owes a great deal of its effect to cleverly utilized bosses, concavities and irregularities of the vault (Plate XIV).

What really decided the actual emplacement of the palæolithic paintings we do not know. It is, however, probable that the wizards' wisdom played its part in determining what should and what should not be adorned with pictures.

Though Neanderthaloid men may have painted their

28

bodies, they did not, as far as we know, create any form of art.[1] 'Modern' men, that is representatives of *homo sapiens* (and generally called, though not quite correctly, Cro-Magnon men), were the creators of art upon this earth. In mid-Aurignacian times we find outlines of hands, lines drawn with three fingers and other marks that tell us of the first experiments with colour and with drawing. As yet there are no pictures, only lines and scribblings. A little later on, however, we can begin to make out figures, such as, for instance, a snake at La Pileta or a bison at Labaume-Latronne.

In mid-Aurignacian times, also, we find linear, but naturalistic, representations of animal forms. Pictures consist entirely of outlines; there is no attempt to reproduce the appearance of the body itself; there is no perspective, no sense of depth. At first only one pair of legs on one side is shown. The horns are slewed round. But by late Aurignacian times greater verisimilitude is achieved. All four legs are depicted and the horns or antlers are represented in perspective. The artists are obviously tending towards an art with plastic qualities. But the road to be trodden was a hard one.

In a picture such as that from La Grèze (Plate II), the outline dominates and the figure has not yet been endowed with plastic quality; still, the form and shape reflect a highly naturalistic art. Indeed, by a series of masterly strokes, the picture has been made to stand out from its background despite the flatness of the design.

The pictures in the Covalanas cavern (Plate I), in the Province of Santander belong partly to the mid-Aurignacian and partly to the late Aurignacian culture-phase that has been named by Breuil and Peyrony 'Perigordian'. At Covalanas, as at La Grèze, the figures are presented in simple outline; however, not only are all four legs shown, but the backward movement of a hind's head reveals, for instance, the artist's endeavour to express that appearance of life and movement which is conveyed by the representation

[1] The author cites as proof of the Neanderthaloids' use of colour in painting their bodies, that ruddled bones are sometimes found in Neanderthaloid burials. (Translator's Note.)

of things on different planes. Still, here also the outline is the whole picture. At Covalanas, also, not a few drawings have dotted outlines. This primitive 'pointillism' is an attempt to render the contour more living, to make it less static and the result is, it must be admitted, a picture full of the suggestion of life.

To the same age as the Covalanas pictures belongs a drawing from El Castillo cave (also in the Province of Santander) (Plate III), depicting a wild ass shot with arrows, its head sagging down towards the ground. The pigment employed is red. There is only an outline, yet the painting is instinct with life: the realistic way the beast droops its head, the neck indicated by a sure, strong line, the long ears standing out from the rest of the figure. Here is already some loosening up of the outline that, as the evolution of palæolithic art proceeds, gradually fades away.

As an example of the transition to the new artistic conventions there is the figure of a mammoth in the Pech-Merle cavern at Cabrerets in the French department of the Lot (Plate IV). It is true that this painting, taken as a whole, still depends much upon its strongly marked outline, but the outline is no longer all. The line of the back is heavily and firmly drawn, but the belly is much more freely indicated. A heavy clothing of hair covers the body and conveys a tactile sensation as distinguished from one solely visual. Towards the end of the Solutrean culture-period mammoths either died out entirely or became very rare in France so that in Magdalenian times this mighty beast was unknown and thus the presence or absence of a given fauna in the rock-pictures will often enable us to date them. The impression made by the mammoth pictures at Pech-Merle is most profound as I noticed from the effect they had upon my students when I took some of them to the cavern soon after its discovery in 1923.

Towards the end of the Aurignacian the movement away from mere outline and towards plastic forms becomes more marked. A clear indication of changing styles is afforded by the charming picture of a horse (*equus hydruntinus*) (Plate XXIV) discovered in 1950 in the Italian cave of Levanzo, an island about ten miles off the Sicilian shores. Graziosi,

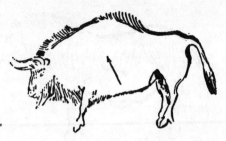

22 BISON STRUCK BY AN ARROW,
MAGDALENIAN Niaux

the discoverer of the figure, dates it to the late Aurignacian
and this dating is also accepted by Breuil. There can,
indeed, be no doubt about the classification of this Levanzo
piece. The outline, it is true, dominates and yet this contour
is free not rigid. The farther hind leg is treated in a perspective that is quite similar to that of Magdalenian
techniques. The backward-turned head of the animal has
permitted the artist to convey an impression of several
planes.

In the Solutrean this movement is accentuated. The
sculptures at the Roc de Sers (department of the Charente),
at the Fourneau du Diable (near Bourdeilles in the Dordogne) and at the Chaire à Calvin (department of the Charente) present animal figures from a well-determined level of
the upper Solutrean, figures in which the outline is no longer
the essence of the representation but in which the bodies are
clearly modelled with light and shade, with appearance of
depth and with a juxtaposition of planes.

In the bison of Le Roc de Sers all the weight and force of
the body is felt, the legs are plastically rendered. Then there
is the composition of the fighting ibexes. It is a scene of light
and shade, of plastic quality, of sense of depth. There are the
really magnificent sculptures of Angles-sur-Anglin (department of the Vienne, France) discovered by Miss Dorothy
Garrod and by Mlle. de Saint-Mathurin from 1950 to 1952.
These carvings (Plate XVII) belong to the Magdalenian
culture-phase III and are astounding in their power and
expressiveness. The palæolithic art objects from Angles-sur-
Anglin belong to the most perfect which have yet been
brought to light.

Mid-Magdalenian art is dominated by a tendency to

23 WILD HORSE,
MAGDALENIAN Niaux

minimize the significance of the outline and to develop, as
much as possible, the appearance of space and depth. The
flat surfaces no longer dominate, but the representation of
space. The artist's eye becomes more sensitive to differences
of context and texture, to surfaces, to the tegument of
things. Lines are less harsh. Spots, blobs, hatching take the
place of one continuous contour line. The animal forms
begin to live, to move. Light and shade are, so to speak,
independent elements. The pictures are much more vivid.

The earlier, or linear style, gives a static representation of
something seen, while the pictorial style gives an animated
representation.

A picture such as that of a horse from the Bédeilhac cave
(near Tarascon-sur-Ariège, Ariège, France) will illustrate
what I mean (Plate V). A head only is shown, but this head
is so represented that in its drawing alone it displays the
distinctive characteristics of the mid-Magdalenian art. The
outline is purposely broken in most places and even where
the lines of the contour are continuous they are nervously
executed. The under-side of the head, for instance, is merely
indicated—just a few strokes thrown on with rapid movements. The eye is but a point. The erect mane is engraved
with a few sure and nervous lines—it is blurred like a
fleeting impression left upon our vision. Here we have the
essence of mid-Magdalenian art—that remains pictorial
even when it is just a drawing.

To take another example. It is a picture from the Montespan cave in the department of the Haute-Garonne in
France (Plate VI). The loosening up of the outline here

gives us a representation of astonishing depth. This also is a horse's head; it belongs to the same period as the Bédeilhac picture but it is executed in quite a different style. Here the representation of outline is completely discarded. The upright mane is shown by means of short parallel strokes most accentuated at the top. The ear is just two notches thrown together but with penetrating effect of depth. The eye, just two incisions meeting at the apex, is depicted in masterly fashion. The upper part of the head is bounded by a waving, almost shrill line. The muzzle is left to the onlooker's imagination. The hair beneath the head is, so to say, sprinkled onto the loam of the cavern. The drawing is, of its sort, perfect. The artist, with full command of his art, represented the head as his eye glimpsed it.

This Montespan picture must be assigned to the same period as the horse's head at Bédeilhac, but the Bédeilhac artist drew with more spirit, his work is fresher, more filled with an appreciation of movement, with a more vivid impression of the animal model. The Montespan artist worked more cautiously, more precisely. His picture is the more carefully finished. Here we have the works of two artists of two different temperaments, and the personal style peculiar to each one is not to be mistaken.

Then, again, we have horses' heads from Niaux and from Les Combarelles (Plate VIII). The Niaux artist has a loose, almost airy style, his lines are dextrously drawn, his representation is dashed off at the command of a rich memory. The Les Combarelles artist was more thoughtful, more serious as is shown by the longer lines, the greater accentuation. The treatment of the eye alone indicates a creator with his own personal art-style.

Quite different again in treatment and in appearance is the horse's head from Labastide in the Hautes-Pyrénées department (Plate XI). The powerful beast is shown with full mane and thick growth of hair on the throat. The strokes are free, but surely executed. The style is easy, but certain. The animal (similar to the still extant Przewalski's Horse of Central Asia) is instinct with the fierce strength of animals that roam the steppe. The impressiveness of the work derives from the effect of the momentary, of the haphazard.

33

The quivering, upstanding mane, especially, lends the whole picture a plenitude of life, a sort of primitive force that is most arresting.

There is at Altamira the head of a young aurochs. It is drawn with only a few strokes, nevertheless the eye is full of expression and the muzzle clearly indicated. An extraordinary feature of this picture is that the outline becomes more and more marked and then—breaks off. The general effect is most remarkable. The beast looks as though it were alive.

Quite as impressive is the figure of a hind (also at Altamira, Plate X). The head is rendered with astonishing clarity and firmness. The artist has solved all the technical problems of his art. The tall ears stand out, as do the upper part of the muzzle and the eye. The outline is loose. All the force of the picture is concentrated in the head—and especially in the eye. This Ice Age engraving might be a drawing executed by one of the 19th-century Impressionist masters.

One of the most famous, and important of all Ice Age paintings is that of a buffalo (again at Altamira—Plate XII). The colours are red, yellow, brown, black and white. The imposing bulk of the beast seems to loom up before us. The broad, bold brush-strokes on the back and under the head can be clearly recognized, as also the finer, more delicate brush-work in the beard. The legs are painted in excellent perspective and the body, itself, developed with great plastic intensity.

The colours immensely increase the impressiveness of the picture which, as it covers bosses and bumps on the ceiling of the cavern, is both picture and sculpture in one, or, perhaps, rather, painting in relief.

The famous collapsed bison at Altamira must rank among the great works of art of all time. The colours are yellow, red, white, blue and black. The beast has been hit. Its head sags. The legs are contracted, the hump abased. Great dexterity of composition is shown in the arrangement of the forelegs, in the disposition of the hoofs, in the representation of the nerveless head. The perspective is perfect. It is hard to believe that this painting was executed thousands of years ago. Here we see illustrated the tasks the Ice Age artists set themselves, the representation of movement, the reproduction of the momentary.

As the light strikes these Altamira paintings they seem to be living, to move. The men who executed them may have had no agriculture, no domestic animals, but they were lords of art.

The most significant of the more recent discoveries of Ice Age art were those made in the Lascaux cavern, accidentally found by some lads in September 1940. The caverns lie in hilly, wooded ground to the south-east of the little town of Montignac in the French department of the Dordogne. For centuries men had trodden this soil, worked in the woods, and sought mushrooms or truffles, but no one had remarked the hole down which the boys' dog disappeared.[1] To find the dog, one of the lads forced himself down through the hole and when he reached the end of a comparatively short chute he saw he was in a great oval chamber on whose walls he could make out, by the light of his pocket-lamp, vast shapes of beasts. Even the younger people in the Dordogne—a paradise for prehistorians—know something about ancient rock-paintings, so, Ravidat, as the boy was called, had at once some idea of what he was looking at. He shouted up to his friends to come on down. When they had feasted their eyes upon the paintings they went back to Montignac and informed their school-teacher of what they had seen. He it was who realized what had been discovered and informed the great specialist, the Abbé Henri Breuil, who was staying not far away, at Brive, whither he had gone before the German advance.

After Altamira, Lascaux is the finest and the richest of all the palæolithic caverns. Both caves were for long ages hermetically sealed up and the pictures have thus been preserved in an astonishing state of freshness.

At Lascaux entrance gates have been built and these give access to the main hall, but the original entrance lay at the

[1] As a matter of fact the actual hole was known, though no one had thought it worth while trying to make his way down it. It is not certain that the tale of the disappearing dog was not a little embellishment added to the sober story of the discovery. When I first visited Lascaux immediately after the late war the dog story had not, apparently, become firmly established. (Translator's Note.)

far end of the caverns.[1] Indirect electric lighting now throws a soft radiance on to the pictures decking ceiling and walls: huge figures of beasts, some of which are over 15 feet long. The visitor is amazed at the majesty and beauty of these subterranean wonders.

Among the many paintings at Lascaux there is one of a pregnant wild mare that is especially striking. The soft, often broken outline is executed with a broad brush, as are also the muzzle of the little head and the arrows directed against the body. The body and the mane are, however, executed by means of a spray and in consequence display a particularly soft, almost floral texture. The Impressionistic character of the art is further increased by this technique.

Very lifelike also is an ancient type of ox (*bos longifrons*) (Plate XX) at Lascaux. The body-colour is something between light and dark red but the head is black. The painting is about nine feet long, but through the figure of this animal can be made out the traces of a more ancient picture. The small head with the slender horns and the long tail lend the animal an almost playful appearance.

Another specimen of ancient ox is depicted as in the moment of attack (Plate XXV). The head is shot forwards, the horns are lowered, the eye is blazing, the nostrils are dilated. A spear has hurtled towards the beast and struck it on the hoof. The whole assemblage is of great dramatic effect.

Particularly charming and surprising are the delineations of smaller animals such as foals that jog clumsily along (Plate XXI). These figures were executed by spray technique and in dark yellows, dark browns and often in black. In one lateral passage there is a frieze of stags' heads. It suggests that the creatures are swimming and indeed just beginning to rise out of the water as they reach a river's bank (Plate XXII). The scene is instinct with life and feeling. In its perpetuation of the momentary this is one of the most enchanting of Ice Age pictures.

[1] The original entrance lay possibly through a collapsed hall at the far end of the lower 'crypt' with the man and bison picture. The blocking of access by roof-falls must have been one of the most frequent reasons for the abandonment of the painted caverns in ancient times. (Translator's Note.)

Lascaux contains also pictures illustrating the transition to late Magdalenian styles. In fact, the gigantic figures of ancient oxen that sprawl and stride over other paintings must date from late Magdalenian times. These pictures, indeed, show a strong tendency towards the linear and they no longer display the plasticity and the freedom of outline that are characteristic of the mid-Magdalenian (Plate XIX).

In one place at Lascaux[1] there is a hole in the wall giving on to a drop of about 30 feet. A rope-ladder has to be used to get down to the gallery at the bottom of this abrupt fall. When we reach the ground again we stand before a puzzling picture (Plate XXIII). There is a bison wounded to death— pierced with a javelin. The intestines bulge down to the ground. Near the beast is the stylized supine figure of a man. His arms are outstretched and his face is that of a bird. He wears a mask. Near him, upon a pole, is a bird. It is not impossible that we may have here represented some sort of shamanistic incantation . . . the wizard sinks into a trance and, then, experiences in his dream the killing of a beast.

24 WILD BOAR, MAGDALENIAN Montespan

[1] The place is to the right in the so-called 'nave' as one approaches it from the main hall. This lower passage is not accessible to the public. The author does not mention that on the left-hand side of this enigmatic assemblage is the figure of a rhinoceros. The author in his text refers to the human figure as that of a man who has 'fainted'. I have brought this down to a footnote because it is arguable that the figure has a broken neck—a supposition rather supported by the ithyphallic condition of the human figure. (Translator's Note.)

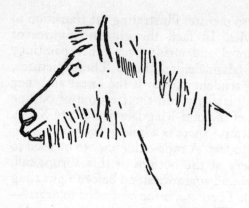

25 HEAD OF A WILD HORSE,
MAGDALENIAN
Montespan (Haute-Garonne)

The bird upon the pole might be symbolical of the ghostly change in the wizard's state. Horst Kirchner has remarked, in this connection, that certain Siberian tribes, to this day, expect their shaman to fall into a trance before the hunt begins and a bird may be the symbol of shamanistic power.

The Montespan cave (Figs. 24–25) contains a considerable number of pictures that are what Wölfflin would have called 'picturesque' (*malerisch* in German). Characteristic of this style of loose outlines and of perspective and plastic quality—which were features of the peak of Magdalenian art—is the engraving of a bear, and still more that of a bison, in the Santimamiñe (also called Basondo) cave in the Province of Santander (Figs. 27–28). Especially charming, again, is the delicate engraving of an ox in Grotte des Eglises,

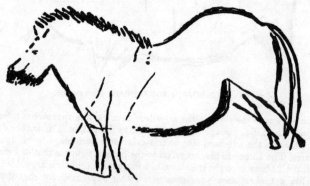

26 WILD HORSE, MAGDALENIAN Peña de Candamo (Asturias)

38

near Ussat-les-Bains in the Ariège department (Fig. 29).
The picture is daring in that a large portion of the outline is
left out and must be supplied by the eye of the beholder.
However, by this device, the drawing gains much in effect.
Its lifelike appearance is also accentuated by the soft treatment of the hair which looks as though it had been sprayed
on. Some of the pictures in a cave near Sallèles-Cabardès
(discovered in the Aude department in 1947) are also mid-
Magdalenian in style.

29 BISON, MAGDALENIAN Ussat, Grotte des Eglises (Ariège

The art of this period likewise displays a feature that, save in palæolithic and in 19th-century art, is hardly to be found elsewhere in or out of Europe. I am referring to a certain way of representing a multitude of figures. An art which appeals wholly to the eye must not show a mass of figures as a collection of clearly distinguished individuals, but the impression must be conveyed of a whole, consisting of parts which merge into each other. When, for instance, Liebermann painted the arrival of the Queen of the Netherlands at Amsterdam, the only clearly defined figure in the crowd is that of the policeman in the foreground. The mass of people behind is nothing but a multicoloured haze. However, palæolithic artists had already hit upon this device when, for instance, they made that Teyjat engraving on bone[1] representing a herd of reindeer (Fig. 31). The herd is there but we see it not as a collection of individual

[1] The scene of the advancing herd of reindeer is engraved upon a piece of bone and was recovered from the Teyjat site, in the Dordogne department.

40

animals but as a mass in movement. The herd is moving to the right. The three leading animals are distinctly depicted, as is one beast to the left. The rest are shown as a mass of strokes and a row of upraised antlers. The significant thing about this picture is that the artist has drawn the scene not as he knows it was but as it seems to the eye—what is seen at a glance, the blurred, flowing, fleeting herd of beasts.

In the case of the first animal and the last, the body is shaded, the surface of the skin is indicated, perspective is reproduced. The great antlers, the legs, the ears are all plain. Less distinct are the second and third reindeer while the remainder are but strokes and antlers. This technique was not, so far as we know, employed again between the end of the Ice Age and about the year A.D. 1900.

Such a device would not have been possible in Egyptian or in Mesopotamian art. There is no such convention in the

30 IBEX, MAGDALENIAN Gazel, near Sallèles-Cabardès (Aude)

41

31 HERD OF REINDEER MOVING FORWARD Teyjat (Dordogne)

arts of China or Japan. We might have looked for some such
treatment in the Roman art of the 1st and 2nd centuries
A.D. but there is no trace of it. The convention is quite
foreign to the Middle Ages, nor does it appear in Renaissance, Baroque, Rococo or 'Romantic' art.

It is also noteworthy that a problem of perspective is
inherent in the representation of a mass of figures. In the
Teyjat engraving the problem is solved thus: in the foreground, to the left, the antlers are larger, the strokes are
firmer, stronger, bolder; after the middle, they become
smaller, thinner, lighter. The mass loses itself over to the
right until the three leading beasts stand out clear and distinct before the herd.

On a piece of bone from Isturitz (Basses-Pyrénées) are
depicted four horses' heads. That nearest to one as one looks
at the engraving is about 12 millimetres long, the second
10 millimetres, the third 8 millimetres and the fourth 5

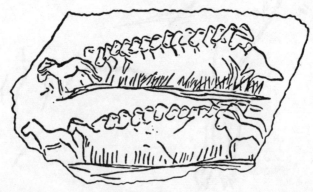

32 TWO HERDS OF WILD HORSES, ENGRAVING ON BONE, MAGDALENIAN Chaffaud
(Vienne)

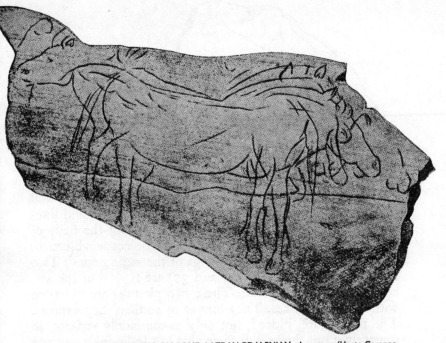

millimetres.[1] An obvious representation of perspective. Again, on a piece of bone from Le Souci, near Lalinde, Dordogne, there are also four horses' heads, one behind the other. The first measures 14 millimetres and the last 4 millimetres. This object is late Magdalenian.

Still another example of perspective in palæolithic art is a drawing from Chaffaud (Fig. 32) (department of Vienne); two herds of horses are depicted but only the first and last members are clearly delineated. The other animals are represented by a mass of hoofs and heads. We see the whole not as an assemblage of individuals but as it appears to our eyes.

After the 'pictorial' phase of Ice Age art there follows another linear style. Small art-objects excavated at Lespugue (Fig. 33), at Bruniquel and at Isturitz (Fig. 34), and

[1] These dimensions are so small that it is not easy to express them in divisions of an inch, but 12 millimetres is about half an inch.

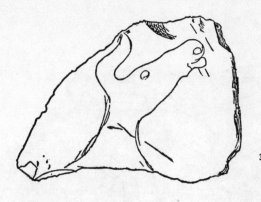

belonging to the most recent strata of the Magdalenian, well illustrate this new artistic style. The rather thin, bold lines are executed with great sureness of touch, but the body of the image is not elaborated. These small objects enable us to date the large-scale rock-paintings of the same period. Two horses at Altamira (Figs. 35 and 37) are typical of the art-conventions of this phase. These two pictures are executed with but few strokes. They hint at more than they express. The figures are, indeed, not only uncommonly striking in themselves but they recall somewhat the India-ink paintings of the Japanese artists, and that both in the abbreviation of the strokes as well as in the sureness of touch.

If the outline pictures of this art-phase of the Palæolithic consist of only a few strokes, these are of great dexterity and

35 GALLOPING WILD HORSE, LATE MAGDALENIAN Altamira

skill—although it is true that there is no more plastic quality, no more depth, no more perspective. Once again, the outline *is* the picture. It may not be fanciful to compare this art with that of Van Gogh, Cézanne and Matisse.

But these outline figures of the late Magdalenian differ from those of earlier times, of the Aurignacian. The Magdalenian outlines are more simple, they extract the picture, as it were, from its background, and present it in an assured manner.

This latest Magdalenian art came to an end with the Ice Age. Palæolithic pictures began as simple outlines. Then came a movement rising to a peak of richly pictorial forms. After that we get a convention of contour outline once more.

One question must occur to us as we review the course and the nature of Ice Age art. What sort of men could they have been who painted such things? Well, they were men who lived in a lowly stage of material culture. They took what nature offered them. The men of the Ice Age produced nothing at all, they only consumed. There were, as yet, no forms of agriculture, no domestic animals—not any pottery. The men hunted and the women gathered plants and fruits. We are, in fact, in an age of hunters and food-gatherers, the earliest phase of human economy. Men lived, it would seem, in small groups—more like large families than tribes as we understand the word. As men must move with their quarry, they had continuously to discover new places in which to live.

36 HEAD OF A HIND, LATE
MAGDALENIAN
Les Combarelles

45

37 WILD HORSE, LATE MAGDALENIAN Altamira

Such a roving, rambling, hunting existence still survives among certain Eskimo, the Australian aborigines, the Bushmen of South Africa, the Veddah in Ceylon and such a way of life lingers, mostly as a memory, with the vanishing Ainu in the northernmost island of Japan.

However, the Ice Age men did have more or less permanent settlements, as is shown by the excavations of palæolithic dwelling-sites at Willendorf, at Wisternitz, at Předmost, and at Moravány in Czechoslovakia, as well as at the Russian settlements such as Kastnskaya on the middle course of the Lena, Kostienki on the Don, Puskari, Buret and Timonovka. Families, it seems, sometimes lived long at these sites, and hunters would repair to them again and again. It is also certain that several caves in France served as homes for Ice Age man.[1]

Not only the primitive character of the Ice Age economy but also the lack of anything making for social differentiation explains the unity of European culture of those remote times. Indeed, the essential cultural content is the same for all Europe—and for northern Asia. The old theory that there was an Eastern art-province distinguished from a Western one seems to be erroneous. The art of the East—of all over Siberia to the Chinese borders—is the same as that of France and Spain. The tools and utensils and instruments tally, in the main, over the whole of this immense area and that down to slight variations such as a special sort of Cantabrian notched point.

Migrations, movements of peoples and wanderings of tribes are indicated by the occurrence in various places of

[1] Especially those with no pictures and which, consequently, were not cult-caves.

46

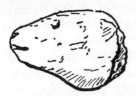

38 (a) HEAD OF A BEAR Unter-Wisterwitz (Moravia)
    (b) HEAD OF A BEAR IN BONE Isturitz (Basses-Pyrénées)

certain sorts of shells, the principal medium of exchange in
those days, though we must imagine 'trade' as being mostly
barter from hand to hand. For instance, at the Kesslerloch
cave near Thayngen in Switzerland were found ornaments
made out of shells that come only from the Mediterranean
and the Atlantic. At Krems, on the Danube, have also been
found shells that occur only in the Mediterranean; while the
shell-ornaments from Linsenberg near Mainz and from the
Ofnet cavern [1] are likewise Mediterranean in origin.

Art-objects also travelled far. In the Isturitz cave (Fig. 38)
was brought to light a bear's head that is almost the exact
double of one discovered at Unterwisternitz in Czechoslovakia. Such finds obviously indicate barter, and consequently travel, over considerable distances. Statuettes of
female figures, closely similar in type and in execution, are
known not only from the Mediterranean, from southern
France, from Germany, Czechoslovakia and Austria, but we
come across them also in Siberia and particularly at the
Malta site on the Yenissei River, near Lake Baikal. The
Aurignacian-type artefacts found at this latter place resemble
those of France.

The art of the rocks, on the contrary, did not spread so far.
It is confined to certain areas. One of these is in south-
central France, especially in the Dordogne department, and
another is in the Cantabrian Mountains of northern Spain.
However, there are painted caves in other regions of France
(such as the Lot department and the Corrèze) and prehistoric caverns with pictures in areas so remote from the
Cantabrian Mountains as the Spanish provinces of Guadalajara and Málaga.

But outside France and Spain only three caves with

[1] And also from Schlossfelsen near Birseck in Switzerland.

palæolithic pictures have been found.[1] One is the Romanelli cavern near Castro, about thirty miles or so south of Lecce in Apulia. This site offers but a few and not very important engravings.[2] Of greater interest is the cave (discovered in 1949 and explored by Graziosi in 1950) on the island of Levanzo off the west coast of Sicily (Plate XXIV). At Schulerloch near Kehlheim in Germany (Plate XVI) was found in 1937 a group of Aurignacian-style engravings consisting of an ibex, faint traces of a trap and a female human figure.

The grouping of the prehistoric painted caves indicates that the men of the Ice Age had their settlements mostly far to the south of the glaciers' fringe. It was in this region that were the cult-sanctuaries of the men of the Late Palæolithic. When men went out hunting in the spring and summer, most likely they took their ornaments, their 'wizards' staves' and their small female statuettes with them. However, the pictures upon the rocks, the pictures that hallowed the sanctuaries, could not be displaced: and Ice Age winters were long while the summers were as short and as hot as those in Siberia today.

Palæolithic art has not been known and recognized for very long. It was during the last century that we first obtained information about these very ancient phases of Man's culture. It was in 1840 that Brouillet, a notary of Charroux who was making geological investigations in the Chaffaud grotto near Savigné in the department of the Vienne, discovered a piece of bone engraved with the figures of two hinds (Fig. 39). In 1851 this piece came into the possession of the Cluny Museum in Paris, but the engraving attracted no attention there. No one knew of anything like it. However, in 1853, Prosper Mérimée[3] sent a sketch of the object to Worsaae, then director of the

---

[1] This is rather too low an estimate and in any case to those mentioned in the text must be added the Addaura cave in Sicily. (Translator's Note.)

[2] The Romanelli cave, however, has a most curious painted rock with signs that Professor Blanc of Rome recognizes as a "sort of very primitive writing". (Translator's Note.)

[3] Prosper Mérimée (1803–1870), who besides being a celebrated writer was Inspector-General of French Historical Monuments.

39 TWO HINDS HIT BY ARROWS, BONE, MAGDALENIAN Chaffaud (Vienne)

Stockholm Museum, who could make no useful suggestions. In 1861, however, Lartet[1] began his excavations in the Dordogne where he found, and published, engravings resembling that from Chaffaud. Whereupon Mérimée informed Lartet about Brouillet's find over twenty years before. Lartet recognized the antiquity of the Chaffaud piece and published a description of it.

Another piece of Ice Age artistry was found at Veyrier near Salève in the Haute-Savoie department, near the Swiss frontier and not far from Geneva. Taillefer had been making geological studies at Veyrier since 1834. When the piece from Chaffaud was published, attention was attracted to the Veyrier engraving which was published both by Alphonse Favre and by Gabriel de Mortillet in 1878.

However, it is to Edouard Lartet that we owe our first real knowledge about the men of the Ice Age. In 1860 he was excavating at Massat in the Ariège while his friend Milne-Edwards[2] was at the same time digging in the Espelugues grotto near Lourdes. Milne-Edwards, moreover, from 1862 onwards, worked in the Bruniquel cavern in the Dordogne. Systematic excavations, indeed, in the Dordogne region really started at La Laugerie-Haute in 1863 and at La Madeleine in the following year.

By 1871 Piette had begun his work at the Gourdan cave near Montréjeau in the Haute-Garonne department. He also excavated the Lorthet and Arudy grottoes in the

[1] Edouard Lartet (1801–1871), French archæologist.
[2] Henry Milne-Edwards (1800–1885) was, despite his name, a Frenchman and was a well-known zoologist; his son Alphonse (1835–1900), a palæontologist, was professor at the Museum of Natural History.

Hautes-Pyrénées. It was in 1874 that K. Merck and Heim got to work on the Thayngen site near Schaffhausen. From the middle '70s onwards every year brought forth its complement of art-treasures from the caves. I have given an account of these discoveries in another book.

It was in 1879 that the Altamira paintings were found. The cave had been stumbled upon by some sportsman whose dog disappeared down what looked like a fox-hole. A Spanish gentleman who resided in the neighbourhood, Don Marcelino de Sautuola, had seen, at Paris, some of the prehistoric engraved bones and stones. He began to excavate at Altamira. One day he took his daughter with him and she it was who first saw the famous paintings. Sautuola knew that the cave was unexplored and had until shortly before been quite unknown, so he concluded that the pictures must be of the same period as the artefacts found in the strata of the cavern, that is to say, of Ice Age date.

In 1880 the International Congress of Anthropology and Prehistoric Archæology met in Lisbon. The most prominent anthropologists of the day were present, but Sautuola did not manage to convince them of the great antiquity of the Altamira pictures. The cave and its paintings were forgotten. No one at the time would believe in the existence of Ice Age art.

It was two later discoveries that demonstrated the authenticity of palæolithic drawings and paintings. First of all came the Pair-non-Pair cavern near Marcamps in the Gironde. The site had been known since 1881 and Daleau, who worked there from that time, found six Aurignacian strata and under the lowest of them a Mousterian layer. He had, however, spent no less than fifteen seasons in the cavern before, on 3rd August, 1896, he made out, for the first time, figures of animals upon the walls, figures which had been completely hidden by mid-Magdalenian strata. Daleau in 1897 published his first report upon his finds, but it was hardly noticed at all.

The second significant discovery was that of La Mouthe. Here, on 11th April, 1895, Emile Rivière recognized engravings upon the cave's walls. It is worth while stressing the fact that Rivière had been working at La Mouthe for no less than forty-nine years before the removal of the accumulation of fillings revealed the pictures. When Pair-non-Pair and La Mouthe were recognized as sites of Ice Age art, attention was drawn to two other caves already discovered. They were Marsoulas in the Haute-Garonne and Chabot in the Gard.

So, by 1896, if we count Altamira, five grottoes with prehistoric wall-paintings or engravings had been revealed. Still hardly anyone of the archæologists of those days would recognize the pictures for what they were. It was not really until the revelation of Les Combarelles (on 9th September, 1901) and of Le Font-de-Gaume (on 12th September of the same year) that attention was again drawn to Altamira. In September 1902, Cartailhac, and a young prehistorian called Henri Breuil, began their systematic exploration of Altamira.

In 1903 were discovered Bernifal near Les Eyzies, La Calévie and Teyjat near Montron in the Dordogne. Then followed, fast one upon the other, the great finds in northern Spain: 11th September, 1903, Covalanas; 13th September, 1903, La Haza; 21st July, 1903, Salitre; and Hornos de la Peña in the same year. El Castillo was explored on 8th November, 1903; Venta de la Perra on 16th August, 1904; Santián (in the Province of Santander) in 1905. 1906 was marked by the discovery of La Clotilde de Santa Isabel, Sotarriza (Santander), Spain; of Gargas in the Hautes-Pyrénées, and above all of Niaux (Ariège) France—and also by the publication of Breuil's celebrated work on the Altamira Cave.

Further discoveries were:

In 1907, El Pendo (Santander) and Pindal (Asturias), Spain.

In 1908, Le Portel (Ariège) and Laussel (Dordogne, France) with wall-engravings.

In 1912, La Pasiega near Puente Viesgo (Santander) and Le Tuc d'Audoubert (Ariège).

In 1913, Isturitz (Basses-Pyrénées).

In 1914, Peña de Candamo (Asturias), Cueto de la Mina (Asturias) and Les Trois-Frères (Ariège).

In 1917, Santimamiñe (Vizcaya) Spain.

In 1923, the important site of Montespan (Haute-Garonne) France.

In 1927, Fauzan (Hérault) France.

The most significant discovery of all this century was that of Lascaux in 1940, while in the same year Labaume-Latronne was explored.

In 1950, Levanzo off the Sicilian coast, and also Etcheberri and Jasisloaga (Basses-Pyrénées).

In 1951 began the revelation of the Magdalenian works of art at Angle-sur-Anglin.

Sites which have yielded only small objects embedded in the strata are not mentioned at all, while only the more significant of the prehistoric caverns have been included in the above list.

The number of painted and engraved grottoes is, indeed, very great: some one hundred and six—seventy in France, thirty-three in Spain, two in Italy and one in Germany. Since several of these caves contain hundreds of paintings, drawings or sculptures, our knowledge of Ice Age art is founded on an abundant material.

The revelation of Ice Age art is due first and foremost to the Abbé Henri Breuil. His explorations, his researches, his published works and his reproductions of paintings created, in fact, a new and most important scientific discipline. The study of prehistoric art owes much also to Count Bégouen and to the late Hugo Obermaier.

Pictures Dating from Between
10,000 and 2000 B.C.

SUMMARY

THE tradition, the significance and the influence of the Ice Age pictures were so great that the art did not die out (rather suddenly, indeed) as was once supposed. The palæolithic heritage lived on for millennia.

There are four principal groups of prehistoric art which are linked up with the traditions of the Ice age. These groups are: those of North Africa, of Levantine Spain, of Scandinavia and of Russia.

All four groups retained for long the legacy of sensorial art; nevertheless, in the course of time, the naturalistic style weakened. This evolution can be clearly seen upon the painted rocks where, when there has been overpainting, the naturalistic pictures invariably are overlaid by schematic, stylized designs. The development in these post-glacial times was, then, the opposite to that during the Ice Age itself, in which the evolution was from the linear to the pictorial which reached its apogee in mid-Magdalenian times. The later Magdalenian culture-phase was, as we have already seen, one of renewed linear technique with which is linked the art of post-glacial times. In no place is this art really pictorial. Even in its earliest form it is strongly linear (and in this it maintains the late-Magdalenian tradition) but as time goes on it loses its essentially linear character and becomes gradually more and more schematized.

This tendency may be observed in all the four groups. There are very often overpaintings so that the relative dating of the pictures is not difficult to determine. There is no single exception to the rule that the naturalistic pictures lie below, the stylized above.

Much discussion has taken place as to whether the Scandinavian rock-engravings really do continue the traditions of the Ice Age. It has been suggested that these engravings resemble more closely Aurignacian than Magdalenian pictures. In this view there seems to be some misapprehension. The developed, naturalistic, polychrome paintings do not occur at the end of Ice Age art but at its peak period. It is the linear art of the late Magdalenian that forms the starting-point for the art of post-glacial times.

In all four groups, in North Africa, in Levantine Spain, in Scandinavia and in Russia, the basic, the original, tradition is that of sensorial art, of naturalistic pictures though presented in a linear technique. It is only with the passage of time that the art stiffens, the forms assume a more harsh appearance until finally the naturalistic mode is quite abandoned. What takes its place is an imaginative art, not imitation but something conceived, something tending to the abstract.

But these four groups we are considering display at first a sensorial art even if its technique is linear. The aim is still the reproduction of things seen, not of things imagined. It is not, indeed, until we get to the New Stone Age and to the Bronze Age that we find a purely imaginative art. Here the essence is quite different, the content, the values entirely changed. This imaginative art reflects a world in which men's preoccupations are no longer exclusively centred upon the Here and the Now.

After the close of the Palæolithic or Old Stone Age, there is a long period, known as the Mesolithic or Middle Stone Age, leading eventually to the Neolithic. This Mesolithic was formerly thought of as a relatively short epoch since comparatively few discoveries of artefacts were made in mesolithic strata. The rock-pictures, however, alone, indicate that the Mesolithic lasted a long time. In northern Europe, indeed, its duration was from about 8000 to 2000 B.C. or a span of six thousand years. In southern Europe, the epoch lasted as long, if not longer, but as it started earlier and ended earlier, the figures would be from about 10,000 to 3000 B.C.

In recent years the number of mesolithic finds has greatly increased and our whole view of the epoch, or culture-phase, has become much clearer. Pottery appears towards the end of this period but remains rare throughout. The main difficulty in obtaining information about the mesolithic way of life arises from the fact that men no longer lived in caves or rock-shelters but in huts half sunk in the ground or beside wind-breaks. Such structures, however, are very perishable and much more difficult to trace than Ice Age Man's homes in the caverns or Neolithic Man's settlements marked by an abundance of pottery. In fact, the mesolithic dwellings were made of wood and thus have left only traces of discoloration in the soil and since the occupation trenches reveal, generally, only small worked flints and very little pottery, the discovery and the recognition of a mesolithic site is much more a matter of luck than anything else.

However, in recent years so many finds have been made that characteristic mesolithic material has become quite easy to recognize. In the Mesolithic, however, regional differences (such as are not noticeable in the Upper Palæolithic) begin to be recognizable. One type of mesolithic object is called 'Azilian' and occurs in France and Spain. It takes its name from the Mas d'Azil site in southern France. Another group is the 'Tardenoisian' (so called from La Fère-en-Tardenois in the Aisne department of France). A third group is the 'Campignian' whose type-site is at Campigny in the French Seine-Maritime department. Campignian is common in Belgium and in western Germany. Still another group, in southern Europe and in North Africa, is known as 'Capsian', from Capsa, the Roman name for the town in southern Tunisia now called Gafsa.

So we have a number of post-glacial cultures that differ among themselves but which have one feature in common— the continuation of the great palæolithic tradition in art and in artefacts.

The Levantine Spanish group is, in style and in content, certainly related to the African group and it looks, indeed, as though the Capsian style has survived until today in the Bushman art of South Africa.

There is a further North African group that consists

mostly of engravings and whose centre is in the Saharan Atlas in the south-west of the Algerian province of Oran.

In many ways, also, the Scandinavian group of rock-engravings shows clearly a connection with palæolithic traditions but in the North the rock-art followed its own peculiar line of development. Related to the Scandinavian rupestral art is that of the Russian engravings by the shores of Lake Onega and of the White Sea. The Siberian group is closely allied to that of European Russia but, being outside Europe, neither the Siberian nor the North African pre-historic pictures fall within the province of this book.

Still, however different, in style, in technique, and in vision these groups may be if we compare them with one another, nevertheless, they all display the movement we have referred to—that from a sensorial form of art to an imaginative one. At the end of the epoch there is stylization everywhere. It is reached sooner in southern than in northern Europe. That is all. In southern Europe there occurs earlier the switch-over from the matter-of-fact, realistic point of view of the hunter to the very different one of the agriculturalist. Agricultures are dominated by the seasons and are bound up with the soil, the sun, the wind, the rain. The agriculturalist's attention is turned towards the divine Powers that bring warmth, fructifying rain, dew—and storms. With the practice of an agriculture men turn their thoughts to a Being above, one that no human will can command. Men's aim, then, is directed towards the moving of this Being in the way they think favourable to them. So we get the sacrifice of field-fruits, we get prayer, we get sacraments. And the more, in such a culture-phase, men reach out in thought to what is beyond their sight and touch, the more their art will be removed from the incidental and will attempt the portrayal of eternal forces which can be represented only in geometrical forms, in circles, in triangles, in squares.

In all the art-groups we have mentioned, progress towards stylization can be clearly perceived, but nowhere is the process so rapid as in southern Europe where conditions were the most favourable for cultivation of the soil.

The North kept longer to old traditions. Agriculture appears rather late. In the great forests men still hunted. In the lakes fish were caught as in the Ice Age. With a palæolithic mode of life went palæolithic modes of thought.

We may, then, sum up thus: the art traditions of the Ice Age did not die out but were carried on. Nevertheless, differences developed, differences that are the reflection of diversified conditions and circumstances. The change-over to new modes comes sooner in the South than in the North, yet everywhere there is the same tendency away from a naturalistic art to a stylized one.

THE ROCK-PAINTINGS OF
LEVANTINE SPAIN

ON Spanish soil there is a group of rock-paintings linked to palæolithic art and known as the Levantine. The pictures of this Levantine group occupy an area from about Barcelona in the north to the province of Málaga in the south. The sites are, for the most part, not very far from the coast, but some of them reach as far inland as Cuenca. By 1952 some twenty-nine sets of rock-shelters were known and some of these display as many as five hundred or even more pictures. There is, therefore, plenty of material for the study of this art.

Although the Levantine paintings are closely linked with Ice Age art, they show, as a whole, features and characteristics which are highly peculiar. In only a few of the sites are there polychrome paintings. Generally speaking the pictures are in monochrome and they are silhouette-like, they have no depth. Yet this art shows a new impetus. The human forms display a sense of movement and of life that is quite alien to the Ice Age art of France and northern Spain. There is, moreover, in this Levantine art a decisive factor—the reproduction of scenes, of assemblages. In Ice Age art there are just isolated figures of animals although occasionally groups or herds are depicted. There is a small engraving on bone from La Laugerie Basse (Dordogne) that shows a figure of a man stealing up upon a bison. There is, also, of course, the scene of the bison, the man, the bird and the rhinoceros at Lascaux (Plate XXIII). Scenes, however, in Palæolithic art are so rare as to be negligible.

In the Levantine Spanish art, however, the scene is developed as a constant and, in fact, a principal aim of the artist. There are many scenes of the chase. There are warriors in processions. There are men fighting (Plate XXVII). Men are shown slaying another man. There are pictures that look like scenes of punishment being inflicted by the group

58

or tribe (Figs. 43 and 55). There are scenes of honey-gathering (Plate XXX) and of the dance.

From one point of view, then, the Spanish Levantine art is richer than that of the Ice Age, even if there has been a loss of depth and of space. But this is a linear art, an art of the draughtsman. The pictorial, it is true, is abandoned, but new values are won.

Discussions concerning the dating of this Spanish Levantine art have not yet quite died down. One of the difficulties in assigning an age to these pictures is due to the fact that none of them has yet been found hidden by fillings or cave-strata. In the regions of the paintings there are no caves from which we might hope to extract small art-objects or artefacts. The pictures are in natural hollows of the rock-face, in rock-shelters. Many of the figures are exposed to rain, sun and weathering. Excavations at the foot of the rocks have yielded but little—a few stone tools and that is all. We lack, therefore, almost entirely, those significant resemblances between small objects and great pictures that we get in northern Spain and in France. It is generally easy enough to date any given stratum at an Ice Age site. The artefacts can be sorted out as early, middle or late Aurignacian or as belonging to one of the phases of the Magdalenian.

For our Levantine pictures we must seek other means of dating. Stylistically the Levantine art resembles that of the Ice Age in that both are naturalistic. The Levantine artists, and those who painted the palæolithic pictures of France and northern Spain, were men who lived in similar economic conditions, those of the hunter and food-gatherer. However, these two considerations by no means prove that the two sets of pictures were executed at the same times.

Men of the post-glacial epochs were also hunters and food-gatherers. The agricultures developed very slowly indeed. And as for the similarity in style, we must confess that that consideration is not conclusive. The Scandinavian rock-engravings are also naturalistic, but none of them can possibly be assigned to the Ice Age, since during late palæolithic times the whole of Scandinavia was buried under a heavy mantle of glaciers.

It may be advanced that the two picture-groups in Spain (that is the Levantine and the Ice Age, mostly centred in the Cantabrian region) correspond to two distinct areas of human occupation, that one does not impinge upon the other and that, consequently, the two arts may have been the creation of two separate human groups which lived at the same time but in different areas. Ice Age art is known as Franco-Cantabrian because it occurs in France and in the Cantabrian mountains. It must be attributed to men of the Aurignacian and Magdalenian culture-phases. The Levantine art is confined to eastern Spain and may be attributed to a population living in a Capsian culture-phase, and 'Capsian' designates a special sort of stone chipping technique markedly different from Aurignacian, Solutrean or Magdalenian.

However, this theory of the contemporaneity of two groups of artists in Spain has, in recent times, been badly shaken. Some considerable time ago there were found cave-pictures in southern Spain [1] which must be referred not to the Levantine art-complex but to that of the Cantabrian north. Moreover, in 1934, there were discovered two caverns [2] not far from Madrid. Their engravings are not, as might, perhaps, have been expected, in the Levantine style but in that of a pure Franco-Cantabrian palæolithic art.

And there is a third site of importance for our problem. In 1929 Cabré excavated the cavern of Parpalló, not far from Gandía in the province of Valencia. It lies right in the area of Levantine Spanish art. It is true that Parpalló contains no wall-paintings or engravings, still from the cave-filling were recovered more than sixty small art-objects, all in Franco-Cantabrian style. The accompanying artefacts are Magdalenian with the exception of one Solutrean stone instrument.

These three instances of Ice Age art occurring in the 'province' of Levantine Spanish art seem to be conclusive.

[1] La Pileta cavern which is frequently referred to as being near Málaga. As a matter of fact La Pileta (near the small town of Benoaján) lies in the extreme west of the province of Málaga and some sixty miles or more from the town of Málaga. (Translator's Note.)

[2] Los Cazares and La Hoz in the province of Guadalajara.

In the Spanish prehistoric pictures we are faced not with two contemporaneous phenomena but with an earlier and a later art. To these considerations we must add that recent investigations have shown the Capsian to be a neolithic culture-phase. In North Africa pottery has been recovered from Capsian sites. Excavations at the foot of the Levantine rock-paintings in the Valltorta ravine have revealed a post-glacial stratum with post-glacial artefacts. The digging at the foot of the Albarracín and Bicorp pictures disclosed similar post-glacial stone instruments together with a neolithic hatchet.

A further reason used to be advanced in favour of an Ice Age dating for the Levantine pictures. On some of the sites, it was thought, an elk, a wild ass, a rhinoceros or a bison could be distinguished. Nevertheless the identifications of none of such figures is certain enough for us to build upon it a whole theory of dating. In any case, the rocks on which these animals have been made out are very few in number.

We cannot maintain, either, that the Levantine art reflects a purely hunting culture. At Villar del Humo (in the province of Cuenca) there is a man leading a horse by a halter (Plate XXXI). A similar scene is shown at Doña Clotilde (Plate XXIX). The world of the Levantine artists was not the same as the world of the Ice Age hunters. There is every reason to hold that the Spanish Levantine paintings are not glacial but post-glacial. They are linked with the Ice Age tradition but they developed in a new and peculiar way.

Moreover, there is a difference in spiritual content. The Levantine pictures are instinct with religious feeling. As was the Ice Age art, the Levantine paintings were created for reasons of magic, of wizardry. Luck must be attracted to the hunter by the representation of killed and stricken beasts.

In the Levantine pictures arrows and missiles are more often shown in the animal figures. The actual chase itself is more frequently depicted than in Ice Age art. If we stand before a complex of these paintings and take into account the landscape, the site and emplacement of the painted rocks, we must conclude that we are faced with an art created for magic, for enchantments.

First and foremost this is indicated by the sites themselves. The pictures occur on certain rocks in certain ravines. Similar rocks and ravines in the neighbourhood were not utilized. There are, indeed, special niches, special high places, painted and re-painted, adorned and re-adorned throughout the centuries. On the great Minateda frieze thirteen layers can be made out, one upon the other. On this rock-face were recorded all the art-phases of post-glacial times, right up to evolved Neolithic. The oldest pictures are those of great beasts, naturalistically treated. Their colours still show through the later paintings the wizards laid upon them. Painting lies upon painting but not in such a way that every portion of the space is utilized. The pictures overlap everywhere; the older beneath; the most recent right at the surface.

In the Cueva de Mas d'en Josep in the Valltorta ravine there is a bison that later was transformed into a wild boar (Fig. 40). But the boar still has a bison's tail and the bison's horns are still apparent. Arrows shoot towards the animal. Maybe the magic of this drawing was so potent, that the lucky hunter would not abandon a place so propitious for securing good fortune in the chase; thus the picture was worked over into the semblance of another beast.

Representations of shamans or wizards are less frequent in Levantine paintings than in those of the Franco-Cantabrian group. Still, forms of medicine-men do occur, as in newly discovered sites in the Gasulla ravine. There may be

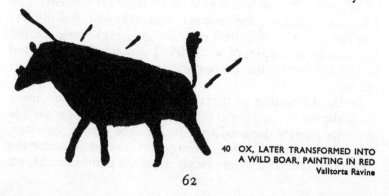

40 OX, LATER TRANSFORMED INTO
A WILD BOAR, PAINTING IN RED
Valltorta Ravine

62

seen a man with a spiky mask and an animal's tail. He is
shown clambering up something that is either a rope-ladder
or a wickerwork trellis. Another shaman wears a great
animal-mask, a bull-mask (Fig. 41). Yet another bears upon
his head elk's horns, while his feet are as bison's hoofs.
Before this last wizard stands a hunter with bow and arrow.
It may be that this is a representation of a magic dance. At
Alpera there is an obvious cult-dance. Nine women are
swirling round a man, but the significance of the scene is
difficult to determine.

In these Levantine pictures there are also scenes that we
must most probably read as magic pictures for encompassing
the destruction of men. In the Cueva Saltadora (of the
Gasulla ravine) is a picture of a man, probably a chieftain,
who is collapsing under an onslaught of arrows. He is still
managing to hold his bow in his hand. One arm rests against
his knee, but the head droops sadly forward and the body
is pierced with missiles. On his head is a crown-like object
that may be an insignia of rank (Fig. 42). In the Gasulla
ravine also is a picture of men shooting at a hunter as he lies
upon the ground (Fig. 43). He props himself up a little on
his arms but his legs are beating the air while the arrows fly
towards him. In the same ravine, also, is a procession of

42 HUNTER HIT BY ARROWS Cueva Saltadora, Valltorta Ravine (Province of Castellón, Spain)

warriors in Indian file most probably performing some cult-dance or ceremony (Plate XXXII).

All these pictures are pictures of enchantments. The Levantine art most certainly belongs to the sphere of magic art. Animals, however, are comparatively rare. Magic is rather exercised upon the hunter than upon the hunted. Therefore the hunter is depicted in movement. He is hurrying, rushing about. He is seen in the excitement of the chase upon these Written Rocks that brought him good luck.

However, we cannot say that in the Levantine pictures magic is the sole motive of art. There is also what we might call 'reporting'. We have pictures that tell a tale. Occurrences are depicted.

The world of post-glacial times was, then, in the main, dominated by the hunt. The chase lay in the forefront of men's preoccupations and commanded their lives. Nevertheless the art had changed.

Man had come to realize himself and to take his place at the centre of things. If the Ice Age was a period when Man's vision was directed towards the outer world, we can seem to sense in this Levantine post-glacial art Man's conquest of himself, first of all in the realization of his bodily appearance, his movements, the rhythm of his gestures. For the first time we get an anecdotal art. We are at the beginning of the old, familiar story of Man and his fate. We have gone a step beyond the Ice Age and beyond mere magic.

We can liken the evolution of Ice Age art to a curve that rises to a culminating point and then falls to the level of the first point plotted on the graph. The post-glacial art stems from the linear art of the last palæolithic phase, yet it does not develop into a 'pictorial' art but moves farther and farther into the stylized until the purely imaginative is reached. So the oldest pictures are the most naturalistic. They are, from the Impressionist point of view, the best pictures. The development is steadily towards the abstract.

This tendency is evident not from any one frieze of pictures but it can be observed in the overpaintings at Cogul, at Alpera (Plate XXVIII), at Minateda (Plate XXVII), at Cantos de la Visera, at Tabla de Pochico, at Cueva del Santo, at Bicorp, at Doña Clotilde, Albarracín (Plate XXIX). Everywhere the evolution is the same, towards a stylization whose end is the schematic, the sign, often astonishingly like a letter or an ideograph or a letter in a script.

Levantine Spanish art gives us no plasticity, no appearance of depth, of light. There is none of the enchantment of

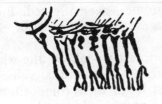

43 SCENE OF AN EXECUTION
Gasulla Ravine

44 HUNTER
Cueva Remigia, Gasulla Ravine (Province of Castellón, Spain)

colour. There is no attempt at the three-dimensional. With the exception of a few of the oldest paintings which are polychrome—such as some at Albarracín—the Levantine paintings are in monochrome—generally red. But no ancient art conveys more sense of movement, of elation, of animated rhythm.

In the Levantine Spanish art we take in the whole complex at a glance. The æsthetic and spiritual value and significance of the paintings lie in their composition, in the relation of the component parts to the whole. Ice Age art built up a picture from separate parts. Often the palæolithic artist drew only the head of an animal, but this head has a life of its own. It is a complete work of art without the body. Sometimes only a leg is shown or a body with no head. So in Greek art a torso has its own life. It is impressive even if an important part of the whole is lacking.

In the Levantine art, however, the whole complex is constructed as a unit whose parts can live no individual life of their own. Limbs are significant only in relation to the whole body and thus they may often appear distorted,

66

45 SPEEDING HUNTER
Gasulla Ravine

46 HUNTER
Cuevas del Civil, Valltorta Ravine
(Castellón)

unreal, unnatural. No attempt was made to reproduce, in detail, the natural forms. What was sought was to convey an impression of violence, of action. The men in these pictures are running, hunting, falling down, jumping, dashing through the air. Their legs are wide stretched. Their bodies are thrust forward. They are reduced to bundles of lines that express nothing but movement, swiftness, dash (Figs. 45 to 51).

There are three main stages in the Levantine art. First we get large, still naturalistically drawn, figures of animals. In the second stage we have silhouettes of animals and of hurrying hunters. The third stage is that of stylized, geometrical figures among which naturalism fades entirely away.

But, as we have seen, from the point of view of composition, the most significant achievement of these mesolithic artists was the presentation of the Scene. For instance, in the

47 HUNTER Cuevas de la Araña   48 HUMAN FIGURE Gasulla Ravine

49 HUNTER Gasulla Ravine

50 HUNTER Cueva Remigia, Gasulla Ravine (Castellón)   51 HUNTER Alacón (Teruel)

Valltorta ravine there is a *battue* depicted (Fig. 52). The hunters are shooting their arrows into a galloping herd of stags and hinds. Behind the beasts must be the beaters, but we have to imagine them. The artist leaves them for us to supply. A layer of calcite sweated from the rock has glazed the whole assemblage.

There is a very charming scene shown in a hollow of the Cueva de la Araña near Bicorp (Plate XXX). A natural hole in the rock-face has been transformed into a beehive.

52 SCENE OF THE CHASE Valltorta Ravine, near Albocácer (Castellón)

Two human figures, probably women, are clambering up ropes to reach the hole. One has a vessel of some sort on her back. She is down below on the rope ladder that is flexed. The other woman has already got to the top. She holds her basket in her hand and is surrounded with huge bees. A vivid picture of men's lives in mesolithic Spain. In Alpera, there is also a painting of a man climbing up a rope (Plate XXVIII).

In the Cueva Remigia of the Gasulla ravine is a spirited hunting scene (Fig. 53). Two men are attacking an ibex. The larger of the two (possibly intended as the one nearer to the animal) has his bow bent and his arrow ready. His right hand is drawn back. His left hand holds several arrows. The left leg is flexed but the right juts out behind as though taut with nervous tension. The ibex is charging at full speed. Under the first man's feet can be made out the figure of another man also shooting at the ibex, while still a third man, who has not yet drawn his bow, is running up to the assistance of the other two. The picture makes an extraordinarily powerful impression. Yet the representation of the human figures is in no way realistic, or naturalistic. There is here expressed the higher reality of imaginative thought, of movement.

From the same ravine we have the painting of warriors on the war-path (Plate XXXII). Five male figures, one behind the other. Each one holds in his right hand a bow over his head while in every left hand is a bunch of arrows. The leader strides ahead. He wears a high head-dress and, in contradistinction to his fellows, he carries arrows in his right hand, his bow in the left. The bows seem to be flourished aloft. The legs jut out sharply. Faces are not clearly indicated but it looks as though we could distinguish a beard, a nose, hair, and, in the case of the last warrior to the

53 HUNTING SCENE Cueva Remigia, Gasulla Ravine (Castellón)

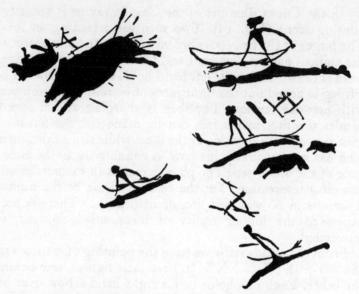

54 HUNTING SCENE Cueva Remigia, Gasulla Ravine (Castellón)

left-hand side of the procession, feathers stuck in the hair. It is a scene of great movement, of action, astonishingly impressive. As far as we know such a painting would have been impossible in Ice Age art.

In the Gasulla ravine is also another very striking picture. It represents a boar-hunt (Fig. 54). A great wild boar is shown in flight. Men are leaping, bounding after it. Their legs are so widely stretched that they make horizontal lines. The bodies are slim, the legs rather thicker and on them we can see the knee-ornaments, the bands that constrict the leg above the calf. This form of garter is one we find again and again in Spanish Levantine art. All the hunters are armed with bows and arrows. The careering beast is pierced with missiles while near it lies another boar on its back—shot to death.

Quite near this hunting-scene there is a picture of man-slaughter. In the background, dimly indicated, a group of men (Fig. 55). In the foreground two women whose figures are, unfortunately, rather damaged though we can make out clearly the arrows in their hands. Before them lies a man pierced through with missiles. Obermaier, who devoted much study to the Gasulla ravine paintings, was of the opinion that this assemblage represents an execution as punishment for some crime. He based his explanation on the fact that the group of men in the background is standing and that, moreover, there are comparable pictures of men being killed by a group of human beings, in three other spots in the same ravine. It may well be that we have here presented some expiation of sin, that of having contravened, perhaps, the Law of the Chase.

In Figure No. 43 we have the same theme—also from the Gasulla ravine. The group of 'avengers' is at the top left-hand side. Bows are held over the men's heads. Below is the body of a man pierced with arrows. A firing squad.

The intention to represent a mass of men together is expressed several times in the Gasulla ravine (Fig. 56). Here is a group of warriors holding bows over their heads. The figures are in movement. They are just strokes one behind the other. In fact, we have here a technique like that of the

55 WOUNDED MAN LYING ON THE GROUND Gasulla Ravine

ARCHERS Gasulla Ravine

Ice Age artists when they conveyed perspective in scenes such as that engraved upon the bone from Teyjat.

There is a melée of warriors at Morella la Vella (Plate XXXIV). The men are in fierce conflict. Two archers are affronted. One to the right and one to the left. They are letting fly at each other. Their bodies are thrust eagerly forwards. Their legs hardly touch the earth. From above and from the right another archer comes hurrying in to help and still others are running up to take part in the fight. The bodies are elongated, slim, gaunt even, yet, all the same, gracile and supple. Everything in the picture is sacrificed to the expression of speed, movement—alarm. Yet the composition is deliberately conceived. There is no discontinuity of line. The strokes are clear and constant indications of the stress that informs the whole picture. And this is not, we feel, just some modern interpretation that we may read into the paintings. The men of the Mesolithic knew quite well what they were doing when they composed their picture so that the bodies of the men hastening from above form one line, this line continuing, with a slight curve, in the body of the principal combatant who is on the left-hand side. It is also obviously intentional that the arrows of the warriors fly forwards parallel and that the men's bodies are represented at the same angle. There is, indeed, something fundamentally 'compositional' which is not always apparent at first sight, but which nevertheless exists in the scenes of Spanish Levantine art.

Three figures of women in the Cueva Saltadora (Valltorta ravine) are most impressive (Fig. 57). The bodies are thin, almost scraggy, but the hips bulge out. The three are bending forward slightly and all in the same direction, but one woman is plucking at another's arm so as to restrain her. On the heads are feathers. A vivid scene from the remote past.

Often in the Levantine pictures the female figures are clothed, as at Alpera, Cogul, Charco del Agua Amarga, Minateda and the Gasulla ravine. The women wear cloche-shaped skirts, while the upper parts of their bodies are also covered.

Among the representations of warriors are some very impressive figures such as that of a hunter on one knee, holding his arrows behind him and looking down into the Valltorta ravine from the Cueva Saltadora. There are also diagrammatic figures in violent movement often rendered with very considerable artistic skill (Figs. 58–59).

Generally speaking, the animal figures are more naturalistically treated than those of men, as we may see, for instance, from the picture of a collapsed stag in the Tormón niche (Fig. 60). At Albarracín there is a painting of a young stag with antlers in velvet (Plate XXXVII). It is very realistic—as is, also, the picture of an ibex with turned head that is in the Gasulla ravine (Plate XXXVI). At Albarracín, again (Plate XXXV), are many naturalistically rendered

57 THREE WOMEN Valltorta Ravine

58 HUMAN FIGURE WITH BOW
Valltorta Ravine

representations of beasts together with figures of men in the typical Levantine elongated manner.

The actual paintings seem to have been executed after the outlines had been traced with a fine, very thin brush. In not a few of the half-finished pictures the outlines can be clearly made out, as, for instance, in the Valltorta ravine and at Minateda. We know that in palæolithic times small feathers were used as brushes and it is reasonable to suppose that they continued to be utilized during the Mesolithic. In the representations of bow-strings, arrows, hair and head-dresses, the lines are often only a few millimetres thick.

In many cases this first sketch was worked in pale red or in grey and then painted over in more vivid pigments. There

59 HUMAN FIGURE WITH ARROW Valltorta Ravine

60 YOUNG STAG COLLAPSED ON THE GROUND
Tormón, Teruel

are instances of this treatment in the Gasulla ravine. The procession of the warriors was, for example (Plate XXXII), first of all, sketched in a faint, but darkish, colour before the actual painting was done in light, bright red. In one case— at Albarracín—the background, that is the rock-surface, was covered with a uniform colour-wash and on this the pictures were executed in several different tints.

In contrast to the large (often more than life-size) Ice Age pictures, the Levantine Spanish paintings are small, sometimes not covering more room than the area of a man's hand. Often the pictures are no longer than one's thumb. There are, indeed, some that could fit on one's thumb-nail— real thumb-nail sketches. From their small dimensions it is obvious that the Levantine pictures could not have been executed with the naked hand alone. The colours most usual are light and dark red and brown. Grey and black are rare and yellow even more uncommon.

At places where the pictures have been damaged it can be seen that the pigments have eaten their way several millimetres into the substance of the rock. Although the paintings are in the open air and thus exposed to variations of temperature, the colours have been preserved marvellously fresh. If moisture be applied to them they stand out sharp and impressive.

The uplands of the central Spanish plateau—where there are also some prehistoric paintings—form a region that is by no means warm. It freezes early and the winters are hard and long. During the summer, rain often follows upon spells of terrific heat. It is more difficult to determine the medium used by the Levantine painters than it is to discover that employed by the Ice Age artists.

Since the rock-faces are nearly all dry there can be no question here of 'natural frescos' as in the damp caverns. The raw pigments—charcoal, black manganese earths, hæmatite, and especially limonite (that is brown iron ore) and ochre—which were reduced to powder, could hardly have been prepared solely with water. We must suppose that fats, blood-serum or white of egg were employed. Chemical tests applied to a series of pictures in the Valltorta ravine have given no certain result. On the other hand such tests, combined with spectrum analysis, have shown that the mesolithic painted pebbles from the southern French site of Mas d'Azil contain hæmoglobin, and porphyrin. We may suppose then, in the absence of any definite proof, that the Levantine Spanish artists also used blood and probably fats as media for their pigments.

The utilization of the natural forms of the rock-surface that was so common in palæolithic times occurs also in the Levantine pictures. As we have seen, the bees' hive in the Cueva de la Araña (Plate XXX), is not a painted hole but an actual hollow in the rock. The hunter who looks down from the Cueva Saltadora rock-shelter into the recesses of the Valltorta ravine, rests his foot against a small boss in the stone. In a hollow of the rock-wall of this same Valltorta ravine is the figure of a beast, all hunched up, stuck with arrows and so placed that one would think he had sought out a hiding place in which to die alone. In other cases, however, the lines just run right over the protuberances as though they were not there. There was obviously, then, no hard-and-fast rule as to the physical nature of a surface to be painted.

If, however, the Levantine art is, in many respects, fundamentally different from the Franco-Cantabrian art of the Ice Age, still they must both be characterized as sensorial, as naturalistic. There is nothing surprising about this. In mesolithic times, life in southern Europe carried on much as in the Ice Age. Moreover, hunting magic is still a main content of mesolithic art. No picture relates, in any way, to an agriculture and but few pictures (and those nearly all dating from towards the end of the Mesolithic) allow us to conclude that there was pastoralism. At Albarracín (Plate XXIX) and at Villar del Humo (Plate XXXI) are figures of men leading horses by halters. Similar pictures can be seen at Canforos near Rodriguero in the Sierra Morena (Fig. 97) and although this site is no longer included in the Levantine group of painted rocks, nevertheless, the Canforos pictures are clearly linked directly with those of Levantine Spain.

If horses were domesticated then surely also were cattle and perhaps sheep and goats. The new economy at the end of the Mesolithic—the first attempt at the transformation of nature and at production—demanded, indeed imposed, a new way of living, for the pastoralist is no longer dependent, or at least not wholly dependent upon the products of the chase. Hunting magic, therefore, no longer occupies the foremost place in his thoughts, no longer informs all his artistic creation. Thus, towards the end of the Mesolithic, the figures of beasts recede more and more into the background. Man himself begins to dominate the picture. With the fading of sympathetic magic the way is opened towards abstract art. The subject of art has been the individual in the real world, but now the artists come to concern themselves with things beyond the Here and the Now. The process begun in Mesolithic times is fully developed in the symbolical art of the New Stone Age and of the Bronze Age.

We can determine with some degree of accuracy the date of the Levantine art's disappearance. The Levantine traditions lived on until the time of the megalithic monuments. One of the stones in the Orca das Juncas dolmen in North Portugal bears a painting that is quite in the style of the Levantine Spanish art. Since this dolmen cannot be dated before 2000 B.C. we may be fairly sure that the Levantine art traditions survived until the second millennium B.C.

The Spanish Levantine paintings have been recognized for only a comparatively short time. It is true that, as we have

79

already mentioned, some of the paintings are mentioned in Lope de Vega's comedy *Las Batuecas del Duque de Alba* which was published in 1598. These same rock-pictures are also referred to by Ponz in a book he published at Madrid in 1778. It is his *Viaje de España*. During the 19th century we come across stray references to the 'Written Rocks'. The local inhabitants were terrified of the pictures and believed that the ghosts of Goth or Moor had limned them. While I was visiting and studying the Spanish rock-paintings I was always having difficulties on account of these superstitions.

The systematic and scientific study of the Levantine Spanish pictures did not, however, begin until 1908, though in 1903 Juan Cabré Aguiló had, quite by accident, during an excursion, discovered the rock-paintings of Calapatá near Cretas in Aragon. He did not, however, dare to publish his find. It was not until Alcalde del Rio, in 1906, issued his book upon Altamira, that Cabré spoke of his discoveries to a journalist through whom the news eventually reached the ears of the Abbé Breuil. In 1908 Breuil, in an article in *L'Anthropologie*, made the first published report upon Cabré's discoveries and in the following year, 1909, Breuil himself visited the Spanish Levantine sites.

The second site to be studied by an expert was Cogul. In 1907 a missionary priest who was on a walking excursion with some boys had seen the paintings while he and his charges were taking shelter during a rain-storm. He wrote a report for the Press and the first of his articles appeared in 1908. Breuil published descriptions of the Cogul paintings both in 1908 and in 1909. Urged on and guided by Breuil, Cabré became the principal discoverer of the Levantine sites. In 1909 he revealed Albarracín near Teruel.

In 1910 Alpera was recognized. Breuil visited Alpera in 1911 and in the following year his article upon the paintings was published in *L'Anthropologie*. Las Batuecas was reported in 1910 and an exhaustive description of the site appeared in 1918–1919. Cantos de la Visera near Yecla (in the province of Murcia) was found in 1912. In 1915 the announcement was made of four new sites, among them the Cueva de las Grajas at Almaziles, not far from Granada.

One of the most important discoveries was that of Mina-teda, near Hellín (in the province of Albacete) in 1914. Morella la Vella and the Barranco (or ravine) de Valltorta (near Albocácer in the province of Castellón de la Plana) were both identified in 1917. In 1919 was found the Cueva de la Araña near Bicorp (province of Valencia). The fine paintings of Tormón, near Albarracín (province of Teruel) have been known since 1926. One of the most significant of the Levantine sites is that comprising the pictures in the Gasulla ravine near Ares de Maestre (Province of Castellón de la Plana).

In 1944 a new rock-shelter, called the Cueva de Doña Clotilde, was discovered near Albarracín and also another, the Cocinilla del Obispo. One of the latest of the sites to be found is that of La Cenia (also in the province of Teruel), which was first described in 1950.

THE SENSORIAL ROCK-PICTURES
OF SCANDINAVIA

In northern Europe too, in Scandinavia, there exists an art that is a continuation of that of the Ice Age. It is remarkable that between Spain and Scandinavia there stretches a huge area—including France and Germany—in which no post-glacial pictures are to be found. Since this area is thickly populated there is not much chance of any picture of the mesolithic style-group being found there—at least above the ground.

In Scandinavia, on the other hand, a rich store of rock-engravings has been discovered. The drawings are strung out along almost the whole of the Norwegian coast nearly as far as North Cape and—continued as the Swedish rock-engravings—this group reaches far inland. It was formerly thought that these half-naturalistic pictures existed only in northern Norway. For that reason they were called 'Arctic' in contradistinction to the Bronze Age rock-drawings of southern Scandinavia with their representations of ships, of swords and of daggers and whose dating is assured by the types of objects shown in the engravings.

In recent years, however, so many drawings of the 'Arctic' type have been recognized in southern Norway, while in the north so many Bronze Age rock-pictures have come to light, that it is no longer admissible to speak of 'Arctic' pictures as opposed to the southern Scandinavian ones. Gutorm Gjessing has, therefore, proposed the term 'Huntsmen's art' to designate what was formerly called 'Arctic' engravings, and this term 'Huntsmen's art' really does indicate the essential of these pictures which are sharply distinguished from those relating to an agricultural way of life. The 'Huntsmen's' group is, generally speaking, sensorial, while the 'agricultural' group is strongly stylized and imaginative.

It was also held that there was a great time-lag as between the two groups. Lately, however, new discoveries have tended to show that the 'Huntsmen's' rock-pictures quite gradually, and without any violent break, merge into the 'agricultural' rock-engravings. This is especially true of Norway, for agriculture has never been there the main source of men's livelihood. Hunting ways lasted long. It was not until 1899 that a law was enacted to prohibit the age-old methods of hunting and trapping game. By this law were forbidden the use of enclosures for capturing elk, stag or reindeer, the employment of pit-traps, standing snares and weighted traps, eel forks and other archaic devices for catching wild animals. The *battue* of game over the cliffs into the sea was also prohibited. Now all these methods of hunting belong to the Stone Age, but they were long preserved in an isolated and remote part of northern Europe.

If, therefore, the traditions of the Ice Age lingered on until our own times, it is certain enough that for long after the beginning of agricultures, the hunters still retained their mode of life, their habits and their customs. Therefore, also, the hunters continued to bewitch the game they would capture. And they exercised their wizardry through pictures. But, as this picture-magic lasted all through the Bronze Age and beyond it, the dating is extremely difficult.

Moreover, there occurred marked changes of style within this art. I should like, therefore, to speak of three successive stages, analogous to those we find in the Spanish Levantine pictures. The first stage of the Scandinavian post-glacial art is characterized by large-scale, naturalistically executed figures of animals. The second phase comprises—and this in marked contradistinction to the hurrying hunters and shadow-show beasts of Levantine Spain—also animal figures, but angular, schematic. The third stage consists of fully stylized and schematized figures (and especially figures of human beings), which are quite removed from any naturalistic representation. However, the development from naturalistic art to abstract art is to be seen as clearly in Scandinavia as in Levantine Spain or in Africa. In Scandinavia, as elsewhere, the proof of the development is to be found in the superposition of drawings. Perhaps the best example of this

—and it is often referred to in the literature of the subject—
is the Pictorial Rock of Bardal. Underlying the Bronze Age
representations of ships are large-scale 'sensorial' pictures
of elks. Between these two main sets of engravings can
be made out a third set characterized by delicate designs
of animals in rather stylized technique.

And Bardal is not the only site where we can see this
juxtaposition. At Sletfjord in Nordland, among the 'Huntsmen's' engravings, are drawings of birds and traps which
are similar to Bronze Age pictures. At Tennes, Nordland
(Fig. 61), there is a human figure so stylized that it can be
paralleled only among Bronze Age engravings, yet in its
actual technique it cannot be distinguished from the contiguous 'Huntsmen's' pictures with their half-schematic
delineations of animals.

At Hammer (Nord-Tröndelag) Bronze Age rock-
pictures of ships and of men on horseback lie over relatively
naturalistic figures of birds. The same thing is to be seen
at Skotröa also in Nord-Tröndelag.

At Bogge and Romsdal (Plate XL) we can easily make
out several stages or phases in the 'Huntsmen's' art. To the
oldest phase belong a large elk and an elk's head. Over these
are less ancient, and more schematized, representations of
animals. On the edge of the cliff can be seen very stylized
animal-forms (much resembling Bronze Age drawings) and
these obviously belong to a third and later stage.

At Rusevik, Sogn and Fjordane most of the pictures can

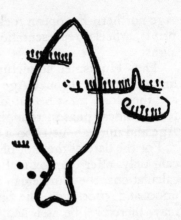

be assigned to the second—or half-schematic—phase, though many transitional forms are to be seen. The superpositions and the overcuttings make it relatively easy to trace the chronological succession of the engravings.

At Meling, Rogaland (Fig. 62), under about fifty Bronze Age pictures of ships, are two figures of fish, 'sensorial' in style, and these must belong to the first phase. At Sporanes, Telemark, some elk heads underlie Bronze Age pictures showing ships and stylized human figures, which, judging from their style and technique are less ancient.

Although the relative chronology is fairly simple to establish—the stylized drawings are the more recent, the naturalistic ones the more ancient—the absolute chronology is difficult to determine. In central and northern Europe the Bronze Age (as Cretan and Egyptian evidence indicates), Period I, begins about 1600 B.C. This period, however, in central and northern Europe (a period that stretches from about 1600 to 1400 B.C.), really belongs, culturally, to the Stone Age. The bronze objects, such as they were, were nearly all imported. It is not until we get to about 1400 B.C., and the start of the Bronze Age Period II, that the real Bronze Epoch can be said to have opened for the inhabitants of central and of northern Europe. The peak-period of the Bronze Age pictures falls in Periods III to V of the Bronze Age, that is to say, during the centuries from about 1200 to about 750 B.C. This epoch is characterized by importations from Italy. To this time we must assign most of the Bronze

Age northern European rock-paintings showing ships, footprints, wheels, representations of divinities and symbolical signs.

The 'Huntsmen's' pictures are more ancient, but they link up with the Bronze Age engravings. The 'Huntsmen's' art, therefore, must be dated to the period before 1600 B.C. for its oldest phases, though it lasts right into the Bronze Age and until about 1000 B.C. if not later.

For the date of the first phase of the 'Huntsmen's' art we can only offer approximations. According to de Geer's calculations, the Norwegian ice-cap was melted by between 6000 and 5000 B.C. The oldest type of 'Huntsmen's' art may, therefore, be assigned to some date before 3000 B.C. But any figures we can give for the beginning of the Scandinavian rock-engravings are only guesses, though the phases and stages of art-evolution can themselves be clearly distinguished. Moreover, not only are the most ancient engravings recognizable from their greater naturalism (deriving from the palæolithic tradition) but they are marked also by technical peculiarities of execution. While the later pictures have outlines composed of a series of 'pecks' or points close together, the lines of the oldest engravings are deeply incised so that even today they seem smooth compared with the rough and weather-beaten surface into which they are cut. The case is the same with the North African rock-drawings.

In the North African rock-engravings, at least, the incisions were made so that they could hold pigments. At Tiout, in the south of the department of Oran, I noticed some traces of colour in the deeply cut lines. In like manner, at Leiknes, in Nordland, red pigment was found in the rock-engraving of the stag's antlers (Fig. 63).

The grooves are often 2 centimetres (that is roughly ¾ inch) wide and 1 centimetre deep. Since the grooves are quite smooth it has been thought that the artists used blunt wooden sticks to finish off their work. It seems, however, more probable that powdered quartz and water were utilized for polishing. Such a technique would indicate a neolithic or New Stone Age dating for the engravings, for if the lines of the animal pictures were polished then we may be

63 STAG, ENGRAVING AND PAINTING
Leiknes, Tysfjord, Nordland

64 OUTLINE ENGRAVINGS OF ANIMALS
Leiknes, Tysfjord, Nordland

sure that stone axes, hatchets and the like were polished also.

It is noteworthy that the most northern rock-pictures are also the oldest. They all display a certain naturalistic treatment. At Leiknes (Fig. 64) there are several superposed layers of drawings. All are naturalistic. 'Agricultural pictures' have been detected in the north only in one single case.

The lowest layer, composed of the most naturalistic pictures, contains also the largest. Amid reindeer and elks and bears, a mighty whale is depicted. This rock-picture also offers a naturalistic feature, in common with the art of the Ice Age, a feature that is found nowhere else in Scandinavian prehistoric art: it is the motif of a beast's head turned backwards as though it were looking behind it. Progressively, the artist's interest in the representation of sudden movement fades away in Scandinavian art. Animals may be shown standing or walking but never is the impression of rapid action conveyed. There is no sense of space. The legs on one side only are represented.

A characteristic example of the early phase is given by the pictures at Sagelven (Plate XXXIX). Two reindeer are shown. The outlines are deeply incised and, despite some simplification, the figures still reflect close observation of nature. The two drawings are on a sheer rock-face above a stream so that to examine them a rope and tackle are necessary.

To this same phase belong also the rock-pictures of Fykanvatn (Figs. 65 and 66). They are in the Glaomfjord, one of the wildest and most inaccessible of all the Norwegian fjords. At the end of the fjord itself a range of crags rises steep and precipitous to Fykan lake. Formerly a great waterfall dashed down here into the waters below, but the cascade is now mostly used up to turn the turbines of a hydro-electric station. Above the Fykanvatn is a glacier. There are the rock-pictures. In separate groups, the engravings stretch for a length of some 225 yards. The polished grooves of the incised outlines $1\frac{1}{4}$ to $1\frac{1}{2}$ inches wide, and nearly $\frac{1}{2}$ inch in depth, stand out distinctly from the sombre mass of rock. Altogether there are twenty-eight animal figures—reindeer, elk and fish—some most realistic and lifelike. One reindeer is more than 13 feet long.

Similar pictures are to be found at Klubba, Nordland. The cow-elk shown in Fig. 67 is nearly 15 feet long. The Klubba pictures lie on the north side of Åmnöy and extend for over a hundred yards along the bleak, bare crags. The

65 REINDEER Fykanvatn, Glaomfjord, near Melöy, Nordland

66 TWO REINDEER Fykanvatn, Glaomfjord, near Melöy, Nordland

grooves of the outlines are rather less deep than those of the
Fykanvatn pictures. Intertwined and intermingled among
the representations of elks, of reindeer and of whales are
long lines leading nowhere, or which, at least, cannot now
be deciphered as representing any known living form.

One of the very finest of the rock-engravings of the oldest
period is that at Böla, Nord-Tröndelag. The picture, which
has often been reproduced, is situated near a waterfall and is
that of a reindeer, particularly well executed. The incised
outline is, however, in several places, rather damaged. To
this first art-phase belong also the elks of Bardal, Nord-
Tröndelag. They are also on a large scale and they lie
under drawings of ships. Somewhat more developed is the
stylization shown in the picture of two reindeer at Hell in
the parish of Nedere Stjördal, Nord-Tröndelag. However,
judging from the technique (the outlines are deeply incised
and give a triangular cross-section) this picture also belongs
to the first phase.

Further rock-engravings of this phase are to be found at
Valle, Nordland (among other figures a remarkably well-
executed one of a bear—Plate XXXVIII); at Strand, Syd-
Tröndelag; at Bogge, Romsdal; at Evenhus near Frosta,
Tröndelag (Plates XLII and XLV); and at Drammen

67 ELKS Klubba, Åmnöy, near Melöy, Nordland

(Plate XLIII) and Rødøy in the parish of Tjøtta, Nordland (Plate XLVI).

These eleven, together with six Swedish groups, make up the seventeen sets of rock-engravings which we may attribute to the most ancient phase of Scandinavian prehistoric art. They all represent gigantic beasts, generally singly. The proportions are lifelike. The lines are deeply incised.

A certain superficial resemblance to Aurignacian Ice Age art for long confused discussions about the Scandinavian rock-pictures. It was held to be impossible that Scandinavian art could be linked directly with that of the Ice Age, that is to say with the naturalistic Magdalenian. The objections to the Ice Age origins of the northern European engravings faded, however, when late Magdalenian art was revealed as having a strong tendency towards the linear. In fact in all three groups, the North African, the Levantine Spanish and the Scandinavian, the earliest pictures are 'sensorially' conceived but the later ones show a progressive stiffening and stylization.

Most of the 'Huntsmen's' pictures belong to the second phase of the art. Rounded contours and outlines are abandoned. The animals are angular—indeed, often quadrangular. Lines, bearing no relation to reality, sometimes criss-cross the beasts' bodies. Instead of a technique of deeply incised grooves, we have the beginnings of the pecking technique. Perhaps the best example of this phase is the rock-picture group at Vingen.

To the third phase must be assigned the stylized figures of men such as appear at Tennes, Solsem, Ovnen (Plate XLVIII), Kvithammer, Rönningen, Trondtveit and Ulveneset. These figures, in their extreme stylization, resemble those of the Bronze Age. In any case they cannot be included in a naturalistic art-category, but they mark the transition to the following epoch, that of imaginative, abstract art.

We can understand Scandinavian prehistoric art only if we regard magic as the determining factor in its creation. Here, again, upon these northern rocks, we have representations of the creatures which nourish Man and upon which he lives—reindeer, elk, bear, whale, seal, birds. Over and above the choice of subject it is the emplacement of the engravings themselves that makes one think at once of hunting-magic.

There is, in the whole of Scandinavia, but one prehistoric cave with rock-pictures. It is at Solsem, Nord-Tröndelag. Since it opens upon a steep and almost impracticable declivity, the cavern can hardly have served as a dwelling-place but only as a cult-sanctuary. The grotto is about 40 yards long and the entrance is obstructed by a huge block of stone. Soon after the entrance the cave takes a sharp turn so that most of the interior is in complete darkness. The cavern is about 20 feet wide at the spot where are the paintings; they represent men with enormous phalli and engaged in a dance, probably a cult-dance. When the fillings of this cave were excavated human bones were found as well as great quantities of those of fish, birds, cattle, sheep, goats and horses. With these was also recovered a small carving of a northern duck (*alca impennes*) (Fig. 68). The thing has a hole bored through it, so that it must have been worn as a pendant. Harpoons and other hunting gear also came to

68 CARVING OF A DUCK   Solsem, Leka Island

light. These objects are neolithic and are probably contemporaneous with the pictures which, on stylistic grounds, may be assigned to the end of the Neolithic or the beginning of the Bronze Age. Maybe the bones are the relics of sacrifices.

With the exception of this cave, however, the Scandinavian pictures are mostly on rock-faces or steep crags over which the game was driven. Vingen, for instance, is still one of the best places in all Norway for stag-hunting. In a novel by J. A. Krogh, set in the period about 1700, it is related that there were even then so many stags in the neighbourhood of the Nordfjord that they did much damage to the peasants' crops. When, in the autumn, the beasts headed off westwards over the mountain ranges towards Culen and Stattland, the peasants would drive the herds over the precipices so that the animals crashed down the crags into the water. Below, men in boats on the lake waited to retrieve the booty. The Vingen rock-engravings stand out just at the place described by Krogh. Clearly these hundreds of pictures chiselled upon the cliffs must exercise powerful magic upon the beasts and lure them down to their destruction. As a matter of fact all the Vingen animal-figures are represented with their heads drooping downwards to the waters below. The engravings depict the deer as they appeared when they were huddled in their herds upon the cliffs' edge and just about to slither down to death.

We could hardly ask for a more decisive proof of sympathetic magic and of the wizardry of the chase.

There are plenty of other examples of hunting-magic in the Scandinavian pictures, representations of pits, snares and enclosures. We can see these, for instance at Sletfjord, at Strand, Vingen and Ekeberg. At Sporanes (Fig. 69) there are even a few pictures of beasts just about to fall into traps. At Ekeberg, too, we have an animal in a snare. Boomerangs are one of the weapons most often depicted. At Vingen, for instance, can be seen beasts springing among a volley of sickle-shaped missiles. Boomerangs of this description have actually been recovered from Scandinavian sites. Such instruments are neolithic.[1]

[1] In Russia, too, boomerangs have been found.

69 ANIMAL CAUGHT IN A SNARE Sporanes

Another proof of the magic character of the pictures is afforded by the representation of internal organs and of 'lines of life'. In many of the engravings there is a line that runs from the mouth, over the breast and there swells out into a rhomboidal or more or less circular object. Often the line continues on to the hindquarters of the animal. Such delineations can be seen at Bogge, Evenhus, Skogerveien, Klöftefoss, Åskollen (Plate XLVII) and Bardal. For pictures of this type, the ethnologists offer us modern parallels.

W. J. Hoffman reports that, among the Ojibway Indians, he noted that before a hunt the medicine-man sings a magic song and then draws in the sand, or on a rock, a picture of the animal to be hunted. He marks the heart with a red blob and draws an arrow piercing it. From the heart to the mouth he makes a continuous line. This symbolizes the life of the beast that must die. Such 'lines of life' are known among many Amerindian tribes. I myself have seen such among the Pueblo Indians in New Mexico, and Arizona, while I was living among them and studying their art. I can testify that Hoffman's observations are correct. The Indians themselves explained to me the meaning of the 'line of life'. Rock pictures in the United States—for instance in Minnesota and in Virginia—also display 'lines of life'. In Siberia and in the art of the Lapps 'lines of life' are of frequent occurrence and it is quite possible that this symbol of the palæolithic and Bronze Age Scandinavians passed on from them to the Lapps.

As in the Ice Age, the next aim and object of the pictures

—after magic for death—is magic for fertility. Fertility magic is especially common in rather later times when game became more scarce. A striking example of fertility magic is offered by a representation of animals copulating on the rock-engravings of Fykanvatn.

Perhaps, however, the most significant indication of hunting-magic, as inherent in the Scandinavian pictures, is the custom, still retained by peoples living around the Arctic Circle of drawing pictures of the chase. In south-western Alaska, in the region of Cook Inlet, and also on the islands of the Kodiak group, Frederica de Laguna found Eskimo pictures strikingly like the Scandinavian prehistoric drawings of the last phase. These Alaskan pictures consist of stylized figures of men, seals, fish and four-legged animals, apparently elks or stags. There are also representations of men in kayaks. The importance of the discovery is enhanced by the fact that the discoverer was able to get information from the Eskimos in the neighbourhood. She learned from several different individuals that only certain people, that is wizards, paint the pictures and that they do this in order to secure good luck in hunting. One of the men interrogated (the nephew of a wizard) explained that the pictures were the work of his uncle, but that there were other artists, too, who formed a sort of secret society. All the pictures served in secret ceremonies (there are harpoons depicted in some of the scenes). The Eskimo added that whale hunters would kill a man by magical means in order to use his fat as poison for their javelins. This report by Frederica de Laguna is of very considerable interest as throwing light upon the meaning of the ancient rock-pictures of the North.

Hallström says that in 1910 he observed Lapps offering up sacrifice before a prehistoric rock-engraving at Seitjaur in the Kola peninsula.

Thus it is as easy, indeed it is easier, for us to determine the meaning of the Scandinavian prehistoric pictures than it is for us to see what is the sense of the Ice Age paintings. It is easier to understand the former because, through the Lapps, the practice of rock-art has been preserved until our days. Moreover, the Lapps are quite ready to give information about the significance of their art. We seem to have here one of the rare instances in which not only the outward forms, but also the spirit of remote ages, have been kept alive until now.

For the history of Man's artistic achievement the Scandinavian rock-pictures are as important as those of North Africa or as the Levantine rock-paintings of Spain. In these two latter groups, it is true, there are scenes so repeated that we must conclude they were very popular; there is movement, there is coloration of the figures, whereas Scandinavian art is static. Only rarely are the animals shown as running. Only seldom is a figure depicted in haste, or, indeed, in movement at all. There are no scenes, no 'anecdotal' art, no groups systematically arranged, no pictorial composition. The few exceptions worth while mentioning are at Forslev (Fig. 70) where we can see a halibut—or some other flat fish—secured on a hook and held by a line with a sinker-lead—being hauled up on to a boat. There is also a figure of a man with a dog on a leash. With the exception of a few copulation scenes of human beings at Bardal and of beasts at Gjeithus these figures at Forslev are the only ones which can be described as by any means 'scenic'. We get groups of men first in the later, stylized art, groups of men collected together, probably, for cult purposes. But on the whole the 'scenic' is lacking. The few representations of groups of figures hardly count.

With regard to the technique of execution we may resume the phases thus: in the most ancient times we get deeply incised lines, polished and smooth so that one can with ease run one's finger round the outline. In the second phase the lines are scratched or chipped while in the third phase they are lightly scratched on the surface.

We may also note that there are Scandinavian rock-paintings also and, indeed, at no less than eleven sites in Norway and six in Sweden, making seventeen in all. The pigments have been subjected to repeated and to different chemical analyses. Dr. F. de Lemos of the University of Oslo concludes that the colour was iron oxide mixed with some fatty organic substance, probably blubber. By exposure to the air this mixture has assumed the appearance of a resinous substance so that we have an explanation as to

95

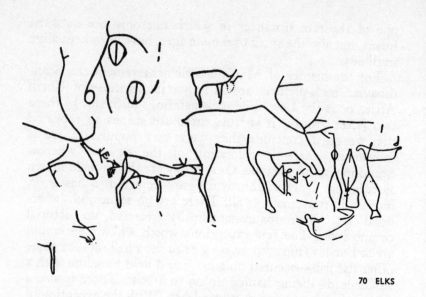

how the pigment has been able to withstand the destructive
forces of the weather. Painting in prehistoric Scandinavia
was, however, used exclusively to accentuate the incised and
the pecked outlines and never to give an appearance of
modelling to the body of the figure. Colour is used in all three
phases of the Scandinavian art.

For the oldest phase we have the animal pictures at
Furuodden or Forberg in Spind and at Vest-Agder. As
examples of the second phase, the engravings at Honhammer,
Möre and Romsdal (where fish are represented): of the
third phase are the pictures at Ovnen, Kvithammer,
Rönningen and Ulveneset. All these show traces of colour.

As in the case of Ice Age art or that of Levantine Spain,
the Scandinavian pictures can be arranged in sets or cate-
gories which lead us to conclude that there were art-schools
each with its own tradition. Thus the engravings of the
northern Scandinavian region are so much alike in style and
execution that Hallström and Engelstad did not hesitate to
speak of 'schools' whose work can be seen upon the rocks.
Often, indeed, one is tempted to recognize the same hand at
different sites. The pictures of Forselv (Fig. 70) and Sletfjord are extraordinarily alike, and those of Tennes much

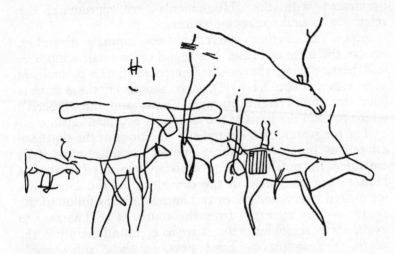

Forselv

resemble those at two former places. In southern Scandinavia the engravings at Åskollen, Skogervejen (Plate XLIII) and Ekeberg (Plate XLIV) might almost be by the same artist. These pictures are closely related in style to the drawings on small objects of palæolithic date.

This Scandinavian art, however, is a linear one. Outline dominates. There is no plasticity. The figures are motionless. Moreover this art displays very clearly its stylistic evolution, an evolution that is paralleled in North Africa and Levantine Spain. However, we must not conclude that because there is a similarity in the succession of art-phases these three arts of Scandinavia, Africa and Spain were, of necessity, contemporaneous. Cultures developed much quicker in the South than in the North. The stylized pictures of Levantine Spain belong to the beginning of the Neolithic, the New Stone Age, while those of Scandinavia fall into the Bronze Age, but in southern Europe during Bronze Age times art began, once again, to be more lively and realistic. Development is much slower in the North where Ice Age styles and traditions survived much longer than in the South. The peak period of the southern European imaginative art occurs in the Neolithic while the same epoch in the North is filled and

97

permeated with the 'Huntsmen's' art represented by relatively naturalistic rock-pictures.

Again the northern carved objects, animals in amber, axes in the form of beasts' heads and other small sculptures still bear, during the Stone Age, a relatively naturalistic appearance (Plate XLVIII). It is, moreover, these objects (that are found right through Russia and into Siberia), which formed the basis of the so-called 'Scythian' art.

The long-preserved naturalistic traditions of the northern art tell us much about the economic circumstances of its creators. In northern Europe Man remained longer a hunter than elsewhere in the continent. In the North the ice melted late. Some tribes and human groups followed the beasts as they retreated from the south. It is thus easy to explain why the older pictures are to be found mainly in the north of Scandinavia. Even now, in those inhospitable regions agriculture is hardly possible. Despite all men's efforts, few crops will grow. Near Vingen, for instance, attempts were made to lay down earth upon the rocky soil and then to sow and to reap. All in vain. The yield was far too scanty. Today at Vingen there are no gardens round the houses. Man's livelihood here must still be derived from hunting.

So, from a survey of Scandinavian rock-engravings we may conclude that there was in northern Europe a special, and late, blossoming of post-glacial art, later than the rock-pictures of North Africa or of Levantine Spain, less rich too, it may be, in sheer power and delicacy of draughtsmanship, but certainly not poorer in the mysterious might of magic.

Pictures of the Second and First
Millennia B.C.

SUMMARY

QUITE different from Ice Age and post-glacial art is the schematic art that begins in Spain between, say, 2500 and 2000 B.C. However, though the two groups are so sharply distinguished one from the other, still, they are linked. The connection is, indeed, so close that, at some sites, the evolution from the older paintings to the younger can be quite clearly perceived. The intermediate stages are represented and the transition from naturalistic to stylized forms is plain. On such rocks as those of Minateda, of Cogul or of Alpera, in the Spanish Levantine province, this evolution is particularly well marked. There is nowhere any exception to the rule that the stylized pictures are the more recent, the naturalistic the older.

The same tendency may also be observed later on and at sites where all, or nearly all, of the pictures are stylized. Take, for instance, the Tajo de las Figuras in the province of Cadiz. Here there are several superposed layers. All are stylized but the most strongly schematic are the uppermost layers. The older ones (often, moreover, executed in different colours and clearly distinguishable from the more recent) are what might be called 'half-naturalistic'. They are, it is true, stylized to a certain extent but still they are a good deal closer to natural shapes and forms than are the later pictures.

The most recent pictures of this group reach such a peak of stylization that no further progress is possible. The pictures are so simplified, so conventionalized, so nearly reduced to symbols that they look, for all the world, like some sort of script or writing. That these pictures did not develop into a real script was due to there having been, during those ages in the Iberian peninsula, no political or ecclesiastical authority and organization which could take matters in hand and utilize the instrument that lay within Man's reach.

In ancient China things took an analogous course. On the so-called 'oracle-bones' (dating from about 1500 B.C. and discovered at Anyang in Honan, the old capital of the Shang-Yin dinasty) are highly conventionalized pictograms that had already had a definite meaning assigned to them by an organized priesthood. Present-day Chinese script has developed from the ideograms on the 'oracle-bones', has kept its ideographic character and has never evolved in the direction of alphabetical writing. Although the signs are, generally speaking, much altered, those for 'man' and 'woman', for instance, are comparatively easy to recognize as modifications of the old Shang pictograms.

Similarly, Egyptian writing was derived from stylized art-forms. In this case, once more, the rock-pictures throw some light upon the origin of writing. There are in Upper Egypt, and out in the desert, a considerable number of sites with semi-stylized pictures typical of post-glacial times and showing a remarkable resemblance to the North African rock-engravings in the region of the Saharan Atlas. These semi-stylized paintings merged gradually into fully stylized forms; indeed, the most recent layers present shapes similar to, nay, sometimes identical with, the pictures of the most highly schematized phase in Spain.

Even in pre-dynastic times (that is to say before 3000 B.C.) there was, presumably, a hierarchy of priests in Egypt and they developed from the rock-picture signs a script that is the first hieroglyphic writing. Gradually, however, the signs for words were transferred to individual syllables. As only the consonants were taken into account and vowels were disregarded, in the case of a syllable that had only one consonant, the 'hieroglyphic' sign came, to all intents and purposes, to represent a single consonant. So it came about that words—or syllables—sounding more or less alike could be represented by one and the same sign even if their meanings were quite distinct. Thus, the sign for an 'eye' serves not only for the word *yart* (that is 'eye') but also for the verb *yirt* that means 'to do'. Likewise, the sign for a 'house' (in Ancient Egyptian *per*) is used also to express the word *peri* (that is 'to go out'). The sign pronounced *ma*, that is, a conventionalized picture of a saw, stands for both 'new' and 'to see' since the two were pronounced alike—*ma*. This ancient semi-alphabetical script was not, however, developed in Egypt. The alphabet that is the ancestor of ours was an invention of the Semitic-speaking peoples of the eastern Mediterranean seaboard.

The very names of our letters—and still more those of the Greek alphabet—are of Semitic origin. Thus the Semitic word for an 'ox' (*aleph*) is clearly represented in the oldest forms of our letter 'A', that is an ox's head and horns, though our 'aleph' is now printed upside-down. The Semitic word for a 'house' is *bet* and our 'B' still shows the contiguous quadrangles that once depicted the ground-plan of a dwelling with two rooms.[1] There is an Egyptian hieroglyph for the leaf of a door. It is formed by a perpendicular stroke and an attached rectangle. In the Semitic scripts a similar sign (called *daleth*, that is, a 'door') is used to express the consonant 'D'. From this the triangular Greek delta derived, of which our Latin 'D' is only a modification. Our zigzag-shaped 'M' goes back to the old hieroglyphic sign for 'water', the word for which, in northern Semitic, is *mem*. The hieroglyphic picture of a snake lives on in our 'N'. Especially interesting is the case of our letter 'P'. In the ancient Egyptians' hieroglyphic writing there was a sign clearly representing a head and pronounced 'tp', that is, a 'head'. The same sign, but more abbreviated, still appears in the Sinai inscriptions. However, as in the Semitic tongues a 'head' is *ras* or *rash*, the vocal value of the signs was changed by the Semitic speakers to 'R'. The Greeks took over the sign with the 'R' value—and with this significance it still is used in the Russian alphabet. On the contrary, in our Latin alphabet we still give the sign the old 'P' value.

It is, thus, fairly clear that in some ancient cultures the stylized pictures of the Neolithic led on into writing. In Europe, also, there were stylized pictures but they did not develop into writing. The decisive factor that was present in

[1] On the famed 'Sinai inscriptions', discovered by Flinders Petrie in 1905, the pictograms for 'ox' and 'house' can be clearly seen.

ancient Mesopotamia, Egypt and China was lacking in neolithic Europe. There was no organized priesthood that could bind definite and fixed meanings to the different signs. Europe played no part in the invention of writing and our remote ancestors had to borrow from the Greeks, who themselves were the debtors of the Semitic-speaking peoples of the Levantine Mediterranean shores.

The art of ancient Europe remained symbolic and did not expand into writing. In that symbolic art, however, a prominent place is occupied by the stylized representation of a man's figure. In Ice Age times we find but few human figures. Man did not feel any urge to represent himself. In post-glacial times, however, Man moves to the foreground as a phenomenon that is achieving, is creating, is accomplishing. In stylized art, on the other hand, Man, for the first time, seems to have thought of himself as a spirit, as a soul. Probably also, at this time, began the concept of the world of external things as a Whole.

Art, like speech and thought, is, at first, rooted in the concrete. A beast is just a certain beast seen; a bison, a reindeer, a horse. Then a beast, an individual beast, is a part of the general concept 'animal'. The sign or symbol for 'animal', however, does not possess the richness of the special picture or representation of one particular beast. The symbol is something generalized and it is, therefore, rigid and, to a certain extent, abstract. Moreover, as an embodiment of a general idea, the symbol became sacred and intangible. It could not be changed. Any modification would take away something of its magic virtue.

The blazon of a family, the coat-of-arms of a country, the trademark of a firm are, with us, symbols which must not be altered lest they lose their significance. A country's flags are saluted and honoured. Disrespect shown to the national emblems is felt to be especially shocking. The emblem stands for the whole complex and who shows contempt for the symbol shows at the same time contempt for the Whole.

Compared with the sympathetic magic of the Ice Age and of the post-glacial epoch, the use of symbolism denotes a considerable spiritual advance. Prominent in this new way of thinking are the concepts of preserving life, of fertility, of

PLATE I. Interior of the Covalanas Cave, with Paintings of Animals in Aurignacian Style. Province of Santander, Spain.

PLATE II.
Engraving of a Bison, Aurignacian Style. La Grèze, Commune of Marquay, Dordogne, France. Length 0·60 metres.

PLATE III.
Painting in Red Pigment, Wild Ass struck by Arrows, Aurignacian Style. El Castillo Cave, Province of Santander, Spain. Length 0·70 metres.

PLATE IV.
Painting in Black
Pigment, Mammoth,
Late Aurignacian Style.
Pech-Merle Cave,
Cabrerets, Department of
the Lot, France.

PLATE V.
Engraving of a Wild
Horse's Head on the
Floor of the Bédeilhac
Cave, near Tarascon-
sur-Ariège, Ariège
Department, France.

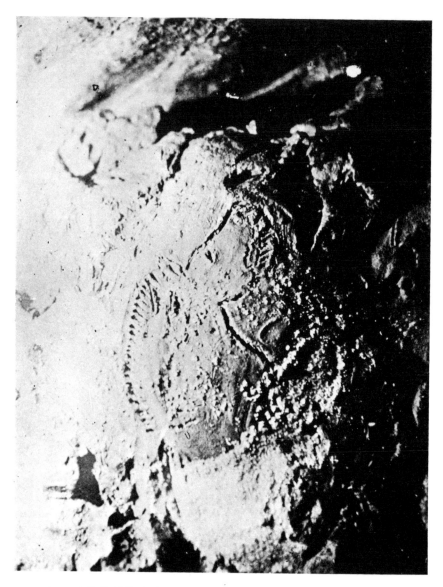

PLATE VI.
Head of a Wild Horse
engraved in the Clay of the
Montespan Cave,
Haute-Garonne
Department, France.
Magdalenian Style.

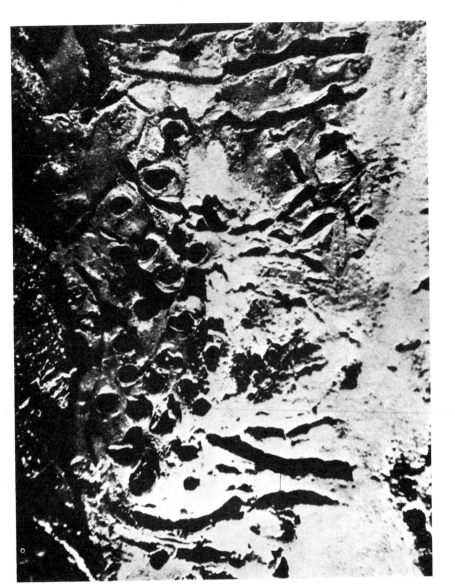

PLATE VII.
Wild Horse pierced with
Holes. Engraving on the
Cave-Wall of Montespan,
Department of the
Haute-Garonne, France.
Length 0·30 metres.

PLATE VIII. Head of a Wild Horse, Detail from a Complete Figure,
Engraving on the Cave-Walls of Les Combarelles, near Les Eyzies, Dordogne
Department, France. Mid-Magdalenian Style. Length of the Whole Figure
1·10 metres.

PLATE IX. Hunter Running. Painting in Red Pigment. Width 13 centimetres. Cueva Remigia in the Gasulla Ravine, Ares del Maestre, Province of Castellon de la Plana, Spain.

PLATE X.
Head of a Hind, Painting in Red, Brown and Black Pigment, Detail from a Whole Figure, Mid-Magdalenian Style. Altamira Cave, Province of Santander, Spain. Length of the Whole about 0·80 metres.

PLATE XI. Engraving of a Wild Horse on a Cave Wall. The Grooves have been filled with White Chalk for the Photograph. Mid-Magdalenian Style. Labastide Cave, Hautes-Pyrénées Department, France. Length about 2 metres.

PLATE XII. Standing Bison, Painting in Red, Yellow, Black and White Pigments, Mid-Magdalenian. Altamira Cave, Province of Santander, Spain. Length 1·95 metres.

PLATE XIII. Stylized Human Figures. Peñón de Aguila, Solana del Pino, Sierra Morena, Spain.

PLATE XIV. Stylized Human Figures. Cueva de los Letreros,
Province of Almeria, Spain.

PLATE XV. Stone engraved with Spirals from the Gavr'inis Gallery-Grave,
Commune of Baden, Department of Morbihan, France. Height 2 metres.

PLATE XVI. Engraving of Ibex and Trap, Aurignacian Style. Schulerloch, in the Valley of the Altmühl, near Kehlheim in Bavaria. Length of Ibex 13·5 centimetres.

PLATE XVII. Sculpture in Relief of a Wild Horse's Head, Stone, Early Magdalenian. Angles-sur-Anglin, Vienne Department, France.

PLATE XVIII. Wild Horse struck by Arrows, Painting in Yellow and Black. Late Magdalenian. Lascaux Cave, near Montignac, Dordogne Department, France. Length 1·40 metres.

PLATE XIX. Portion of a Painted Wall, Cattle, Wild Horses and Stags, Painting in Red, Brown, White, Black and Yellow, Mid- and Late-Magdalenian. Lascaux Cave, near Montignac, Dordogne Department, France. Length of the Section shown 5 metres.

PLATE XX. Large Ox painted in Red Pigment with Overpainting in Black. Lascaux Cave, near Montignac, Dordogne Department, France. Length 2·80 metres.

PLATE XXI. Five Small Wild Horses, Brown and Black Pigment. Lascaux Cave, near Montignac, Dordogne Department, France. Length of Frieze 3·50 metres.

PLATE XXII. Frieze of Stags' Heads. Lascaux Cave, near Montignac, Dordogne Department, France. Length 5 metres.

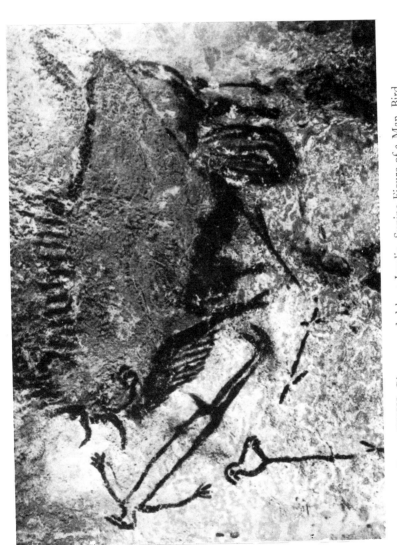

PLATE XXIII. Bison wounded by a Javelin, Supine Figure of a Man, Bird upon a Pole. Lascaux Cave, near Montignac, Dordogne Department, France. Painting, Length 1·35 metres.

PLATE XXIV. Horse with turned Head, Engraving in the Style of the Late Aurignacian. Levanzo Island, off the Sicilian Coast. Height about 25 centimetres.

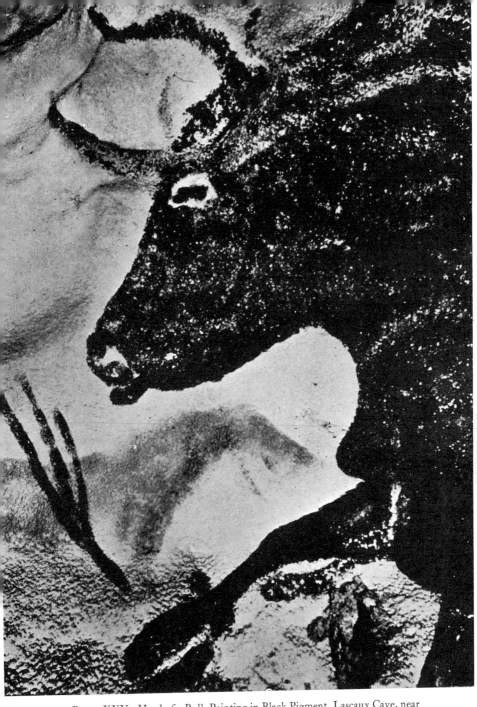

PLATE XXV. Head of a Bull. Painting in Black Pigment. Lascaux Cave, near Montignac, Dordogne Department, France. Length of the Whole Figure 3 metres.

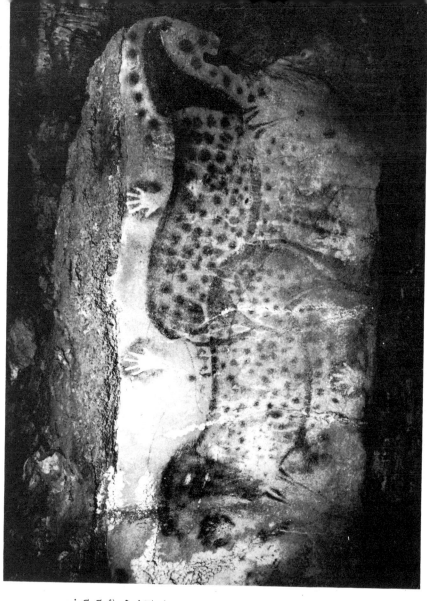

PLATE XXVI.
Wild Horses, Painting in
Black, Stencils of Human
Hands. Pech-Merle
Cave, near Cabrerets,
Lot Department, France.
Length of the Painted
Surface 3 metres.

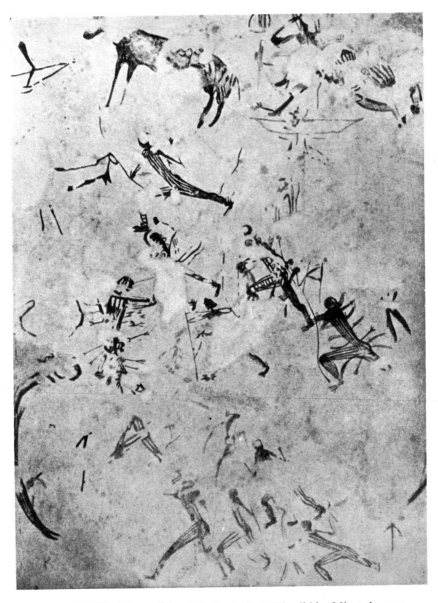

PLATE XXVII. Men at War, Painting in Red, Mesolithic. Minateda, near Hellín, Province of Albacete, Spain. Height of the Section shown about 1 metre.

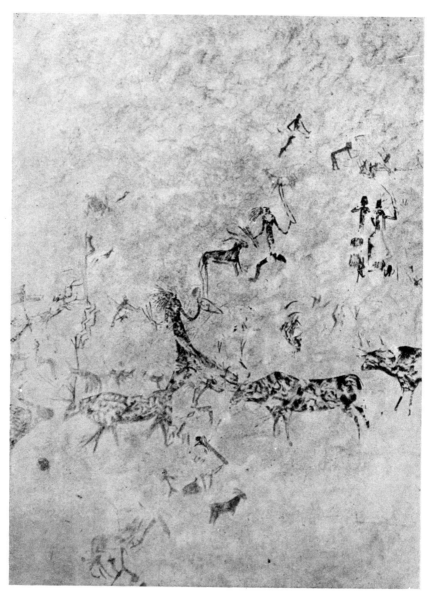

PLATE XXVIII. Men and Beasts, Painting in Red and Black Pigment.
Alpera, Province of Albacete, Spain. Height of the Section shown about
1·50 metres.

PLATE XXIX. Man leading an Animal by a Halter, Stylized Figures of Men, Tree with Falling Fruit, Painting in Red. Doña Clotilde site, Albarracín, Province of Teruel, Spain. Section shown about 2 metres long.

PLATE XXX. Human Figures climbing up Ropes and gathering Honey surrounded by Bees, Painting in Red. Cueva de la Araña, near Bicorp, Province of Valencia, Spain. Size of Section shown about 0·50 metres.

PLATE XXXI. Man leading a Horse by a Halter, Painting in Reddish Brown Pigment. Villar del Humo, near Cañete, Province of Cuenca, Spain. Length of the Section shown about 0·50 metres.

PLATE XXXII. Procession of Warriors, possibly a Cult-Dance. Gasulla Ravine, near Ares del Maestre in the neighbourhood of Albocácer, Province of Castellón de la Plana, Spain. Width of Section shown 0·13 metres.

PLATE XXXIII. Rock Engraving. 0·40 metres. Tanum, Bohuslän, Sweden.

PLATE XXXIV. Archers in Battle, Painting in Red Pigment. Morella la
Vella, Province of Castellón de la Plana, Spain.

PLATE XXXV. Animals and Men, Painting in Red, Brown and White Pigments. Barranco de las Olivanas, Albarracín, Province of Teruel, Spain.

PLATE XXXVI. Ibex with Head turned, Painting in Red Pigment. Gasulla Ravine, near Ares del Maestre, Province of Castellón de la Plana, Spain. Width 14 centimetres.

PLATE XXXVII. Stag with Horns in Velvet, Painting in Red Pigment. Barranco de las Olivanas, near Albarracín, Province of Teruel, Spain. Length 15 centimetres.

PLATE XXXVIII. Bear, Engraving. Finnkåg in Åfjord, Valle, near Lödingen, Nordland, Norway. Length 2·26 metres.

PLATE XXXIX. Reindeer, Engraving. Sagelven, Nordland, Norway. The Animal on the Left is 2·35 metres long and that on the Right 2·75 metres long.

PLATE XL. Elk and other Animals. Engraving. Bogge, Romsdal, Hedmark, Norway. Length of the Elk 1·97 metres.

PLATE XLI.
Stylized Stag. Height
48 centimetres. Detail
from Plate L. Tajo de
las Figuras, Laguna
de la Janda,
Province of Cadiz,
Spain.

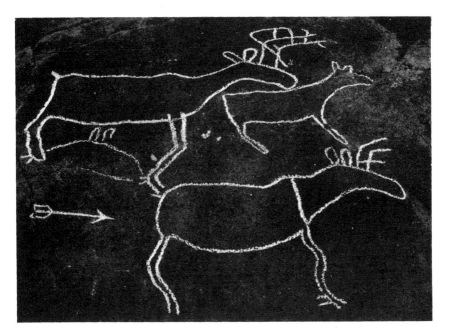

PLATE XLII. Elks, Engraving. Evenhus, Commune of Frosta, Nord-Tröndelag, Norway. Length of the Upper Animal 1·28 metres and of the Lower Animal 0·67 metres.

PLATE XLIII. Whale, Engraving. Skogervejen, near Drammen, Buskerud, Norway. Length 2·28 metres.

PLATE XLIV. Elk, Engraving. Ekeberg, near Oslo, Norway. Length 0·65 metres.

PLATE XLV. Rock Engravings. Evenhus, Commune of Frosta, Nord-Tröndelag, Norway. Length of the Elk in mid-Foreground 1·14 metres.

PLATE XLVI. Human Figure with Snowshoes. Rödöy, Tjötta, Nordland, Norway. Length 35·5 centimetres.

PLATE XLVII. Elks and Fish, Engraving. Åskollen, Drammen, Skoger, Vestfold. Norway. Length of Large Elk at the Top 1·81 metres.

PLATE XLVIII. Stylized Human Figures, Painting in Red Pigment. Ovnen, Trondtveit, Nissedal, Telemark, Norway. Height of Figures 30 centimetres.

PLATE XLIX. Rock-painting. Peña Tú, Llanes, Province of Asturias, Spain. Height of the Idol 1·04 metres.

PLATE L. Rock-painting in Red, Brown, Black and Grey Pigments. Tajo de las Figuras, Laguna de la Janda, Province of Cadiz, Spain.

PLATE LI. Rock-painting in Red Pigment, Ibex and Human Figure. Tajo de las Figuras, Laguna de la Janda, Province of Cadiz, Spain. (Detail from Plate L.)

PLATE LII.
Stylized Human
Figures. Cueva de
la Graja, near
Jimena, Province
of Jaén, Spain.

PLATE LIII. Stylized Human Figures. Barranco de la Cueva,
Aldeaquemada, Sierra Morena, Spain.

PLATE LIV. Stylized Human Figures. Piedra Escrita, Fuencaliente, Sierra Morena, Spain.

PLATE LV. Stylized Human Figures. Cueva de la Sierpe, Fuencaliente, Sierra Morena, Spain.

PLATE LVI. The Dolmen de Soto, Trigueros, Province of Huelva, Spain. Width of the Arch of the Head 22 centimetres.

PLATE LVII. Stylized Human Forms. Polvorin, near Coruña, Province of Coruña, Spain.

PLATE LVIII. Engravings: Men, Daggers and Animals. Cemmo, Val Camonica, Italy

PLATE LIX. Engravings: Animals and Daggers. Cemmo, Val Camonica, Italy.

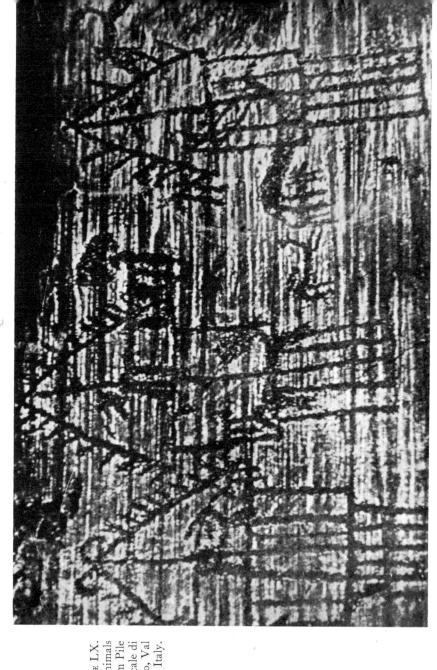

PLATE LX.
Engraving: Animals
and above them Pile
Dwellings. Scale di
Cimbergo, Val
Camonica, Italy.

PLATE LXII. Engraving: Rider. Fucine, Val Camonica, Italy.

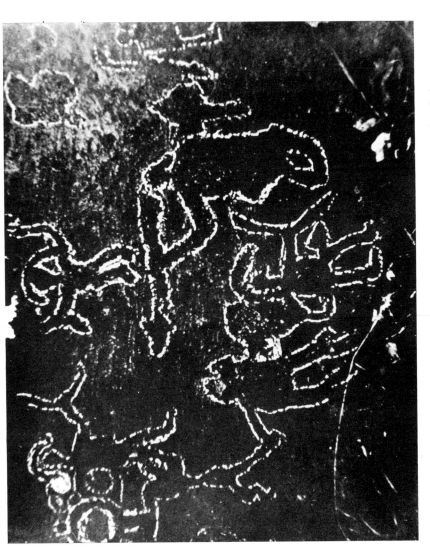

PLATE LXIII. Engraving: Representations of Men. Convai, Val Camonica, Italy.

PLATE LXIV.
Engraving: Stags.
Cemmo, Val
Camonica, Italy.

PLATE LXV.
Sorcerer (?).
Vallon des
Merveilles,
Mont-Bégo,
Tende, France.

PLATE LXVI. Stone engraved with Conventionalized Representation of a
Human Visage. Allée Couverte Coudée, Pierres Plates, Commune of Loque-
mariaquer, Department of Morbihan, France. Height 82 centimetres.

PLATE LXVII. Stone from the Mané-Kérioned Gallery-Grave, Commune of Carnac, Department of Morbihan, France. Height 69 centimetres.

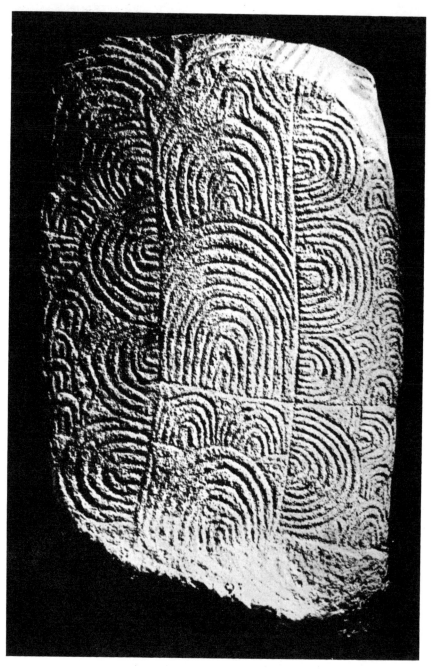

PLATE LXVIII. Stone engraved with Spirals from the Gavr'inis Gallery-
Grave, Commune of Baden, Department of Morbihan, France. Height
2 metres.

PLATE LXIX. Stylized Human Figures. Clonfinloch, Offaly, Ireland.

PLATE LXX. Engravings from the Gallery-Grave of Sess Killgreen, Co. Tyrone, Ireland.

PLATE LXXI. Engravings on the Stone from the Gallery-Grave of Knockmany, Co. Tyrone, Ireland.

PLATE LXXII. Engravings from the Gallery-Grave of Lochcrew, Co. Meath, Ireland.

PLATE LXXIII. Engraved Stone from Anderlingen, Province of Hanover, Germany. Height 1 metre.

PLATE LXXIV. Engraving on Stone representing probably a Textile. Stone
Cist from Göhlitzsch, Province of Saxony, Germany.

PLATE LXXV. Engravings in the Gallery-Grave of Bredarör, Kivik, near Hvitaby, Scania (Skåne), Southern Sweden.

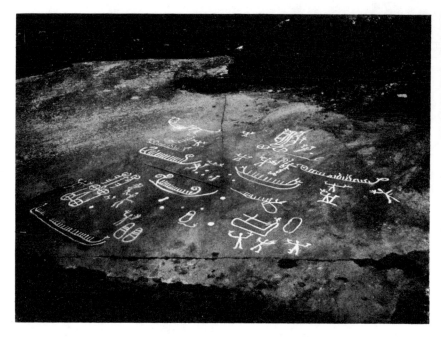

PLATE LXXVI. Rock-engraving. Rished, Commune of Askum, Bohuslän,
Sweden. About 3 metres long.

PLATE LXXVII. Rock-engraving. Stora Massleberg, Commune of Skee,
Bohuslän, Sweden. About 1 metre high.

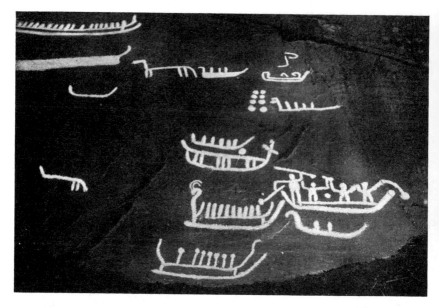

PLATE LXXVIII. Rock-engraving. Torp, Commune of Hogdal, Bohuslän, Sweden. 2 metres.

PLATE LXXIX.
Rock-engraving.
Hede, Commune
of Kville,
Bohuslän, Sweden.
5 metres.

PLATE LXXX. Rock-engraving. Tanum, Bohuslän, Sweden. 0·60 metres.

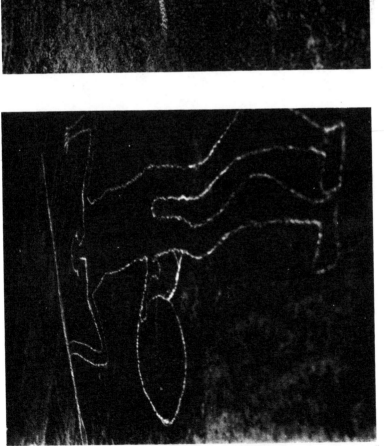

PLATE LXXXII. Figure of a Divinity (?). Tanum, Bohuslän, Sweden. Height 0·80 metres.

PLATE LXXXI. Figure of a Divinity (?). Tanum, Bohuslän, Sweden. 3 metres high.

PLATE LXXXIII. Scene of Wizardry (?). Besovnos, Northern Cape of Lake Onega, Russia. Length 0·51 metres.

PLATE LXXXIV. Stylized Ship. Perinos, Southern Cape of Lake Onega, Russia. Length 0·24 metres.

PLATE LXXXV. Rock-engraving of a Cult-Figure with Superposed Cross. Besovnos, Western Cape of Lake Onega, Russia. Height of the Figure 2·46 metres.

PLATE LXXXVI. Hunter. Besovnos, Western Cape of Lake Onega, Russia. Height of Human Figure 0·25 metres.

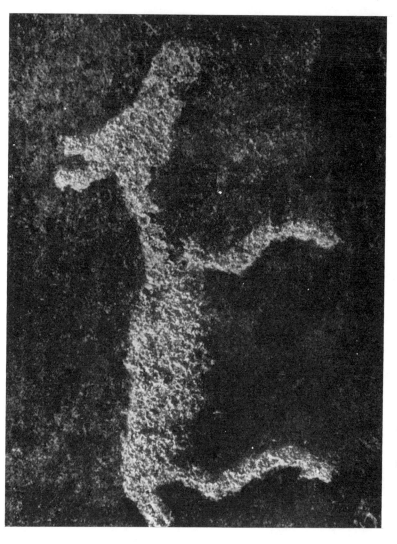

PLATE LXXXVII. Engraving of an Animal. Perinos, Southern Cape of Lake Onega, Russia. Length 0·25 metres.

PLATE LXXXVIII. Rock-engraving of an Animal with Conventionalized Figure of Rider (?). Perinos, Southern Shore of Lake Onega, Russia. Length 0·29 metres.

PLATE LXXXIX. Rock-engraving of Human Figures on Snowshoes. Zalavruga, White Sea, Russia. Height of the Left-hand Side Figure 0·32 metres.

PLATE XC. Rock-engraving of a Swan. Kladovets, Besovnos on Lake Onega, Russia. Height 0·54 metres.

PLATE XCI. Rock-engraving. Perinos, Southern Cape of Lake Onega, Russia. Size of the Swan 0·16 metres.

luck, of health, of living. Men's thoughts are directed to the permanent elements that encompass existence and determine it.

Ever and again appears the zigzag line that means 'water' and from which our letter 'M' is derived. Almost as often we find the signs for the stars and heavenly bodies whose periodical movements now begin to interest men. First of these luminaries is the moon (which in one passage of the Edda is called the 'Knife of Time')—the word 'moon', indeed (that is related to the Indo-European root *ma* or *mami*), means originally 'to measure'. This concept may also be observed in Psalm 104[1] where the passage occurs "He appointed the moon for seasons . . .".

The agriculturalist needs to study the stars in order to understand the year. Man's first scientific creation was a calendar to show the succession of seed-time, of growth and of harvest. An agriculture demands a systematic division of time. Calendars are the things of priests and wizards, for they know the changes of the year, they fix and determine the weeks and the months, the lucky and the unlucky days. So, in the rock-pictures occur, again and again, signs for the sun and the moom. These signs are among the most mysterious known to man, for in them lurk powers and influences both uncanny and vague. These symbols are signs of knowledge of the unknown.

Another sign is very common in the symbolic rock-art of prehistoric Europe. It is a sign to be found all over the world. It appears in the Bushman's paintings as well as on the rock-pictures of the Americas, of Asia and of Egypt. It is the sign for 'rain'. It is formed essentially in the same manner everywhere. A cloud is indicated either by a straight, a bent or a wavy line—a zigzag or an oval from which the rain falls. The rain itself is indicated by perpendicular lines below the 'cloud'. This sign, then, often bears a likeness to a comb and is sometimes so designated in literature about rock-pictures.

The Pueblo Indians in America still use this symbol in their religious ceremonies and during a visit to Taos, in New

[1] Psalm 104 dates from the time of the Babylonian Captivity, that is, 597 to 537 B.C.

71 FIGURE OF A DEMON
El Ratón, near Hoz de Guadiana

Mexico, I had the opportunity of asking old and experienced
Indians about the meaning of this sign. They all asserted,
unhesitatingly, that the sign signified rain. The uppermost
horizontal line is the rain-cloud and the perpendicular lines
below are the rain-drops.[1]

The symbolical, abbreviated representations of the human
figures present a special problem for us when we examine the
rock-art of the last two millennia B.C. In fact these figures are
not just stylized. They are caricatural. The men have huge
heads, big eyes, often three arms, an enormous phallus and
thick bellies. The faces, especially, are always uncanny and
terrifying. However, many of these representations of human
figures have no head at all—as, for instance, in a rock-
picture at El Ratón not far from Hoz de Guadiana (Fig. 71).
Each hand and foot, moreover, is replaced by five curved
lines or 'claws'.

Breuil, to whom, more than to any other man, we owe our
knowledge of the Spanish rock-paintings, offers no explana-

[1] I also asked the same Indians about the meaning of the zigzag lines and they
told me that they meant 'water'.

tion for these singular quasi-human figures. He notes, of course, the progressive stylization and abstraction which he links up with the beginnings or writing, but the signification of these fantastic 'human' figures is not apparent in what he writes. Perhaps, in order to get some idea as to what these figures mean, we must make comparisons with non-European material. The explanation is to be found where pictorial art developed into pictorial script.

On the Chinese 'oracle-bones' we find, again and again, signs similar to those in the Spanish rock-pictures—suggestions of human bodies, horrible heads, huge eyes, several arms—and also strokes instead of heads. These ideograms are the literal ancestors of those which today are used to signify 'ghost' or 'spirit'.

The suggestion I offer here for the first time affords, in my opinion, a key to the understanding of the rock-pictures during the second and first millennia B.C. The figures are not those of ordinary men. They are those of ghosts. They are not ordinary beasts that confront us on the Written Rocks. They are ghostly beasts. All these rock-pictures of the second and first millennia are witnesses to a general belief in spirits permeating all the realms of existence. If the style and the technique of execution vary as from area to area and from region to region in Europe, still, all these pictures display a single dominating theme—they all relate to the world of spirits and are therefore marked by an estrangement from the real world around us.

If we can say that the first great epoch of prehistoric art is characterized by hunting—and sympathetic-magic, so the art from the third millennium onwards might be called that of the epoch of animism and myth. The men of this period developed concepts of mysterious and superior Powers, of a nature that is living and animated down to its smallest components, and also beliefs in survival after death and in the influence of the spirits of the dead.

Right up to our own times there has survived a belief in brownies, in elves and fairies, in kobolds and ghosts and in other mythical beings whose stories give us information about times past, times we cannot easily visualize. A belief in ghosts is, indeed, far from being extinct. In the *Erzgebirge*, for instance, where I am writing these lines, it is the ghosts and the spirits which still fix the suitable days for buying and for selling, for marriages and other celebrations. Ghosts flit through the dales, perch upon trees, ride the clouds, invade houses. The spirits are particularly active between Christmas and the New Year—in the so-called *Unternächten*—when they watch over treasures and often afflict men and affright them with apparitions and strange noises. Sometimes the ghostly visitants take off their heads or appear as half-beast, half-man. They are objects of terror, but, if we know the means, they can be conjured and driven back to whence they came.

But the spirits bring not only sickness and death. Some of them, such as the brownies, are helpful and do men's work while they sleep. For the animist the whole world of nature is filled with such spirits. They cause all things to grow, to ripen and to decay. They descend on to the earth from their dwelling-places in the stars.

Swedenborg, for instance, in his book *De mundo spiritum et de statu hominis*, assigns to the ghosts an abode betwixt heaven and hell. The Apostle Paul speaks (Ephesians ii. 2) of the "princes that rule the air" and in Ephesians vi. 12 of "Powers and Figures, the dark rulers of the world, the evil spirits in the air".[1]

The realm of the ghosts for the Egyptians and for the Greeks also lay in the West, the region of the setting sun. St. Jerome speaks of the Devil as dwelling in the West. In early Christian times persons who were being baptized were required to spit towards the West as they abjured the Devil and all his works. If in Christian churches the sanctuary is at the east end, it is because this orientation towards the rising sun symbolizes Christ—but it also symbolizes aversion from the realms of the demons.

It is from the realms of the ghosts, however, that the rock-pictures of the second and first millennia draw their significance. Æsthetically and artistically these pictures

[1] The author takes his quotations from the German translation of the New Testament. In the English version Ephesians vi. 12 reads ". . . powers, against the rulers of the darkness of this world, against spiritual wickedness in high places . . .". (Translator's Note.)

belong to the sphere of abstract art. They lack depth, spatial quality and plasticity. They lie entirely within the domain of the imagination, in a region that is spaceless. The inner significance of the pictures can be learned only by him who is able to live in this world of spirits.

The forms under which the spirits are represented are forms derived almost certainly from those of the wizards in Ice Age pictures. The wizard's appearance developed into that of the gods.[1] In the rock-pictures of Spain there occurs a female idol, a female divinity. In the pictures of Scandinavia it is a male form that is always clearly distinguishable. There is the God of the Lance, originally Tyr, and later Odin. There is the God with the Hammer, Thor (or Donar), and there is the very ancient God with Bow and Arrows, he that in the Edda is called Ull.

In the rock-pictures of Russia there is also a God with a Lance who slings the lightning flashes and is named Perkunos or Perun. In the Spanish pictures we find, again and again, a figure with bow and arrows. It may represent a divinity, but one whose name remains unknown to us.

In both northern and southern Europe religious ideas are rooted in the concept of fertility; in the agricultural South, however, this concept is associated with women, with the *Magna Mater*, or Great Mother, and it is expressed not only in symbolical figures but also in the matriarchal social system. There is a train of myth that binds together woman, earth, water, serpent, moon, oxen. In the North, where agriculture is of little importance and where pastoralism and stock-raising dominate, the idea of fertility is more associated with male animals, with the copulating male that creates life. So male divinities hold the commanding position. Their symbols are the Javelin and the Axe, the Horse and the Ram, the Wheel and the Ring. And in the forefront of the heavenly bodies stands not the moon, but the sun.

This essential differentiation between North and South cuts very deep and the ideas it fosters are still powerful today. The sun is the unchanging, the symbol of domination,

---

[1] In postulating that the wizard's figure developed into that of gods and spirits, the author does not, of course, necessarily state that the *idea* of a deity arose from the *idea* of a wizard. (Translator's note.)

the moon is a dying and a reviving star, symbol of deities that die and rise again such as Isis, Ishtar or Demeter. Perhaps it is no coincidence that in southern Europe today the cult of the Madonna is the main religious manifestation.

It is clear, then, that the rock-pictures of the second and first millennia B.C. are especially significant for the history of religious evolution. From these drawings and paintings we may learn how men's spirit wandered from magic to animism and then to the belief in gods.[1] In this prehistoric art we may perceive how Man's thoughts about the eternal things developed and evolved.

The rock-pictures are the most valuable documents we possess for learning about Man's spiritual development in Europe.

[1] It is only just to the author to point out that in another of his works (*Auf den Spuren des Eiszeitmenschen*) he maintains that Neanderthaloid men (say in the earlier phases of the last or Würmian glaciation and many millennia before the time of the stylized and schematized art of southern Europe) held a belief in some sort of divinity. He is also inclined to think that monotheistic ideas precede polytheistic ones, a position that would not be assumed by all prehistorians and anthropologists. (Translator's Note.)

THE IMAGINATIVE ROCK-PICTURES
OF SPAIN AND PORTUGAL

THE essential characteristic of the Spanish and Portuguese
rock-paintings of the second and first millennia B.C. is that
they are imaginative. The last phase of the Levantine
Spanish art ends in stylization, but the paintings of the
second and first millennia carry on the tendency and perfect
the process of extreme schematization. The drawing is now
flat and angular. The figures represented have no appearance
of reality. They are abstract expressions. The peak-point
of stylization is reached about 600 B.C. After that, there
is a change and slowly there is a return to naturalistic
forms.

These 'imaginative' rock-pictures are scattered over the
whole of the Iberian peninsula. As we have seen, the art of
the Ice Age is represented from many different parts of
Spain even if the centre of the art was in the Cantabrian
region. Levantine Spanish art flourished particularly in the
eastern coastal areas but it also extended far into the interior
of the country. Still, Ice Age and Levantine art sites in the
south of Spain are rare.

The stylized pictures, however, have one centre in the
Sierra Morena mountains. It puts out arms, wide arms, that
extend on the one side to Murcia on the eastern coast, and
on the other side to Badajoz near the Portuguese border. A
second centre is situated right in the south, between Gibraltar and Cadiz. A third centre exists in Galicia round
about Corunna and Pontevedra.

Still, pictures of this same sort are to be found in many
other parts of the peninsula and one can say that no region is
without them. It seems, therefore, most probable that we
have to deal here with something that lasted for a very long
time. It is at first surprising to note that the main centres of
this art lie in the south and not in the north or in the east

where we find the Ice Age and the Levantine paintings. We may, quite justifiably, demand why this schematic art did not flourish on the same sites as that of the Palæolithic or the Mesolithic. It is true that there is a fairly large number of sites with rocks that were painted and repainted throughout the ages. There are a good many sites where there is so much repainting, so much superposition, that they show distinctly the evolution towards a highly stylized art.

There must, however, be some special reason for the stylized art being found mainly in the south. This reason is to be found in the strong influences which, at this time, were streaming from the Eastern into the Western Mediterranean. In the east, at Troy, in Cyprus, on the Ægean islands, in Crete and in Sicily, there was evolved, during the third millennium B.C., a type of idol-image which, in its geo-metrical, almost Cubist form, showed only a remote re-semblance to the human body. These flat stone—or plaque—idols were imitated in Spain. They are, from the provinces of Cádiz and Málaga (Fig. 72), images which correspond closely with images from Troy. The figurines from Troy, again, have their prototypes in all Asia Minor

72 IDOLS (a) Aljezur, Algarve, Portugal
          (b) Idanha a Nova, Estremadura, Portugal
          (c) Herdade dos Cavaleiros, Ponte de Sor, Portugal

and back to Mesopotamia. There was, then, a culture-wave, an artistic-wave that spread from Mesopotamia as far as Spain. And this wave, which we know through its material relics, its sculpture, its pottery and its painting, must have corresponded to a stream of ideas, of animism, of belief in spirits, in the might of ancestors, a stream that gushed forth from the cultural centres of the Near East.

In Spain, it is true, we find idols—in the South—like those of the Eastern Mediterranean but the local populations in the Iberian peninsula transposed these sculptured forms to the rock-paintings since painting was more familiar to them than glyptic art. However, the pictures and the idols show a parallel development. Each influenced the other. It is, thus, possible to date the rock-pictures with some considerable degree of accuracy.

The idols we have referred to are found at Troy in towns II to VI. Troy II, in the old chronology adopted by Dörpfeld in 1902, used to be dated from 2500 to 1900 B.C. The American excavations of recent years have caused us to revise the chronology, so that now Blegen dates Troy II from 2500 to 2300 and Troy III to V (that Dörpfeld gave as from 1900 to 1500) from 2300 to 1900 B.C. Again, according to Blegen, Troy VI lasted from 1900 to 1350 B.C. This dating is established by comparisons with material from Mycenæ. Blegen holds that the Homeric Troy is Troy VII that flourished from 1350 to 1200 B.C.

As far as the dating of our Spanish rock-paintings is concerned, it does not really matter very much which system of chronology we adopt. What is important is that the idols appear during the time between 2500 and 1350 B.C. We may assume that this type of idol would occur rather later in Spain than at Troy.

By a happy chance the rock-pictures of Peña Tú (Plate XLIX), near Llanes in the province of Asturias, offer a means of dating. Here, painted upon the rock-face, is one of the idols which so often occur as 'Cubist' sculptures in Spain and Portugal. Also on the Peña Tú rock are stylized figures of men and, most especially, the representation of a dagger with five rivet-holes. It is this dagger that dates the pictures. It is a dagger of a sort that often occurs in Period I of the Spanish Bronze Age and a specimen exactly like the weapon figured on the Peña Tú rock is known from an excavation at Fuente Álamo in the province of Almería. This latter site is one of the most important of those showing the so-called 'El Argar' culture.[1] The dating of this El Argar culture is now well determined. Formerly, indeed, a very high antiquity was assigned to it, but now we consider that the El Argar culture-period extended from about 1600 to 1300 but may have lasted until 1200 B.C. The dating is established by numerous finds of Egyptian beads that were a common article of export into the Western Mediterranean. In Egypt itself, these beads can be dated with certainty. The most ancient appear about the reign of Queen Hatshepsut (14th century B.C.) and they are especially common at the time of King Amenhotep IV[2] in the 13th century B.C.

Beads of this type have been found at Fuente Álamo and they occur also at other important sites of the El Argar culture, such as at Almería or the Cuevas de Almanzora. The beads, then, allow us to date, with a considerable degree of accuracy, the El Argar culture which forms part of Period II of the Spanish Bronze Age. From all this it may be concluded that the idol depicted upon the Peña Tú rock was executed some time between 1600 and 1200 B.C. Most of the Iberian rock-pictures, of the highly stylized sort, resemble in manner the Peña Tú paintings, and must therefore be referred to this same period from 1600 to 1200 B.C.

But, on the other hand, a great many pictures are earlier than these and must be assigned to Period I of the Spanish Bronze Age (say from 2000 to 1600 B.C.)—the so-called 'Alcalá' culture. This period is characterized by bell-beakers in pottery and by tombs of what is called the 'gallery-grave' type. The Spanish gallery-graves are undoubtedly of Bronze Age date; enough daggers and hatchets have been discovered in the tombs to prove that. There are, moreover, in these megalithic tombs, drawings and engravings of Period I Bronze Age weapons. We may take

[1] El Argar is the province of Almería.
[2] Also known as Akhenaten or Ikhnaton the 'Heretic Pharaoh', who introduced the worship of the Sun Disk. (Translator's Note.)

73 POTTERY VESSELS WITH REPRESENTATIONS OF STAGS AND EYES Los Millares

it then that the date of the Alcalá culture is satisfactorily determined.

One of the principal sites of the Alcalá culture is at Los Millares near Gádor in the province of Almeria.[1] Here, upon a plateau, there was a settlement and near it is a necropolis with hundreds and hundreds of graves, partly passage-graves and partly corbelled tombs. Most of the small objects recovered here consist of flat copper hatchets (with a somewhat curved cutting edge), of chisels, awls, knives, nails, arrowheads and saws, all made out of copper or of bronze with a high percentage of copper. Amber objects are common. There are remains of textiles and, again, the plaque-idols. The alabaster vases were imported from Egypt. The prevailing form of pottery vessels is that of the bell-beaker. On one piece of pottery (Fig. 73) there are stags represented just in the style of the Spanish rock-pictures of this period. On this same vessel, that is now in the Ashmolean Museum at Oxford, there are also depicted two eyes exactly in the same manner as we may see in the rock-pictures. This find from Los Millares indicates clearly that some of these rock-paintings date back to Period I or the Alcalá phase of the Spanish Bronze Age. Other discoveries of decorated pottery vessels confirm this dating. There is, for instance, a fragment of bell-beaker pottery from Las Carolinas near Madrid (Fig. 74). It bears representations of stags—and of the solar disk—quite in the style of the rock-pictures. This object (excavated by Obermaier) must be dated to Period I of the Bronze Age.

[1] The Alcalá that gives its name to this culture-period is, however, not in Spain but in the southern Portuguese province of the Algarve. (Translator's Note.)

113

74 (a) Left: FRAGMENT OF A POTTERY BOWL WITH REPRESENTATIONS OF STYLIZED
FIGURES Las Carolinas, Madrid
(b) Right: FRAGMENT OF A POTTERY BOWL WITH FIGURES OF ANIMALS Setubal,
Portugal

In Vélez Blanco was found another pottery vessel belonging to Period I and displaying drawings of anthropomorphic idols but distorted into forms of an hour-glass or of a double-axe. This particular sort of stylization and representation of the visage of the *Magna Mater* (which seems to be what is depicted) is found in Brittany (Fig. 75), in England and Ireland (Fig. 76) and as far as Scandinavia (Fig. 77). This symbolical drawing resembles the engravings in the megalithic monuments which indicate the colonial expansion of the bearers of the Megalith culture.

Here, then, are some of the finds that help to date the rock-pictures. Their peak-period occurs after 2000 B.C. and may be set in the centuries between that date and 1200 B.C. The paintings cover both of the Bronze Age periods in Spain: Period I from 2000 to 1600 and Period II from 1600 to 1200.

No doubt some of the rock-paintings are older than 2000 B.C.—especially those which may be called semi-naturalistic in style and that represent the transition from realistic to

75 PORTION OF A POTTERY VESSEL
Camp de Peu-Richard

76 POTTERY VESSEL
England

77 POTTERY VESSEL WITH REPRESENTATIONS OF EYES Hammer Herred

schematic art. However, for these, presumably older, pictures we have no excavated objects to serve as time-clocks. Pictures such as those at the Laguna de la Janda and at the Tajo de la Figuras (Plates L–LI) must in their lower—and semi-naturalistic—figures, be ascribed to a date before 2000 B.C. Perhaps some of them are as old as 2500 B.C.

All these stylized rock-pictures have a religious content—again taking the word 'religious' in its widest sense. The ideas that were associated with these pictures were ideas whose origin and development were religious. Into a world of hunters (which had been the world of Spain) there streamed in from Asia, about the beginning of the second millennium, new modes of thought, modes based upon animism, upon the belief in spirits such as is so well exemplified in ancient Babylonia. These new fashions in thought are, however, linked with astral myths. The symbol of the moon becomes very prominent.

The idols are not represented in human form but they are spirit-figures, uncanny, often ghastly. Men were anxious and preoccupied about their surroundings, about mysterious Powers and their influence: therefore these Powers are objectivized. The Powers that surround men, the Powers for which there is no explanation, are embodied in the form of ghosts, of spirits.

For northern Europe we can find some philological confirmation for what we have just advanced. The German word *Geist* (and Old English *gast*) are, apparently, related to the Old Norse *geisa* that means 'to rage' or 'to rave'. This word *geisa* is cognate with the Gothic *usgaisjan*, that is, 'bring outside of oneself'. The basic meaning of *Geist* is, then, the 'angry' or the 'raging'. The peaceful spirits were, in Old High German, called *hiuri* and the dangerous ones *unhiuri*.[1] The words *hold* and *unhold* (that is 'gracious' and 'ungracious') are designations for demons and spirits. The German word *Gespenst* (that is 'spectre') is related to the Indo-European root SPON, with which is cognate the Old German word *spanan*, that is, to 'allure' or to 'entice'.[2] Another Middle High German word for 'spectre' is *gewas*—related to the Indo-European root *dhves*[3]—with which we may compare the Old Slavonic word *dusa*, that is, 'soul' and the Celtic designation for the spirits that St. Augustine has preserved for us: "*quosdam daemones, quos dusios Galli nuncupant*".[4] In Isodore of Seville, also, there is a reference to dusii among the Gauls.

It is likely that the Greek word θεός, that is, 'god' (derived from an older form θϝεσός), is also connected with the root *dhves*. The link between the words used to designate 'god' and those employed for 'spirit' may be observed also in German. The old German name for the gods is *Asen*. The Old Norse *ass* and the Anglo-Saxon *os* mean also 'god'. The earliest occurrence of this word, that I know of, is in Jordanes.[5] The passage reads: "*iam proceres suos quorum quasi fortuna vincebant, non puros homines sed semideos id est anses vocaverunt*", or: "they called their forefathers, whom they influenced through luck-bringing magic, not mere men but as semi-gods, that is, *anses*." The word is remotely derived from the Indo-European root *an*, that is, to 'blow'. The *Asen*, then, are originally the spirits of the wind that, later on, become semi-divine souls, and last of all, gods.

The rock-pictures reflect a state of things that is revealed by the philological parallels. From the mass of spirit pictures stand out some figures that we may recognize as the

---

[1] From this were derived the Middle High German *ungehiure* and the modern German *ungeheuer* that is 'dreadful' or 'prodigious'.

[2] *spanan* is represented today in the German words *abspenstig* (that is 'alienating') and *widerspenstig* (or 'refractory').

[3] *dwesti*, in Lithuanian means to 'blow together' while *dwase* is the word for 'breath' and 'spirit'.

[4] *De Civitate Dei*, XV. 23.

[5] *De Origine Actibusque Getarum*, Chap. XIII.

78 FIGURES OF DEMONS (?)
Cueva Negra de Meca

ancestors of representations of the gods. The belief in gods
stems directly from animism.

For the world of Iberia in the Bronze Age we have no
such philological information as we have for the North.
But the picture offered us by the arts is a very similar one.
Side by side with simple line-drawings there are paintings
in which a dæmonic, a spectral character is clearly visible.
At a site called El Ratón in the neighbourhood of Helechosa
are two delineations (Fig. 71) of headless human figures. In
one of them the fingers and toes grow out into plant-like
structures while the other figure, instead of a head, shows
four rays. Many of these pictures remind us of the fantastic
pictures of Jerome Bosch.[1] There is, for instance, at Alpera
(Fig. 78), a four-legged figure furnished with huge crab-like
claws. Comparable paintings occur at other sites in the
neighbourhood of Alpera.

At Cantos de la Visera (Murcia), La Cueva de la Graja
(Jaén) (Plate LII), Los Lavaderos de Tello (Almería) and
the Estrecho de Santonge, also in the province of Almería,
we may see similar, strange quasi-human figures which, in
their remarkable, unnatural and curious forms may be at
once recognized as spirits.

From one great spirit-figure in the Cueva de los Letreros,
near Vélez Blanco (Fig. 79), there grow out two mighty
horns and from one of these head-ornaments issues a heart-
shaped leaf. One hand is pointing downwards and the
other upwards. Both hold crescents. Above the figure are

[1] Jerome Bos or Bosch, 1460–1518.

117

the sun's disk and yet another lunar crescent. This spirit, then, would seem to have had some connection with the heavenly bodies.

An uncanny charm is radiated by a figure at Cimbara (Aldeaquemada) (Fig. 80), that represents, no doubt, a fertility-spirit or rain-spirit. The body is formed of one stroke, to the right and the left of which other strokes project. The head is huge and on it the eyes and nose can be made out only with difficulty. A curious sign over the head accentuates the weird impression made by the whole. From the figure issue rows of dots which may, perhaps, represent the effulgence of the spirit's might and power. Indeed, below these dots are comb-like signs that signify rain-clouds.

79 FIGURE OF A DEMON
Cueva de Los Letreros

80 SPIRIT SHAPE
Cimbara

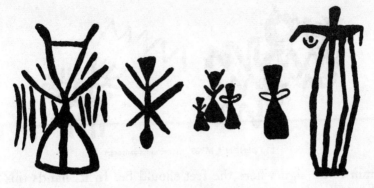

81 CUBIST HUMAN FIGURES Los Gavilanes

Curiously enough this figure reminds one very strongly
of signs on the Chinese oracle-bones.[1]

At Los Gavilanes, near Fuencaliente in the Sierra Morena
(Fig. 81), is to be seen an hour-glass or 'diabolo'-shaped
figure[2] from whose upraised arms issue streams of power.[3]
Nearby stands another figure whose eye hangs under his
arm and whose body is made up of four perpendicular lines
which, judging by other and similar figures, are to be
interpreted as streams of water. Here we have the Spirit of
Fertility, the *Magna Mater*, that sends down rain and
creates the fruits of the field. This character of fertility-
deity or spirit, is emphasized by the rain-clouds close to the
figures.

Often these rain-spirits are found above water-signs, as
at the Estrecho de Santonge (Almería) (Fig. 82), where,
among the wave-lines, little figures may be seen squatting
and holding their hands above their heads. Near them is a
quasi-human figure indicated only by a circle for a head,
outstretched arms, a perpendicular stroke for the body and a

[1] The author adds here a passage comparing the modern Chinese ideogram for
'spirit' with figures among the stylized rock-pictures of Spain. "The human
body is represented by five strokes . . . as on the oracle bones, so in the Spanish
pictures we have an invocation to the spirits of the air that bring down blessings
and good luck. . . ." (Translator's Note.)

[2] 'Hour-glass' or 'diabolo'-shaped human bodies are especially characteristic
of some Saharan rock-paintings. (Translator's Note.)

[3] Just as shown in the Chinese ideograph for 'spirit'.

82 DEMON SHAPES Estrecho de Santonge

rain-cloud sign where the feet should be. In its hands this figure holds two stars—perhaps a sun and a moon.

The moon-sign is very often associated with the figures, for example, at Covatilla de San Juan (in the Valle de San Juan near Horcajo) (Fig. 83) where the bodies are surcharged with crescents placed diagonally upon them.

A spirit-picture at Puerto de Males Cabras (Fig. 84), near Alange, affords an excellent illustration of the transition from the hunting-magic to animism. The figure has two gigantic eyes and upon its head bears great horns. In its hands are a bow and arrow and it is shooting at a stag-like animal. A sign nearby may represent a boomerang. Here we can see the ancient wizards of the palæolithic pictures merging into the spirits of animism.

Horned ghosts are frequent, such as that upon the rock called El Esfanislado near Cabeza del Buey (Fig. 85). A type of spirit-picture which occurs again and again is that with several pairs of stags' antlers one above the other. Often we get strange figures dancing that look like plants (Figs. 88, 90), or insects (Fig. 89). Others defy all identification and might be the work of modern abstract artists (Fig. 87).

83 CUBIST FORMS Covatilla de San Juan

84 HUNTER WITH STAG
Puerto de Males Cabras

85 FIGURE OF A DEMON
El Esfanislado

86 ABSTRACT FIGURES   Nuestra Señora del Castillo

The spirits on the frieze at Reboso de Nuestra Señora del
Castillo (near Almadén) (Fig. 91) have short legs, small
bodies and fingers elongated like wings. The creatures
might be bats. Figures composed only of a face (though
sometimes with a pendent stroke to indicate the body) can
be seen at Peñón de Águila (Solana del Pino) in the Sierra

87 ABSTRACT PAINTING La Batanera   88 ABSTRACT FIGURES Cueva de los Letreros

89 ABSTRACT FIGURES El Navajo, near Solana del Pino, Fuencaliente, Ciudad Real

90 ABSTRACT FIGURES Cueva de los Letreros

91   FIGURES OF DEMONS   Nuestra Señora del Castillo

Madrona (Fig. 92). One of these figures can be paralleled in Portuguese, French and Irish passage-graves.

Admirable composition is often displayed in these abstract figures as, for instance, in those of the Cueva del Mediodía del Arabi near Yecla in the province of Murcia (Fig. 93). To the right-hand side is a figure with a triangle for a head, while the flexed (and apparently sitting) body is composed of wavy lines. The left-hand spirit-figure has a triangular head while the body is a line from which arms and legs project. Quite to the left is a dream-figure such as might have been painted by Klee, Baumeister or Miró. In the same Cueva del Mediodía (Fig. 94) are forms of spirits and ancestors that depict a fairy-tale world. The bodies are slender, delicate, waving or vacillating, unreal, floating in space and dissolving into fleeting, insubstantial images.

The figures at La Sierpe, Fuencaliente (province of Ciudad Real) (Fig. 95), are more set. Human forms are no

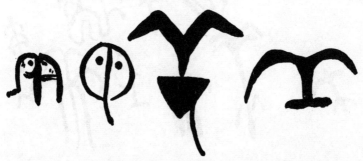

92   ABSTRACT FIGURES   Peñon de Collado del Aguila, and Covatilla del Rabanero

123

93 ABSTRACT FIGURES Cueva del Mediodia del Arabí

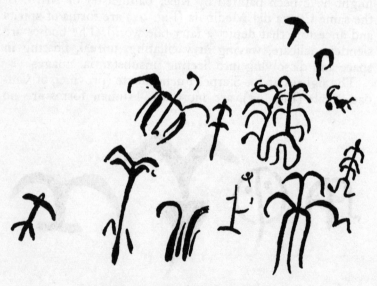

94 ABSTRACT FIGURES Cueva del Mediodia del Arabí

124

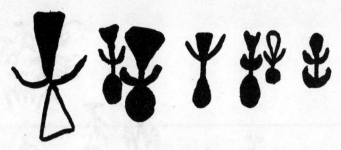

95 ABSTRACT FIGURES La Sierpe

longer recognizable as such. They have been merged into abstractions. The heads are triangles; the bodies ovals, circles, crescents—strange fantasies, dream thoughts of an unreal reality (Plate LV).

Just as abstract are the shapes and forms on the Piedra Escrita (Fig. 96), also at Fuencaliente. One cannot stand before the paintings without being powerfully affected by their coloration, their surface tension, the art of composition they display. The pigments used were light red, brown and yellow. There is no shading, no plasticity, but the forms are rendered tense by the cunning of the construction—line, wedge and triangle and oval. These are pictures of great æsthetic and spiritual significance—for those who can interpret the abstract. There is here a richness of life in some dimensionless space. An enchantment of waving forms. A transcendental frenzy, a swirl of things intangible, incomprehensible, mysterious, dæmonic (Plates LIII, LIV).

In many of the Spanish pictures vehicles are depicted. Their wheels project on the right and on the left. The carts are not seen in perspective but are viewed, as it were, from above, as for example, on the frieze of Los Buitres near Peñalsordo in the province of Badajoz. The predominating vehicle seems to be the two-wheeled cart still so common in southern Europe. The four-wheeled carts were probably used mostly, or solely, to carry about the sacred pictures of the gods and ghosts.

The æsthetic value of these paintings must be assessed by quite other standards than those applicable to the naturalistic pictures of the Ice Age. These schematized and

125

96 ABSTRACT FIGURES La Piedra, Escrita de Fuencaliente

highly stylized Spanish prehistoric pictures lack all plastic
and spatial quality and perspective, but these things were
also wanting in the post-glacial paintings. Now, however,
the proportions have lost all contact with reality. The stags,
for instance, are just strokes with four lines for legs and with
tall antlers. The human figures, or those of forefathers and
ghosts, are often only heads, sometimes only eyes with a line
pendent from them.

All the significance of these pictures lies in the symbolical
expression they give of a mysterious, dark realm that exists
not for the senses but for the spirit, for the imagination. The
æsthetic value of this art, must not, then, be judged by its
greater or lesser approximation to a representation of natural
forms. The importance of these highly stylized paintings
lies, as does that of all abstract art, in composition and in the
metaphysical expression of ideas.

The colour used in these pictures is predominantly red.
Brown, however, was also utilized, as were yellow and white.
Pigments were applied with a brush to the rock-face. The
traces of brush-work can, indeed, be seen in the finely-
drawn lines. The colours were pounded to a powder and

126

certainly mixed with some fatty substance. They are, in fact, similar to the colours used in oil-painting today. The rock-pictures of Galicia, on the other hand, are deeply incised into the surface of the stone.

We may deduce from these rock-pictures that the men who made them still lived in a hunting economy but it was one in which the chase was steadily taking a second place to pastoralism. In the Cueva de los Canforos, near Peñarubia, in the Sierra Morena, are figures of men leading beasts by halters (Fig. 47). These pictures are still semi-naturalistic and therefore must belong to the earlier phases of the art. It follows, therefore, that pastoralism must have been practised during these earlier phases. Later, under influences from the East, an agriculture must also have appeared. The many star pictures indicate an agricultural way of life, as do the frequent water- and rain-symbols. The more stylized the art becomes, the more the hunting symbols give way to signs and devices associated with the life of the agriculturalists.

These rock-pictures afford us, also, much information about the trade and commerce of remote times. We are in the epoch of the Alcalá culture—the first phase of the Spanish Bronze Age. It was the age in which there came to western Europe certain significant borrowings from the Near East, such as, especially, the great passage- and gallery-graves that are so common in Palestine, Syria and Egypt. These megalithic monuments stem from the Near Eastern sepulchres whose construction was dictated by a belief in a life beyond the grave, in continued existence after bodily death.

With this stream of culture is borne along also the cult of the Mother Goddess, the *Magna Dea*, the *Mater Magna*. It

97 HUMAN FIGURES LEADING ANIMALS BY HALTERS Los Canforos de Peñarubia

127

is understandable that there should be female statuettes in Spain that are completely identical with many of the idols in the Eastern Mediterranean region. From about 2000 B.C. Babylonian thought and Babylonian religion streamed out over the whole Mediterranean area and, later on, reached Brittany and Ireland. Further witnesses to the culture-influences of the Near East are the spread of the spiral (a fertility symbol common to the whole Eastern Mediterranean including Crete), of the axe (both simple and double) and the wheel-sign representing the fourfold nature of the earth's surface (north, south, east, west). We have already noted that, through the beads found at Fuente Álamo, we can date this period to between 1500 and 1400 B.C.

The Spanish return for imports from the East consisted mostly of metals in which the men of the Eastern Mediterranean were, at this time, displaying much interest. The existence of metallic ores must have been discovered, in Spain, very early on. Copper objects appear before 3000 B.C. at El Garcel (near Almería) and we know that before 2000 B.C. there was a brisk trade in Spanish copper, tin and bronze to the Eastern Mediterranean lands. When, about 2350 B.C., Sargon of Akkad subdued Sumeria, Spanish commerce with the Eastern Mediterranean was interrupted and Spanish mining declined. Later on, after about 2200 B.C. the east–west Mediterranean traffic picked up again. In the Near East more and more metal was being used while mining operations in Spain were developed. It looks reasonable to assign the rock-pictures to this period. It was the time of the rise of four great empires, those of the Mitanni, of the Egyptians, of the Babylonians and the Assyrians, whose rulers were connected by intermarriage and by treaty. A fifth power was Crete.

Commerce in the Mediterranean was safe. The merchant fleets could sail without fear. This is the period of the spread of a portion of the glory of the East to Iberia and beyond to the north-west of Europe.

The period came to an end with the annihilation of Cretan might by the Achæans about 1400 B.C. and with the decay of Egyptian domination after the reign of Amenhotep IV in the middle of the 14th century B.C. The realm of the

Mitanni was destroyed by the Hittites. Trade with the Eastern Mediterranean was interrupted again and once more Spanish mining declined. The rock-pictures throw not a little light upon these mighty commotions.

The systematic and scientific study of these rock-paintings began in 1910. As we have mentioned, the re-discovery of the rock-pictures at Las Batuecas served as a starting point for an exploration of many other sites.

Breuil visited Las Batuecas in 1912 accompanied by Louis Siret and Cabré. On this trip the pictures at Vélez Blanco (Almería) and at Jimena (Jaén) were also recognized. The visitors excited the interest of the local population in the paintings and Breuil was informed about the 'Written Rocks' at Fuencaliente (Ciudad Real). The Peña Escrita site had, indeed, been noted from the end of the 18th century and had been described as early as 1866 by Góngora but knowledge of the site had not trickled through to the world of prehistorians and archæologists.

In the same year Obermaier, Breuil and Wernert undertook another journey of exploration and this time a whole series of painted rocks was discovered in the Sierra Morena.

From 1912 onwards, Breuil set out each year, on an expedition of discovery and covered the provinces of Albacete, Alicante, Valencia, Burgos, Oviedo, Málaga and Granada.

In 1914 Breuil, accompanied by Miles Burkitt of Cambridge, revisited most of the sites and on this occasion Estrecho de Santonge was found. In 1915, together with Federico de Motos, Breuil discovered the Piedra de los Mártires. Between 12th May and 23rd June, 1916, further outstanding finds were made under Breuil's direction: the sites of Almadén, Peñalsordo, Cabeza de Buey, Hornachos, Alange and Mérida. On this same prospecting trip were recognized also the Portuguese rock-pictures of Nossa Senhora da Esperança.

Since the Spanish prehistorians have busied themselves more and more with the stylized rock-paintings, discoveries have become increasingly numerous.

Closely related, in style and content, to these rock-paintings are the engravings on the megalithic monuments. In his book on the megalithic monuments of Spain[1] Leisner indicates that there are engravings in the dolmens and passage-graves (such as those at Pedra Coberta) which resemble in style those of the Levantine Spanish art. Still, the great majority of these engravings is in the mode of the stylized rock-paintings. In the Dolmen de Soto at Trigueros (province of Huelva) (Plate LVI) there are similar engravings (especially of eyes with eyebrows and nose) to those both in the Mediterranean region and in Brittany, Ireland, England and Scandinavia.

A peculiar and special area of Spanish rock-art is centred in Galicia. Here the engravings are on rocks in the open air. A more ancient and a less ancient series may be detected. The older, quite stylized, is Bronze Age (Plate LVII). The younger, which is of the Iron Age, shows a naturalistic art beginning again. These Galician engravings are linked (despite many points of difference) with the stylized and abstract art of prehistoric Spain. Obermaier devoted a volume to the Galician pictures.

[1] Georg Leisner, *Die Megalithgräber des iberischen Halbinsel*, Berlin, 1943.

THE ROCK-PICTURES OF ITALY

UP TO NOW, rock-engravings have been discovered at four different sites in Italy and the pictures are closely linked, in content and in treatment, with the stylized pictures of Spain.

The first site, not far from Ventimiglia, is so rich that the man who devoted most time to the study of the engravings counted more than fourteen hundred figures. The pictures were mentioned as early as A.D. 1600 and since 1877 have been the subject of an abundant literature. With these are closely related the rock-pictures of Albenga and Voltri, smaller and less well-known sites.[1]

An important complex of prehistoric rock-engravings was made known in 1931. They are in the Val Camonica, near Capodiponte, not far from the shores of the Lake of Garda. The pictures are about 2,600 feet above sea-level. To this same group belong the rock-pictures in the Ligurian Alps some 6,500 feet up.

From the technique of the pictures it is obvious that they are of Bronze Age date. The animals (especially the stags) much resemble, in their stylized forms, the figures of the Spanish rock-art of the second millennium B.C. The human figures are represented in shortened, abbreviated designs of just a few strokes. The Bronze Age dating is confirmed by the frequent occurrence of daggers belonging to Period I of that Age. There is a number of javelins, often with long handles, shown as being hurled by men.

On account of this latter circumstance, earlier students of the engravings—such as Montelius, Déchelette and Bicknell—assigned them to the first phase of the Bronze Age. It is, however, apparent that many of the engravings

---

[1] These rock-engravings 'not far from Ventimiglia' are in fact some considerable distance from that town, and are now not even in Italian territory. The Mont-Bégo site (with the engravings) was ceded to France together with Tende, after the 1939–1945 war. (Translator's Note.)

are of later times—Middle and Late Bronze Ages. Battaglia has pointed out the figure of a rider that appears to resemble those on 6th-century Greek vases. He assumes, therefore, that some of the engravings are of as late as the 6th century. The mass of the pictures would fall, then, into the centuries stretching between the first phase of the Bronze Age and the 6th century B.C.

An absolute dating is afforded by the types of objects represented, especially by the daggers belonging to the so-called 'Remedello' culture in Italy which (again because of parallels with Mycenæ and Egypt) must be dated to the times between 1800 and 1600 B.C. Thus, for instance, at Mont-Bégo, not far from Tende (Fig. 98), in south-eastern France, there is a dagger shown upon the rocks that is quite similar to daggers recovered at the Loreto Aprutino and Ripatransone sites (Fig. 99). The rock-pictures of this group belong, then, as do the Spanish, to the middle of the second millennium B.C. and they survived until about 600 B.C. Style-analysis and archæological research lead us to the same conclusions.

98 ENGRAVING OF A DAGGER   Mont-Bégo (Tende)

99 DAGGER   Loreto Aprutino

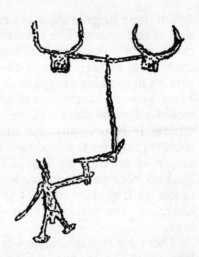

100 Ploughman   Mont-Bégo (Tende)

The first investigators of these pictures were much struck by their emplacement. They are in the Alps, in the mountains of Liguria, to the north of the Lake of Garda, and we may well suppose that further discoveries of rock-pictures will be made in the Italian mountains.

The human figures are depicted as ploughmen (Fig. 100), as men walking behind carts, men leading animals into folds or pens, shepherds with sticks. We see a span of oxen attached to a plough, we see women hoeing and men in huts. This is an agricultural world even if in it there survive hunters with their hounds, for hunting lives on through all economies and has lasted until today. There are warriors on foot and wielding clubs. There are men armed with lances and axes. Men bearing quadrangular or rounded shields. There are mounted men armed with lance and shield.

What induced men in these ancient times to climb and clamber up into the high mountains and there to create rock-pictures that should relate to hunting, to agriculture and to war? Surely it must have been some realization of the existence of a divinity, of some godhead that lived on the summits and must be reverenced in the high places. Upon the peaks Man is nearer to the ghosts, to the spirits; up there Man is more closely in communion with the unknown, mysterious and weird Powers that determine and decide Man's fate.

133

On these heights there can never have been practised any sort of agriculture. The summits were cult-places, just as the caves were cult-places, hidden from the gaze of ordinary men. It is enough to visit these rugged, barren and wild ravines in the hills to realize that no one ever dwelt up here. Here were the sanctuaries to which men repaired when they would sway the divine Powers to the advantage of human affairs. It is not only the site and emplacement of these rock-engravings that indicate the religious nature of their art; it is revealed by the pictures themselves. As in the Spanish rock-paintings, there are signs of the sun, of the moon and of the stars. The constellations are brought closer to Man and can influence his thought and his feelings.

There are representations of human footprints which are lacking in Spain but are very common in Scandinavia. These most probably indicate the presence of the gods. The footprints mean that the godhead has manifested itself in a living and tangible form.[1]

There are also spirit-figures, uncanny forms with strange heads or with no heads at all—and masked figures. All these shapes and representations serve to integrate the Italian rock-paintings into the same ghostly world as that depicted upon the Spanish Written Rocks. A world of wraiths and ancestors, a world of animism, a world in which the first gods arise.

If, however, the style of the Italian rock-engravings is, on the whole, the same as that of the Spanish conventionalized prehistoric art, the Italian group displays a number of obvious peculiarities. First of all, the pictures are not painted upon the rocks, but pecked into the stone. The whole surface of the figure is subjected to pecking—and not just the outline as in earlier times. The effect of this treatment is to make the designs stand out boldly from their backgrounds. The stone still shows clearly the marks made by stone or metal hammer as it struck tap after tap. The older the

[1] On the great holy rock of Jerusalem where Solomon's temple once stood and where now is the Mosque of Omar, there are to be seen most ancient engravings of footprints. Maybe it was here that Yahweh appeared to the remote ancestors of the Jews.

134

pictures the more careful, the deeper and more accurate the hammer-strokes.

The relative chronology inside the epoch can be, in a measure, determined by a study of the overcutting and reworking of the pictures themselves. The oldest layers of drawings show javelins characteristic of phase I of the Bronze Age. Over these are representations of stylized animals often so disposed that they almost entirely hide the daggers and javelins—as in the Val Camonica. Often the pictures of weapons were transformed into animal figures— an indication, maybe, that men no longer understood the significance of the older signs and symbols.

The animal figures must have been executed in Middle or Late Bronze Age times. The most recent pictures are very lightly and faintly pecked in. To this last group belong the pictures of riders that we have already mentioned and which may be assigned to the 6th century B.C.

Another feature of the Italian group that is not found in the Spanish is scenic composition. If it is not common in Italy, at least it does exist. For instance, in the Val Camonica there is shown a vehicle drawn by two horses. Probably a cart for carrying sacred images. Underneath the cart is a masked dancer and over the axle animal figures in the Hallstatt style.[1] They must have some ceremonial, some cult meaning. While these animals and the horses are shown in profile, the vehicle is quite schematized and is depicted as though viewed from above. But the four wheels are circular and affixed one to each corner of the vehicle.

This very interesting drawing must, on account of the animal figures, be assigned to the Hallstatt period. There is also an instructive picture of pile-dwellings. The piles are clearly distinguishable, as are the beams, the thatched roofs and the ornamentation of the roof-ridges. It is just the form of this roof-ridge construction that shows the picture must be dated to Hallstatt times (Plate LX). This engraving (as also the vehicle picture) is superposed upon earlier drawings of beasts and men. In this later period the art-style showed a return to realistic traditions even if the figures were still stylized and schematic. The drawing of a horse and rider

[1] That is the Hallstatt Iron Age culture about 750–400 B.C.

(Plate LXII), for instance, is still 'linear' and stiff but it is a good deal more lifelike than the rock-pictures of neolithic and early Bronze Age times. The horseman has one arm raised while by the side of the horse runs a dog. In similar style is a group of warriors (Plate LXIII) who seem to be celebrating a victory—in any case they are dancing. In the lower part of the picture are four men holding hands. The first man bears in one hand a spear and in the other a bow. The large figure in the middle also carries a spear while on the left-hand side of the picture can be made out several more men with bows in their hands. The outlines are only lightly engraved and there is no modelling at all.

In contrast to these drawings are those of the Cemmo height in the Val Camonica (Plates LVIII, LIX, LXIV). They are of early Bronze Age date. Whole rows of engraved animal-figures occur here, together with carefully executed representations of triangular-bladed daggers. A similar weapon to this was excavated at Montemerano near Saturnia. Of the same date are the very stylized human figures to be seen on the left of Plate LVIII. The rows of beasts and of daggers—which are arranged either above or close to each other—produce, in their stylization and their symmetry, a pronouncedly ornamental effect. Two very lifelike stags remind one of the 'popular' art of later times.

It is very interesting to note that above, or near the Val Camonica pictures, inscriptions have been identified. Alltheim has studied these 'runes' and classifies them in three groups: the first, from 350 to 181 B.C., in indigenous northern Etruscan script: the second, from 181 to 90 B.C., which can be identified by the isolated occurrence of Latin letters: and the third, after 90 B.C., executed when the Latin alphabet had won the victory over all rivals. In the Val Camonica, also, are drawings which belong to early and mid-medieval times and even to later periods.

By their technique alone (they are executed with rather delicate tools) these later engravings are clearly distinguishable from the earlier ones. Together with the earlier and later Gothic inscriptions are representations of keys, Christian crosses, drawings of warriors and pinnacled medieval cities characteristic of the times when the struggle between Guelf and Ghibelline was raging. The fact that crosses and keys—Christian symbols—and inscriptions were added to the rock-pictures indicates that these were regarded as heathen places, the abodes of ghosts and devils whose evil actions and influence must be counteracted by exorcism. The feeling lived on for long that the prehistoric pictures were magical. We shall see that the Russian rock-engravings were rendered innocuous by means of super-posed crosses.

The world represented by this art is one of pastoralism and agriculture. Instead of scenes of the chase we get figures of oxen, swine and horses, representations of men's huts and their fields upon which the medicine-men called down blessings. Once again the signs for water and for rain appear. Near these symbols are ghost-pictures, figures wearing masks such as to this day are still worn upon cere-monial occasions in certain Alpine valleys. Several prehistoric cultural traditions have survived as the customs of today . . . fantastic and uncanny is the expressive visage of the Mont-Bégo wizard (Plate LXV), a powerful figure holding swords in his hands.

From their valleys and villages men climbed on certain feast-days up into the hills and there sought from the eternal powers fertility for their fields and blessing upon their houses. In doing these things men were following the example of their forefathers who had offered up sacrifice before the sacred stones. Bowls have been found, just like those on the Scandinavian rock-engravings, bowls that served to hold water, oil or blood from the sacrificial victims.

If we reflect for a moment upon the formulæ of blessings still used today in churches, if we remember the processions in the fields and the prayers for rain or fine weather, then the spiritual ideas held by the men who executed these pictures may seem less foreign to us than the magic concepts which inspired the naturalistic paintings of the Ice Age, although æsthetically the Ice Age art seems so near to us.

THE IMAGINATIVE ROCK-PICTURES
OF FRANCE

THE French neolithic and Bronze Age pictures on the rocks
have been seriously studied only within recent years. As late
as 1924 E. Hernández Pacheco published a book in which
he stated that highly stylized prehistoric pictures existed
only in Spain. Nevertheless, careful search has now brought
to light many other stylized and abstract drawings of neolithic and chalcolithic date. In 1924 G. Vézian published
engravings found in the Ariège. The first systematic study
of this art was undertaken by A. Glory in a work entitled
Les peintures de l'âge du métal en France méridionale. The
researches concern principally the Ariège department and,
thus, that part of southern France which touches the
Spanish border.

Fairly recently discovered were the paintings in the
l'Hermite cave near Ussat-les-Bains, some three miles
south-east of Tarascon-sur-Ariège (Fig. 101). Here is to be
seen a highly stylized, almost abstract, figure which may still
be recognized as that of a female with strongly marked genitalia. In this same cave Garrigou and Godal dug up several
skeletons with one of which a Bronze Age pottery vessel
was associated. Also near Ussat-les-Bains is the Grand-
Père grotto that contains stylized paintings in red pigment.

The Grotte de la Vache (Fig. 102), two miles south of
Tarascon-sur-Ariège, possesses paintings of stylized human
figures to which Breuil made reference as long ago as 1935.
Especially important here is the representation of a *Magna
Mater*, since there are figures exactly like it on some
Spanish sites, such as Aldeaquemada. Figures of human or
quasi-human appearance occur, moreover, at Baulou, at
Baichon (commune of Miglos), at Lavelanet, at Mont-
ferriet and in the Peyort cavern near Prat—all in the
Ariège department of southern France.

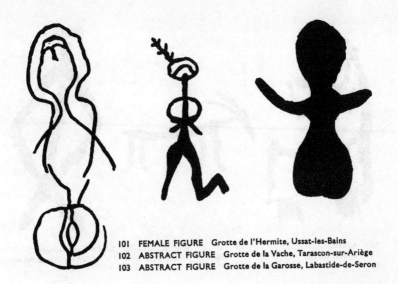

101 FEMALE FIGURE Grotte de l'Hermite, Ussat-les-Bains
102 ABSTRACT FIGURE Grotte de la Vache, Tarascon-sur-Ariège
103 ABSTRACT FIGURE Grotte de la Garosse, Labastide-de-Seron

In the La Garosse grotto, near Labastide-de-Séron (Ariège department), has been discovered a human figure that corresponds very closely with the Spanish prototypes (Fig. 103). The same thing may be said of pictures in the Abri Hilaire, in the Neukirch and Alain caves and also of the stylized pictures in another region, namely those at Ollioullets and Evenos in the Var department of south-eastern France.

The Grotte Dumas (Fig. 104) in the same region shows a painting which looks very like that of the idol on the Peña Tú rock in the Asturias (Plate XLIX). Stylized figures of animals and men are to be seen both in the Grotte Sainte-Estève and in the Grotte Monier, also in the Var (Fig. 105). Excavations in these caves brought to light a remarkable stylized human figure carved in stone, and also bronze objects and pottery vessels which can be dated to period II of the Bronze Age. There is the picture of a human face in the Chélo grotto (Fig. 106) and six stylized human figures in the Toulousanne rock-shelter (Fig. 107) (both in the Var). The engraved rock-drawings in the caves of Sainte-Eulalie, near Ussat-les-Bains, of Le Grand Père and Peyort at Prat were discovered by Glory. J. L. Baudet has reported

104 ABSTRACT FIGURE
Grotte Dumas

105 (a) Left: ANIMAL FIGURE Grotte Sainte-Estève
(b) Right: ABSTRACT HUMAN FIGURE Grotte Monier

upon rock-pictures (human faces and symbolical signs) in the Ile-de-France.

In addition to these pictures upon rock-walls there are, in France, a great number of engravings in barrows, megalithic graves and monuments. Such barrows cover the whole country and are, in France, much more common than in Germany. If we look, however, at a map showing the distribution of these monuments, we shall notice that they are most often to be found on, and near, the coasts. There are two areas where the megalithic remains are particularly common—around Marseilles on the Mediterranean coast,

106 HUMAN FACE Grotte Chélo

107 STYLIZED HUMAN FIGURES Toulousanne

108 ENGRAVINGS OF STYLIZED HUMAN FIGURES Ile de France

and in Brittany, in the extreme north-west of France. Thus, the two departments of the Finistère and the Morbihan in the north and that of the Aveyron in the south are especially rich in barrows. According to a list published in one of Déchelette's books, there are 487 of these tombs in the Aveyron, 400 in the neighbouring department of the Ardèche, 353 in the Finistère and 312 in the Morbihan. As we move east these monuments get fewer and fewer. The departments on the German and Swiss frontiers have, altogether, at the most, ten or twelve of such graves.

The reason for this striking distribution has been much discussed. But there is only one satisfactory explanation for the arrangement. The barrows are closely associated with the trade-routes of tin export. Just as at one time during the Neolithic salt became the most important mineral substance on earth (to such an extent that it is precisely in the neighbourhood of the salt mines that the finds of prehistoric objects, of certain periods, are the most numerous), just as in our own times coal and petroleum are raw materials that arouse diplomatic complications and even wars, so tin was of paramount importance for men of the Bronze Age. Pure tin, on account of its softness and malleability, is useful only for ornaments. If, however, tin be mixed with copper, the resulting alloy (about 90% copper and 10% tin) is the hard metallic substance we know as bronze. Thus, during the Bronze Age, no weapons, no instruments, no tools could be made without the use of tin. It is, therefore, natural enough that important cultural centres should have grown up where tin was to be found.

Of course, in the Europe of those days, the existence of tin in south-east Asia was unknown; still, the ancient authors report that tin was brought in from afar. Herodotus (about 490 to 424 B.C.)[1] calls the land where the tin was found the 'Kassiterides'. It was for him a fabled region, as it appears to have remained for other ancient writers, such as Diodorus, Strabo, Pomponius Mela and Pliny.[2] In none of the old Greek or Latin authors is there any hint at Asiatic tin.

[1] Book III. 115.
[2] In passages which occur respectively in Diodorus, V. 38, in Strabo, 120: 147: 175, in Pomponius Mela, III. 6. 46 and in Pliny IV. 19.

According to all reports the metal that was so precious was imported from the 'Kassiterides'.[1]

In Bronze Age times tin was mined in three areas: Galicia in north-west Spain, Brittany and England, including Wales. Thus these three areas were in close contact with one another. The ships that passed through the Strait of Gibraltar and coasted round Spain, touched at the shores of Galicia, of Brittany and of southern England. Often the ships pushed on to Ireland where there was gold to be obtained. The populations of these regions were, in fact, included in the fabulous concept of the 'Kassiterides'.

The monuments and the art-objects and the utensils found along this trade-route are all alike. The rock-pictures of Spanish Galicia (that are rather aberrant in Spain) reappear, almost unchanged, in the gallery-graves of Brittany, of southern England and of Ireland. In all these areas are found the same geometrical designs upon bronze hatchets, the same crescent-shaped plaques used for adornment (the so-called *lunulæ*), the same decoration on gold goblets, the same concave-base arrowheads of flint. Some authorities[2] have even spoken of a colonization of Ireland from and through North Spain and Portugal. Anyway, it is in these coastal regions that the majority of the megalithic monuments is to be found.

At first this trade route was exclusively maritime. Later on, land communications were established with Brittany and thereby were linked together the two French regions most rich in gallery-graves, namely the north-west and the area of the southern course of the Rhone. Moreover this line of communication can be plotted by means of the megalithic monuments.

We have, indeed, interesting literary evidence which proves the importance of this overland trade-route even as late as the times of Augustus. Diodorus Siculus (V. 22) speaks of the tin mines in the Belerion promontory of Britain—clearly an allusion to Cornwall. He writes: "It is a

[1] It has been suggested that *Kassiterides* may be derived from the Elamite *kassi-ti-ra*, that is, 'from the land of the Kassi'.
[2] Such as John Evans, Déchelette, Åberg, Mahr and Bosch-Gimpera.

stony soil in which there are deposits of earths and it is from these that, by smelting, pure metallic tin is obtained. The metal is run into regular moulds and brought to an island called Iktes (the Isle of Wight?) near Britain. Since, at ebb-tide, the way to the island is dry land, the tin can be laden on to carts and transported in quantities to this island. There traders buy the tin from the natives and bear it over to Gaul. The metal is carried on horses overland through Gaul and takes thirty days to reach the mouth of the Rhone." The route referred to is the same as that we should infer by looking at a map of the distribution of the megaliths. By this same way and road came the bell-beakers from Spain to France and England.

We are enabled, therefore, to determine the chronology of the megaliths and at the same time that of the pictures they contain. Just as in Spain there are no megalithic monuments which can be assigned to the Stone Age (even the bell-beakers first appear in Spain early in the Bronze Age, that is to say about 2000 B.C.), the gallery-graves of France, England and Scandinavia, which are usually assigned to the Neolithic, must be included in the Bronze Age. This is also true for the German barrows and megaliths. Over thirty metal objects have been found in them and if, generally speaking, metal is rare in this epoch, that is because it was not, until later, actually worked in northern Europe. Instead of making use of the rather vague terms 'Neolithic' or 'Bronze Age' it is better to use dates. The megalithic graves date from between 2000 and 1400 B.C.

These figures are vouched for by a series of finds whose meaning is indisputable. Among these discoveries, the most important are those from Bygholm near Horsens in South Jutland: they consist of four flat copper axes with rounded blades, three copper armlets, a dagger-blade with median ridges and also portions of a pottery vessel of a type found in the earliest gallery-graves. It is certain that the objects belonged together since the green patina of the copper has eaten into the surface of the pottery. The copper objects are of Italian origin and are characteristic of the so-called 'Remedello culture' which (judging from a whole series of parallels with Mycenæ and Egypt) must be assigned to the period between 1800 and 1600 B.C. Obviously, then, we must date the older gallery-graves of Denmark and Germany to this epoch.

It is true that, generally, the period from 1800 to 1600 B.C. is regarded, in Germany, as Neolithic; however, bronze was already used, even if it had to be imported.

For the dating of the megalithic graves of Brittany the most important evidence is that from the Parc-Guren gallery-grave near Carnac in Morbihan department. Here, in 1926, Le Rouzic found a bell-beaker, a triangular copper dagger and an Egyptian bead of a special shape, tubular and formed of several connected rings (Fig. 109). Such beads, according to H. C. Beck, are a Cretan imitation, in copper, of Egyptian faience beads well known from finds—for instance in a grave at Abydos: this site is rather accurately dated, since in it was discovered a *scarabæus* bearing the cartouche of the Pharaoh Amenhotep III (about 1412 to 1376 B.C.). The oldest known examples of these beads may be assigned to the reign of Queen Hatshepsut (about 1501 to 1480 B.C.). Beads of this form were found to be particularly abundant in the palace of Tell el Amarna and the fashion for them seems to have lasted until the 19th Egyptian dynasty (that is the 12th century B.C.). This copper bead, then, helps us to date the peak-period of the Brittany gallery-graves as that of the middle Bronze Age (that is, from about 1500 to 1000 B.C.), while some of the older Breton megalithic monuments belong to the Old Bronze Age, that is, to the period between 1800 and 1500—the epoch marked by the occurrence of the bell-beakers.

This dating of the tombs determines also that of their engravings, which belong to the second millennium B.C. and especially to the centuries between 1800 and 1300 B.C.

Taken as a whole, these engravings bear a great resemblance to the rock-pictures of Spanish Galicia, although they also display a certain relationship with the stylized paintings of southern Spain. In the gallery-graves, indeed, there are some engravings in whose deep grooves traces of colour may sometimes be found.

These tombs were not only places of burial but they were also places where sacrifices were offered to ancestors and to spirits. The cult-character of the old graves has remained alive in the memory of the inhabitants of these regions. Thus in Brittany the megalithic monuments are termed *Salle des Fées, Clapier des Fées, Caves des Fées, Fours des Fées, Fuseaux des Fées, Pierres du Diable, Tombeaux des Géants.*

The members of the Council of Arles (in A.D. 452) were moved to make pronouncements not only against tree-cults and the cult of springs and wells but also against that of the 'stones'—that is to say the megalithic tombs. The members of the Council of Tours (in A.D. 567) forbade priests, on pain of excommunication, to perform cult-ceremonies at trees, springs or 'stones'. It was, in those days, in fact, a common occurrence for Christian ecclesiastics to officiate also at heathen cult-rites.

Comparable injunctions were pronounced at the Councils of Nantes (in A.D. 658) and Toledo (in A.D. 681 and 682) and also, in A.D. 789, by Charlemagne himself.

But another, and probably more efficacious, way of combating surviving heathen customs was to exorcize the demons and to transform the graves into Christian cult-sites. The exorcism was effected by the addition of a crucifix or by the engraving of Christian signs and symbols. As early as the 12th—or even the 11th—century, the gallery-grave at Saint-Germain-de-Confolens (in the Charente department) was turned into a Christian chapel. One of the megalithic roof-stones is now supported by a pillar, while another of them forms the altar. The megalithic tomb of Plouaret (Côtes-du-Nord department) was consecrated as the Chapelle des Sept-Saints.

The dominating megalithic grave in the neighbourhood of Carnac is the hill of Saint-Michel. It bears, today, a church, erected in 1664 on the site of a much more ancient sanctuary built by Irish missionary monks. The chapel stands right upon the gallery-grave as though to symbolize that it has lost its power and has been put to Christian uses. This great tumulus, that is a prominent object for miles around, is about 85 yards long, 60 yards wide and 45 feet high. A host of legends is connected with the place. It is said that treasure lies hidden in the hill and that on the eastern side silver coins may often be seen. Another tale has it that Cæsar died near Carnac and was buried in the heart of this hill. He had golden shoes upon his feet and his body was placed in a sarcophagus of pure gold, while near it was heaped up a great treasure. It was so that his rest might not be disturbed that Roman soldiers heaped over the grave a huge mass of stones and earth.

It appears from the excavations that, in fact, some chieftain or prince was buried beneath the tumulus. Galles and Lefèbvre (who undertook the first excavations here in 1852) found, in the burial chamber, thirty-nine stone axes, ten of which were carved out of jadeite. Two of them were pierced with holes and all of them were stuck upright in the ground so that their blades pointed upwards. Further finds were a string of ninety-seven beads and ten pendants and also the remains of a string of ivory beads. The floor of the chamber was covered with flat stone slabs and bore the remains of charred bones. In 1900 and in 1906 Le Rouzic and Charles Keller continued the researches, begun by Galles and Lefèbvre, and proved that the hill covered a necropolis with several galleries and chambers—all vaulted. Some great leader had been interred here with his followers and many animal sacrifices had here been offered up.

Likewise a very considerable number of menhirs—great monolithic uprights—has been christianized. Generally a small cross was fixed on the summit of the stone. On the Champ-Dolent menhir near Dol (department of Ille-et-Vilaine) the crucifix is of considerable size. In the Finistère department are not a few of these 'christened' menhirs. A pillar at Grouanes Coz (obviously a former menhir) carries an ancient Romanesque crucifix, as does another pillar at Goulven—but this latter is a menhir that was transformed into a stele in Gaulish times and presumably bore the image of some Gaulish divinity.

In the megalithic tomb-engravings we come across, once

more, most of the old cult-symbols that appear on the rock-pictures of Spain—the zigzag 'water' line (a symbol of fertility) and the wavy or serpentine line, with the same significance. A snake is a creature which disappears into the earth and, like Nature itself, in springtime emerges once more. This most ancient symbol of eternal life appears in the mystery cults of Greece and Crete where it is represented in association with a woman—as in the Old Testament. It is, thus, not surprising that we should find serpents depicted upon rocks and in rock-pictures which were wrought by men much influenced by the complex of Eastern Mediterranean beliefs and ideas. Snakes can be seen upon a menhir at Manio (in the commune of Carnac), on the walls of the Kermaillard gallery-grave, on the stones of the Mané-Lud and Petit-Mont tombs, as well as upon one of the walls of Gavr'inis.

Frequent are representations of the sun and the moon, as, for instance, upon the stones of the Marchands, Mané-Lud, Petit-Mont, Tachen-Paul and Mané-Kérioned gallery-graves, as well as upon a small stone at Kerpenhir. There occurs, too, a sign of a great wheel with eighteen spokes that seems also to symbolize either the moon or the sun.

Representations of axes are of very frequent occurrence. Simple axes can be seen at Gavr'inis and upon the stones of Mané-Lud. More common even are hafted axes, visible upon so many of the megalithic monuments and especially on those of Gavr'inis, Mané-er-H'roëk, Mané-Lud, Mané-Kérioned (Plate LXVII), Mané-Rutual, Petit-Mont, Pierres-Plates and Lufang. On the walls of the Mané-Rutual tomb (and on those of some others) we find representations of the eyes that are so common on the socketed axes of Bronze Age times. Such an axe was, indeed, found inside the gallery-grave of Er-Grah (in the commune of Locmariaquer in the Morbihan department). At the chapel of Saint-Jean (in the commune of Locoal-Mendom) there is, over the door, a stone set in the wall and it displays the sign of the hafted axe. It comes doubtless from some gallery-grave.

The axe has, from very remote times, been a hallowed object, a symbol of might. The axe, in fact, retains its sacred

110 ENGRAVING OF A SHIP
Petit-Mont Dolmen

character in Christianity where it serves as a defence against the baleful power of demons. An axe will be laid upon a threshhold or hung above a door. Thus men and beasts will be protected from dangers. The ancient custom of immuring an axe over the door of a Christian church had also a definite cult significance.

In the megalithic tombs of Mané-Lud, of Kerveresse, of Petit-Mont and of Lufang are representations of ships and these have not yet been found in the Spanish art of this period. Unique in Europe is an engraving upon the Petit-Mont stone (Fig. 110). This drawing represents a ship with a large cabin on its deck. Le Rouzic, who devoted much study to the engraved stones of Brittany, compares this picture with those of ships in Egypt. The engraving does, indeed, resemble those of Egyptian ships found on the Atlantic coast.

At Petit-Mont and also at Roch-Priol we have representations of human footprints such as are to be found in Italy and especially in Scandinavia. They indicate, most probably, the presence of divinities.

Much discussion has taken place concerning the U-shaped signs (Figs. 111–112) common on the French megaliths. This sign occurs repeatedly upon the stones of Mané-Lud. It is possible that the signs represent ships, but it seems more probable, as Déchelette suggested, that the symbol is that of the Holy Horns. In all the Mediterranean area the bull was a sacred animal. Minos, the legendary Cretan ruler, was half-bull, half-man—the Minotaur. The sacred significance of the horns spread from its Mediterranean centre to Hungary and to the regions of the pile-dwellings in Central Germany.

Bulls' horns owe much of their significance to their

149

III ENGRAVING OF SHIPS (?)
Mané-Lud Dolmen

likeness to the crescent moon. The bull-divinity is probably
originally a moon-deity. The bull-cult seems to have had its
origin in Asia (we may remember the old legend of Europe
borne upon the back of a bull) and the goddess Ishatar-
Astarte is associated with the moon. Ideas of fertility are also
bound up with moon-worship. The phases of the moon, it
was thought, had not only an influence upon the weather but
also, according to ancient beliefs, directly upon the growth
of the crops. Those goddesses who owe much to the shape
and the attributes of Astarte (that is to say, Venus and
Diana) wear crescents in their hair. The moon's crescent at
the feet of the Madonna indicates that the figure of the
Mother of God incorporates features from several different
ancient Mediterranean deities.

The idea that the U-signs represent horns is strengthened
by the fact that on the Mané-er-H'roëk stone there are
delineations of bulls with very prominently marked horns.
Horns and axes are, of course, typically Cretan symbols.

Yet another sign is spread all over the area of the megalithic monuments and that is the spiral (Plate LXVIII). It
is, indeed, one of the most widespread symbols in the Eastern
Mediterranean area. In Crete and on other Mediterranean
islands, the spiral is undoubtedly a symbol of fertility. So
many of the female statuettes bear spirals near or on the
genitalia that the sign may, originally, have depicted the
womb. On pottery the sign occurs again and again,
especially upon vessels designed to carry water, for water is,
of course, one of the principal factors in fertility. Again, it is

possible that the spiral may have been the stylized representation of a snail. Snails are mysterious creatures that slip in and out of their shells and which appear and disappear. Many of the female statuettes bear spirals upon their breasts. We may agree with Arthur Evans and with Montelius that the spiral survived from the Palæolithic, through the Neolithic to the Bronze Age and later spread to the isles and to Egypt.

There are spirals upon IVth-dynasty[1] Egyptian scarabs and spirals are especially common during the XIIth dynasty that was contemporaneous with the peak-period of Cretan prosperity.

The spiral-motif dominates the Hungarian and German Bronze Age and it is noteworthy that before the second phase of the Bronze Age (that is before 1400–1200 B.C.) the spiral-motif is not found in Germany. The fact that, on the other hand, the spiral often occurs in Brittany and on the engraved stones of Ireland and England, merely confirms that the spiral-motif spread from the Eastern Mediterranean, through Spain and Portugal, along the coast to the tin mining regions of Brittany and the British Isles. The way to Germany, however, lay overland and through Hungary.

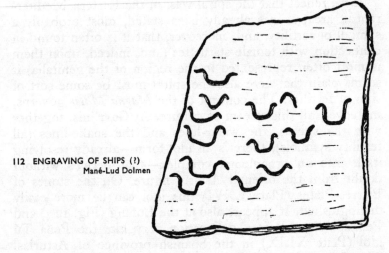

112 ENGRAVING OF SHIPS (?)
Mané-Lud Dolmen

[1] From about 2650 to 2500 B.C.

On the Gavr'inis tomb the spiral-motif is to be found on almost every stone and in ever-varying forms—as concentric semicircle, as wavy line, as spiral curve, and in groups of concentric arches one above the other (Plate LXVIII).

Many theories have been launched to account for the symbolism of these stones. Thus, Déchelette, in an article in *L'Anthropologie* on the idols of the Eastern Mediterranean and of Spain, explained the spirals as the representations of eyes and eyebrows of female divinities. In the following year (that is in 1913) G. H. Luquet, in the same review, saw in the spiral a stylized representation of the human body—derived from Crete. In 1921 Eugen Stockis attempted to interpret the Gavr'inis spirals as lines of human fingers. This view looks much too materialistic and, in its lack of feeling for the ancient world of symbols, is hardly worth discussing.

As a matter of fact, it is most probable that such signs as the spiral, which occur again and again during millennia, have, in the course of time, undergone great changes of signification. It is, thus, most difficult to ascertain their original meaning. Nevertheless, we shall not go far wrong if we look for the interpretation in the realm of religious symbolism.

If we reflect that the spiral was, in the Eastern Mediterranean area, as has already been stated, most probably a symbol of fertility, and, moreover, that it is often found in connection with female statuettes (and, indeed, upon them is most often represented in the region of the genitalia) it seems plain that here also the spiral must be some sort of sign of fertility. The concept of the *Magna Mater* governs, moreover, all this stream of culture. At Gavr'inis, together with the spirals, the water-lines and the snake-lines (all fertility symbols), there is an idol-form—already resolving itself into an ornamental complex—that derives without doubt from the oriental Astarte figure. On the stones of Pierres-Plates (Plate LXVI) this idol can be more easily distinguished. It appears also at the Lufang (Fig. 113) and Penhape sites. It is a delineation very like the Peña Tú idol (Plate XLIX) in the Spanish province of Asturias. The Breton engravings must be, therefore, more or less

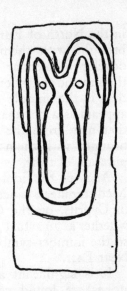

113 STYLIZED HUMAN FIGURE Lufang Gallery-Grave

contemporaneous with the Peña Tú pictures—datable, we may remember, from the type of dagger represented.

Macalister, the Irish prehistorian, has drawn attention to the fact that these representations of idols show seven eyes. His remark is quite justified. If we count the number of eyes on the Pierres-Plates stones, for instance, we find that they are seven. This number indicates, most probably, that we have here proof of Mesopotamian influences. The earliest division of time seems to have been based upon observation of the moon's phases. Thus the basic number is nine. Three times nine for the three phases of the moon, that is twenty-seven. There remain over three days which made up the fourth, short week of three days only. This count is preserved in old sayings, legends, games: the Nine Norns, the Nine Children of Heimdall in the Edda—and, maybe, the very ancient game of ninepins.

The Babylonians appear to have been the first to arrive at a division of the month into even periods—and thus to regard the number seven as sacred. Since these remote Mesopotamian epochs the number seven has come more and more to the fore. What may originally have been nine dwarfs, nine-league boots, nine kids became seven dwarfs, boots and kids. The number seven has probably dominated in the North of Europe since the time of the Romans who brought with them over the Alps the knowledge of a developed calendar that combined the movements of both the sun and the moon. If in Brittany, during the Bronze Age, that is the middle of the second millennium B.C., seven appears as a dominating number, then, we must remember that men from the Near East came into this region and brought with them their knowledge concerning the computation of time.

And as the idol-form itself comes from the Eastern Mediterranean (since its prototypes are to be found at Troy, in Cyprus, on the Greek islands, in Sicily and in Spain, whether as an actual plaque-idol or as a picture or engraving) so the number-symbolism it displays derives also from the Near East.

It is significant also that in Ireland—where engraved stones are found very like those in Brittany—there has survived the legend of a seven-eyed goddess.

The Irish tale bears the name *Táin Bó Cúalnge*—that is, *The Cow-Raid of Cualnge*. In this the hero, Cu-Chulaind, has seven fingers on each hand, seven toes on each foot and seven pupils in each of his gigantic eyes.

In the legend called *Tochmarc Emere*, the hero has in one eye four pupils and in the other three. Curiously enough in the idol-pictures engraved upon the Pierres-Plates on one side there are four circles and upon the other side three. And this occurs not once only but in five separate places. No doubt some special significance must be attached to this.

In another Celtic story there is a robber called Ingcel who kills King Conaire. The miscreant had but one eye; still, that eye had seven pupils.

The stories of the Christian saints offer examples also of this ancient saga-like feature of the seven pupils. The life of Saint Colum Cille was written by Manus O'Donnell. In this book is related how the holy man visited another Irish monk called Baithin in order that they might discuss sacred things. Baithin lived alone and he was horrible to behold. It was said of him that he had seven pupils in each eye.

This sign of the seven pupils must originally have signified an ability to see everything. The symbol was incorporated in a human form. As this was at first a female form, it may not be mere chance that some of the stones in Ireland bear the name of 'The Hag's Chair'. A stone reproduced by Macalister bears upon one side the engraving of a cross. This was called the 'Witches' Seat' and if we enquire who this witch was, then the folklore of Ireland tells us that it is the female divinity still living in tale and fable: Frau Holle in German and in Irish An chailleach Bheara—that is, the 'Witch of Bere'.

So in this complex we can discover a number of elements. The dispersal centre lies in the Near East; then we have some female divinity in idol form, the symbols of the spiral, the sign for water, the hammer, and, also, the number-symbolism from Babylonia, the U-shaped signs of the moon's crescent, and then stories, still extant, of heroes with seven pupils to their eyes.

Pottery vessels from the Brittany area throw further light upon these matters. There are such vessels from the Conquel passage-grave near Quiberon. The objects are now in the National Museum of Antiquities at Saint-Germain near Paris. On this pottery are shown concentric arches such as are to be seen at Gavr'inis and also the zigzag lines signifying 'water'. We have here an indication that the spirals on the stones were not put there just by chance but that they had a definite meaning and were repeated upon pottery vessels which were buried with the dead.

Another symbol is a large wheel, as appears in the gallery-grave of Petit-Mont. The disk has eighteen spokes (a multiple of nine) and most probably represents the sun or the moon, or at least one of the heavenly bodies.

From the purely æsthetic point of view the engravings are interesting because they are so like modern abstract paintings. The designs of Klee, Baumeister, Picasso or Nay are very ancient symbols that Man has used from most remote ages.

The quality of the engraving varies from place to place. In some cases it is deep and firm, in others (less ancient) it is lighter and freer, the rock-surfaces, in fact, are just scratched. Here and there specks of pigment have remained in the grooves.

All the pictures, without exception, belong to the sphere of the imaginative, of the imaginary, of the abstract. They are symbolical and have no relation to reality at all.

The engravings are as significant for the history of trade as they are for that of art. They tell us of sea-voyages from Crete, from Egypt, from Asia Minor and from the Greek Islands, through the Strait of Gibraltar to Brittany, Ireland and England.

With these voyages, which brought tin to the Eastern Mediterranean and to Mesopotamia, not only Egyptian beads spread far and wide but also those ideas and concepts having their origin in the Near East. The *Magna Mater* complex reached northern Europe and the idol-forms of the Eastern Mediterranean are reflected in Brittany.

These engravings of Brittany are, then, of very great significance, for they tell us not only about a whole chapter of Man's art, about the migration of symbols, about trade-routes that linked north Europe with the Levant, but they give us information about the development and the shaping of Man's spiritual life.

THE ROCK-PICTURES OF IRELAND

THE rock-pictures of France, the engravings in the gallery-graves of Brittany, are continued, one can say, in the eastern regions of Ireland. There are tombs and pictures like those of Brittany. The connection between the two arts is, indeed, so close that no difference can be established between the art-motifs of the two areas. In Ireland also are spirals, concentric circles and semi-circles, star-shaped signs, representations of ships, zigzag lines and pictures of idols. Ireland is, after France, one of the richest countries in megalithic monuments; indeed, their number is relatively greater for Ireland than for France.[1]

The barrows, and many of the art-motifs, indicate a clear link with Mediterranean regions. The megalithic tombs, it may be argued, are, in fact, but the poor relations of the vast pyramids of Egypt. Any number of objects excavated and recovered at the Irish megalithic sites proves that Ireland was in constant contact with Brittany, with Spanish Galicia, with the south of Spain and so with the Eastern Mediterranean. The ships from Asia Minor, from Crete and from Egypt made for the places where there was merchandise to buy, that is to say, Galicia, Brittany and southern England for tin, Ireland for gold.

No land in central or northern Europe was so rich in gold as Ireland. The places to the north and south of Dublin seem to have been the first to be washed. Ireland's capital, indeed, owes its origin and growth to wealth that came from the mines. Right up until about the year A.D. 1800 gold was still produced, especially in Co. Wicklow. It is in this county, as well as in Co. Meath and round about Drogheda, that is to the north of Dublin, that most of the rock-pictures occur.

[1] Déchelette counted 4,458 for France and Macalister 898 for Ireland. France is seven times as large as Ireland.

157

The peak-period of Ireland's gold production was during the first phase of the Bronze Age. Irish gold was exported in all directions, to south Europe and to Mycenæ (that covered most of its needs with Irish gold), but also to England, Germany and Scandinavia. A favourite object of exportation was the *lunula* or crescent-shaped article of jewellery which was fabricated in Ireland and then found its way abroad, especially to northern France and to the north of Germany and to Scandinavia. In later phases of the Bronze Age these *lunulæ* developed into crescent-shaped necklaces with designs in high relief and with studs by means of which the ornament was fastened behind.

Another article of export was an ornamented gold plaque. A considerable number of these reached Germany but most of those found have been discovered in Ireland itself. Furthermore, the Irish goldsmiths exported gold shells, that were probably used to adorn horses' harness, and, likewise, gold vessels (a number of which are known in Germany) which bear, as Menghin pointed out, decorative designs similar to those on Bronze Age Irish pottery.

These ready-made goods appear not to have been exported to southern Europe. Their place was taken by small coils of gold wire—about one inch in diameter—which are, also, very common in Irish Bronze Age sites. Some of these coils were found in Belfast and associated with a socketed hatchet. Therefore, they can be, with some certainty, dated to the Late Bronze Age and more especially to the epoch between 1000 and 900 B.C.

In Germany, gold vessels have been found at Eberswalde (Province of Brandenburg), Terheide (near Wittmund, Province of Hanover), Ladergaard (near Hadersleben, Schleswig-Holstein) and Werder (near Zauch-Belzig, Province of Brandenburg).

Irish gold production lasted all through the Bronze Age. In Ireland itself the greatest treasure of prehistoric gold objects—and indeed one of the most important finds north of the Alps—is the Clare Treasure, that was probably a trading-stock. The value of the cache was about £3,000 (gold) and consisted, for the most part, of very thin bracelets and of semicircular rings with the shell-shaped, flattened bezels which are of frequent occurrence in Ireland.

It was, of course, Irish gold that attracted Cretan and Egyptian ships to Ireland. For the return voyage they also loaded up with English and Breton tin. A bar of tin three feet long was dredged up in Falmouth harbour in Cornwall, that is the 'Belerion' of Diodorus Siculus. The Mediterranean ships did not bring back manufactured articles but raw materials, which were then worked up at home according to the needs and the tastes of the Eastern Mediterranean market. It is, however, probable that the many elegant little rings found in Ireland were used as money.

By the time of the Emperor Augustus, the trade-route (as we have seen from the passage in Diodorus Siculus) ran overland from Marseilles. Before that city was founded, however, only the sea-route was used. It was indeed the study of the rock-pictures which brought out this fact. It was the Clonfinloch Stone (Plate LXIX) that first led Breuil and Macalister to realize the link between the Spanish and Irish rock-pictures. In this connection we may add that the ancient reports about the Kassiterides mention that this people lived "beyond the Pillars of Hercules".

The most ancient report on the sea-route to Britain is attributed to the Carthaginian Himilco, who is supposed to have visited Britain about 500 B.C. and to have written an account of his adventures. Himilco's book, if indeed it ever existed, has not survived, but Rufus Festus Avienus, in the 4th century A.D., makes reference to Himilco and says he wrote that the men of Albion were rich in tin and lead and that the men of Tartessos, in southern Spain, carried on trade in tin with the men of the northern lands. Furthermore, the Carthaginians, also, used to visit these northern coasts. Avienus, on his own account, explains that the Phœnicians brought tin from the Kassiterides to the Spanish port of Corbilo. It is not known where this Corbilo was, but we may guess, from the number of rock-engravings in that province, that it was somewhere in Andalusia. The Phœnicians had, in fact, for long a monopoly of the tin trade. It was later on, after the Greeks had spread westwards in the Mediterranean and had founded Marseilles, that they made an attempt to break into this lucrative commerce. Pytheas, a native of Marseilles and a cultivated man, undertook, so he related, the first Greek voyage of exploration in northern Europe. He sailed from the Mediterranean in the 3rd century B.C. The ostensible objects of the journey were to determine the position of the pole, to measure (with an apparatus called a gnomon) the height of the sun at the time of the summer solstice and to study the ebb and flow of tides. No doubt he also wished to investigate trading possibilities in tin and amber. He seems to have reached southern England. Possibly he may have gone as far north as the Orkneys and Shetlands and may have crossed the North Sea and reached the coasts of Norway, Germany and Friesland.

Pytheas's book *Concerning the Ocean* appears to have been much read. It is lost, but geographers of later times cite Pytheas and from these quotations [1] it would seem that the Greek mariner mentioned warm springs in Britain (those of Bath?) and that he also told of a goddess (that the Latin authors who quote him call 'Minerva') whose temple was at the hot springs. A flame in this temple was never extinguished but was fed by lumps of black substance like stone (this is coal). Pytheas also mentioned deposits of tin, especially upon an island he called Mictis, six days' sail away from southern England.

In these early days, tin ore was recovered from surface workings. The first stories about tin-mines and about real mining operations we find in Poseidonius (about 130 to 50 B.C.) who, it seems, visited Cornwall in the 1st century B.C.

We have several clues for the dating of the Irish megalithic graves. It has been known for long that the engravings at New Grange, near Drogheda, resemble those of the Gavr'inis gallery-grave in Brittany. The same spirals and the same concentric circles as are found in these two monuments we see again in the beehive-graves of Mycenæ and Orchomenos and these latter belong to a date round about 1500 B.C. The New Grange and Gavr'inis engravings must, therefore, have about the same dating. But the most

[1] E.g. Strabo (I, IV, 3: IV, 5, 111, 11, 11, IV, V, 5) and Pliny (*Natural History*, IV. 95; XXXVII. 35).

conclusive evidence for dating is, again, afforded by beads. Beck and Stone have calculated that fifty-two Egyptian beads have been found in England and nine in Ireland. The beads are of a type manufactured between 1500 and 1300 b.c. Similar beads have been found in the Parc-Guren gallery-grave (in the Morbihan department) and at Fuente Álamo near Almería in Spain. The beads, therefore, afford proof of the existence of the trade-routes.

There is also another, and peculiar, sort of bead. It belongs to this same period, is found along the trade-routes and nowhere else in Europe. The beads are of a greenish colour and made from a substance called *callais*. This is a phosphate of alum but the source of the material, despite much search, has not yet been found. The beads were cut into the shape of an olive and pierced lengthwise so that they might be strung. They were used, almost always, for making necklaces, armlets and bracelets. These *callais* beads have turned up more in Brittany than elsewhere. Indeed, beads of this sort have been discovered there in almost every megalithic grave. They also occur in great numbers in Spain and have been found in England. Cartailhac, a considerable time ago now, and, after him, Déchelette, saw some connection between these beads and the early Bronze Age trade-routes.[1] In this connection it may be noted that *callais* beads have been frequently found in the neighbourhood of Marseilles (where the number of megalithic monuments is very considerable) and that beads made from this substance disappear completely from the second phase of the Bronze Age onwards.

In England, also, there have been finds of Iberian idols: for instance, in a grave at Folkton, Yorkshire, where three of such objects were found, two of which show, by means of eyebrows and eyes, the delineation of a human visage. The same type of visage is to be seen on idols in the gallery-grave of El Soto, in Spain, the Lufang gallery-grave in Brittany (Fig. 113) and upon the Knockmany (Plate LXXI) and

[1] It was the mineralogist A. Damour who named the substance *callais* (in 1864); the name was suggested by a passage in Pliny where he calls *callais* a precious stone, resembling turquoise and stated to have come from the Caucasus; but the *callais* of the Bronze Age beads is, in point of fact, quite a different substance from that referred to by Pliny.

Lochcrew Stones in Ireland (Plate LXXII). The rock-pictures of Ireland and England are, as we may remember, the last outposts of a movement that spread out from Spain, over France and Brittany and had its starting-point in the Near East.

If this movement was essentially a movement of trade, it exercised, at the same time, many and varied cultural and religious influences. The idol that is found so far and wide, the image of a goddess, is, doubtless, a variant of the Astarte figure, the Eastern deity of fertility and love and (since birth and death are always linked) also of death.

Macalister tells us of a death-goddess in the Bronze Age art of Ireland, a divinity that lived on as the witch Bere. All sorts of legends cling to these Irish stones. Witches, kings or spirits are buried under them. The water that gathers in the depressions of their surface was collected, on certain nights, and used to promote the fecundity of women. Ideas of fertility still are attached to these ancient monuments.

And legends also long survived in England. This was the story told about the Rollright stone circle. A certain king had determined to make himself Lord of all England. When he came to Rollright Hill, there appeared to him a witch who lived there. She owned not only the hill but all the neighbouring land. The king was only a few steps from the summit of the hill from which he would have been able to descry, in the valley, the village of Long Compton. At this moment the witch stopped him and told him to take seven long strides while she said:

"If Long Compton thou canst see
King of England shalt thou be."

The king was just about to break out into a shout of joy when, before his eyes, the earth rose into a great wall and the witch transformed him and his men into stone. The witch, however, herself turned into an elder tree, in which form she still watches over her victims. When, however, the tree blossoms it may be cut (for preference on the last night of the year) and the witch will bleed and lose her magic power. One day, in fact, the magic will be broken, the king and his men will spring to life again and will conquer the whole land.

162

It is said that the custom long prevailed for soldiers, due to go overseas, to chip pieces off the largest stone, the King Stone, and to use them as amulets.

Near the Rollright stone circle is another called the Whispering Knights. These stones are soldiers who, at midnight, move down to a spring to drink and, for a few minutes, resume their human forms, join hands and dance. In Cornwall, the stone circles are called Dawensmen, that is 'stone dance'.

The great graves-area of Lochcrew, with its thirty hills, is called in Irish, Sliabh nec Caillighe, that is 'Hill or Mount of the Witches or Goddesses'. Menhirs in Ireland are termed *Fear Breagah*, that is, 'False Men' and they are linked in legend with giants, witches or the devil. The religious origin of these monuments and of their engravings is still evident from the superstitions that lurk about them.

On these stones of Lochcrew, Co. Meath (Plate LXXII), we find once more the zigzag lines that indicate water. Again we see the star-signs and the moon-symbols (notable, also, on the Sess Killgreen Stone (Plate LXX) in Co. Tyrone). Repeated here in Ireland are the spirals and concentric semicircles (as at Lochcrew, Sess Killgreen (Plate LXX), Knockmany (Plate LXXI) and New Grange), human idols, delineations of the human visage (as on the Stone of Knockmany). On the Stone of Clonfinloch (Plate LXIX) are engraved human figures which closely resemble those on the Galician rocks. All the signs and symbols, in fact, that are to be found in France and in Spain occur also in Ireland.

It is interesting to compare this art with the modern art-movement known as Cubism. In the prehistoric pictures the human figures and faces have become very stylized, have lost all their links with reality—have become fully imaginative. It is not, therefore, surprising that the older generation of prehistorians could not recognize human forms, at all, in the paintings, nor, again, is it remarkable that the symbols appeared quite incomprehensible.

In fact, the signs became comprehensible only when they were studied, not at one or two sites, but as a complete complex in which the development from the naturalistic to the highly stylized and conventional can be observed. The stylized form, just taken by itself, is much too far removed from reality to be recognizable. We must have the evidence of a great number of evolutionary shapes and signs which allow us to mark the transition, observe the transformation.

The stylized art of the megalith builders is of the highest importance for the light it throws upon economic history. The engravings tell of widespread trade in tin and gold; of contacts along the whole of the European coast. From these pictures we may learn that not only common economic conditions reigned but that also a common fund of ideas existed along this trade-route that put out secondary lines to Scandinavia and to Germany. The German megalithic monuments are the very last representatives of a culture that, beginning in the Near East, curved round Spain, traversed France, influenced Ireland and England and touched the lands around the North Sea.

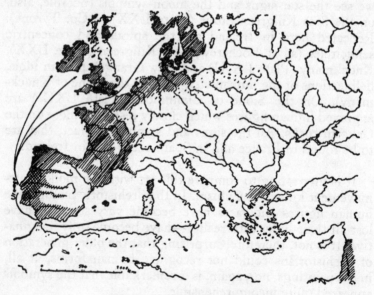

SPREAD OF MEGALITHIC MONUMENTS

THE ROCK-PICTURES OF GERMANY

On German soil there are but five known gallery-graves or stone cists. Pictures of the Bronze Age have not been found upon rocks in the open air and as very careful exploration and prospecting have been undertaken all over the country it is hardly likely that any will be discovered.

The three most important sites lie far apart; in the provinces of Hanover, Saxony and Hesse-Nassau. Moreover, the stylistic differences are too great for there to be any close link between the three.

The Anderlingen Stone (in the Province of Hanover) (Plate LXXIII) is, both in style and content, closely related to the Scandinavian rock-pictures. Three human forms are depicted, two of which are quite clear. One figure holds aloft an axe while the other raises both hands to heaven. In almost all the descriptions of this stone it is taken for granted that we have representations of the three gods of the Germans. The deity with the axe, in the middle, can certainly be identified with Donar (or Thor). The figure with the upraised arms appears often on the Swedish rocks, where he most often holds a lance or spear and may, therefore, be recognized as the god Tyr. The third of the Anderlingen figures is much effaced. Maybe it represents one of the older gods such as Ull, who (armed with a bow and arrows) is often to be seen in the Swedish rock-engravings. The Anderlingen figures are not mere outlines but are carved into the stone, although not deeply. The date would be the second phase of the Bronze Age, that is to say from 1400 to 1200 B.C. The dating is, moreover, confirmed by a typical hatchet and by other objects of this period which have been unearthed nearby.

On the stone cist of Züschen, Province of Hesse-Nassau (Fig. 114), is a picture which can be explained only if we compare it with Italian prototypes. There are oxen drawing

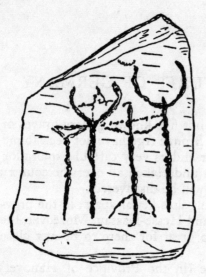

114 ENGRAVING OF STYLIZED OXEN
Züschen in the Fritzlar District

a cart, seen, without any attempt at perspective, as from above. The large horns of the cattle are especially prominent. The exact sense of the picture cannot be now determined but some religious concept lies behind this engraving for otherwise men would not have taken the trouble to ornament the interior of tombs with such drawings. Comparisons with the Italian rock-pictures indicate that this stone cist was made at the end of the Neolithic or during the first phase of the Bronze Age—say, from 1800 to 1400. The typical late neolithic pottery vessels—collared flasks, beakers and so forth—found in the cist confirm this dating.

Similar objects enable us also to date the stone cist of Göhlitzsch (Plate LXXIV) to the same epoch. It should, however, be borne in mind that the Late Neolithic is contemporary with phase I of the Bronze Age, as is proved by a whole lot of copper and bronze objects found associated with late neolithic pottery.[1] However, despite this dating, the style of the Göhlitzsch cist is exceptional in Europe. It is true that the dancetty ornamental-motif—here used almost to the exclusion of any other—is not unknown from elsewhere.[2] But the way this motif is used at Göhlitzsch and

[1] Though neither at Züschen nor at Göhlitzsch were any bronze objects found.
[2] Compare the water-symbol that lives on in our letter 'M'.

166

the manner in which the design is arranged have no parallels in other places. Matthes, therefore, suggested that this engraving is really the representation of a wall hanging. So, with the copy of a neolithic loom, he had a carpet woven from the designs on the cist. In any case, this theory is a plausible one. The whole handling of the engraving leads one to think that we have here the representation of a textile of some sort. The main horizontal line that runs above the whole, and is slightly sagging, really does evoke the impression of a hanging.

If, therefore, the Göhlitzsch engraving has no very great æsthetic significance, maybe it is of considerable importance for the history of Man's material culture.

To complete our list of the German Bronze Age pictures we must mention the covering-slab of a grave-cist found at Dingelstedt, district of Oschersleben, in Saxony. Engraved on this stone there are objects which have been identified as a ring, an axe and perhaps a belt. At Schülldorf, district of Rendsburg, in Schleswig-Holstein, was discovered a stone punched with eleven cuplike depressions and also engraved with a stylized human figure.

From all this it will be clear that no centre of rock-painting or of rock-engraving existed in Germany. The reason is plain enough. The main trade-routes of the time ran along the Atlantic coasts and Germany was little influenced by them. The second principal most ancient trade-route, the Amber Way, that led through Hungary to North Germany, brought, it is true, to Germany the spiral as a motif in bronze objects, brought also female statuettes and images of cattle—also in bronze—but brought no tradition of rock-engraving which is, of course, unknown in Crete and at Mycenæ.

The art of the rock-pictures had its roots in Spain so only the trade-route that passed through Spain carried with it the tradition of the Written Rocks.

THE IMAGINATIVE ROCK–PICTURES
OF SCANDINAVIA

No group of prehistoric European rock-pictures is so large as that of the stylized rock-engravings of Scandinavia. From the south to the centre, both of Norway and of Sweden, the whole countryside is dotted with Written Rocks. There are, however, certain main centres. The first is in Bohuslän, the next in Östergötland, the third in Uppland and still another in Skåne (Scania)—that is arranging the areas according to the number of the sites. There are so many pictures in Bohuslän that in the locality of Tanum alone some two hundred and eighty engraved rocks can be counted. Indeed, the number of pictures is so great that no systematic presentation of the whole material has yet been possible, but there have been published comprehensive monographs dealing with Bohuslän (by Baltzer), with Östergötland (by Nordén) and with Skåne (by Althin).

The drawings have long been known and, indeed, studied, Reproductions of them were made as far back as 1627. The pictures are on rocks whose surfaces have been smoothed by glacial action and lie upon faces that are sometimes flat, often slightly inclined, but almost never occur upon the sides of cliffs or precipices. The drawings are mostly from 16 to 20 inches wide. There are, however, figures of the gods that are 5 and even 7 feet high, such as the representation of Tyr near Tanum (Bohuslän). The pictures of ships are, on an average, about 20 inches long, but, in a few cases, we find ships of as much as 7 or 7½ feet in length.

All these pictures are stylized, without any appearance of depth and their execution is very firm. Beasts, men and ships are not viewed as in space but as though flattened upon a surface. However, despite all this, the rock-engravings show clearly that they have their roots in the post-glacial Scandinavian art of the 'sensorial' type. Often, indeed, the representations of animals in the 'imaginative' group are very like those of the older category. Transitional forms are, in fact, to be noted, so there can be no doubt that Scandinavian 'imaginative' art is rooted in the so-called 'Huntsmen's' art of post-glacial times.

It is, thus, significant that the principal art-motif of Spanish, Brittany and Irish Bronze Age art appears but seldom and, as it were, incidentally, as though the Scandinavian area were the periphery of a much vaster region. It is true that the spiral is found in Scandinavia; it is true, also, that occasionally we find the symbols of the sun and the moon, the zigzags and diamond patterns; but, generally speaking, the whole character of this Scandinavian group is different from that of the pictures farther to the west and to the south-west. From this one fact alone, we may infer that the tin-route did not extend as far as Scandinavia, since what resemblances there are between the northern pictures and those in the British Isles, France or Spain are resemblances due to secondary radiations of art-influences from Ireland.

The principal subjects of this Scandinavian rock-engraving are ships and figures of divinities (Plates LXXVI–LXXIX). The pictures of ships are to be counted by their thousands and they permit of a reliable chronology being deduced from them. Men are shown in the most varied activities: ploughing (Plate LXXX), dancing, jumping (Plate LXXIX), waging war. The figures of the gods are shown with their symbols (Plates LXXXI and LXXXII), axe and spear, bow and arrow. There are also drawings of weapons shown singly, hatchets and swords (Figs. 115 and 116), shields, and then four-wheeled carts with horses (Fig. 117) and oxen, trees—and animals of all sorts: horses, reindeer, stags, elks, seals, snakes and birds. There are also symbolical signs such as sun-wheels, footprints, circles (Fig. 118) and, for the most part, all jumbled up without any apparent order at all. Nevertheless, groups, or even scenes, do emerge from many of the pictures. We can make out a divinity raising his huge hands as he stands before a fleet of ships. At Tanum there is a human pair embracing while a god with a hammer blesses the couple. Often there are men

115 REPRESENTATIONS OF SHIPS AND DAGGERS Leonardsberg (Norrköping)

crowded round the ships or moving around a maypole. Again and again cult-processions (Fig. 123) are depicted in which the same groups of men, in the same attitudes, occur. Often it is hard to say where one group ends and another begins. Indeed, these pictures present many puzzles and it is likely that generations of specialists must devote their time to the study of this rock-art.

The first to carry out research in this field saw nothing in the pictures but the product of men who were just amusing themselves or who were indulging in a natural urge towards pictorial expression. This was the view held, for instance, by Richard Andree, but it is one which can scarcely be supported by the facts which are that these immensely numerous and widely scattered drawings all show the same peculi-

116 SHIPS AND DAGGER Ekenberg (Norrköping)

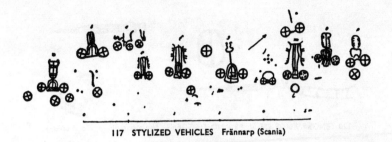

arities of style and subject. Furthermore, it is hardly probable that Man in such early times would have given himself all the trouble to engrave upon granite—with all that that implies—unless his work had some real significance and meaning at the back of it. Sometimes, also, it was stated that the object of the engravings was to 'decorate' the rocks. This idea, I think, can be rejected out of hand. It is difficult to conceive why scattered boulders and stones (often in remote sites far from fields or dwellings) had to be 'decorated'.

Still another and third explanation was that the drawings are mnemonic signs—a sort of writing, in fact. Men, in this manner commemorated and communicated the most important events of their lives. The pictures, then, would be monumental inscriptions. This view for long held the field and was supported by such specialists as Brunius, Holmberg, Sjöborg and Ekhoff. Against this supposition it has been

118 ENGRAVINGS OF FOOTPRINTS, SPIRALS AND SHIPS Järrestad (Scania)

119 MAN WITH HORSES Herrebro (Östergötland

171

120 ENGRAVINGS OF SHIPS AND DAGGERS Himmelstadlund (Norrköping)

advanced that the innumerable pictures of ships could hardly have been the memorials of specific events. Moreover, nowhere has a sea-engagement been identified. Furthermore, the arrangement and the marshalling of the engravings is, everywhere, far too haphazard and arbitrary for it to reveal anything in the nature of writing.

The more recent students of this art are unanimously of the opinion that the Scandinavian engravings are of religious origin. The most thorough exposition of this view has been made by Oskar Almgren in his book *Hällristningar och kultbruk.*[1] There are, however, two sets of interpretations; one is that we have represented in these pictures, first and foremost, a cult of the dead, and the other is that the engravings relate, above all, to fertility-rites. Research, to date, makes it more probable that the fertility cult explanation is the right one.

The dating is relatively easy to determine owing to the many representations of objects—especially axes and shields —specimens of which have been excavated (Fig. 120). The pictures of ships are especially helpful for the dating, since, on the copper razor-blades of Bronze Age phases IV and V, there are engravings of ships which reoccur in precisely the same shape in the rock-pictures. Moreover, real ships have been dug up and these are of the same type as those on the Written Rocks. Nordén drew up a list of all the types for which we have reliable dates. From this work it is clear that a few only of the drawings can be assigned to the first phase of the Bronze Age (i.e. 1600 to 1400 B.C.) and these are, mostly, of axes, daggers and simple sorts of ships. The very

[1] Published in Sweden in 1927: German edition (as *Nordische Felszeichnungen als religiöse Urkunden*) 1934.

172

numerous pictures of the second phase (1400 to 1200 B.C.) are at once recognizable through the occurrence in them of hafted bronze axes, of a certain type of sword, of spirals, and of ships with prominent stems. To this period, also, must be assigned the representation of men with sun-wheels in their hands.

The third phase is characterized by hatchets and swords. A Nordic hilted sword bearing the cartouche of Pharaoh Seti II—who reigned in the early years of the 12th century B.C.—was discovered in Egypt. Phase III must therefore include this century. The majority of the pictures, however, must be assigned to phase IV (1000 to 900 B.C.) and to phase V (900 to 750 B.C.) of the Bronze Age. There are also some engravings that date from about 400 B.C. and even a few which were executed in the first centuries of our era.

The peak-period is that between 1400 and 750 B.C. and we may conclude that most of the engravings were made round about 1000 B.C. The absolute dating of these periods is arrived at by checking off the numerous Italian imports— bronze buckets, cups and helmets—which, in Italy itself, can be fairly accurately dated.

The early Scandinavians, then, were making their rock-engravings at the same time that the Spanish stylized paintings and the rock-pictures of Brittany and Ireland were being executed. This period marked, indeed, the apogee or culminating point of the European rock-pictures. It was a time of developed animism when many spirits and divinities ruled both the earth and the lives of men. These Powers must, through cult-ceremonies, be made favourably disposed towards Man. Out of the mass of figures—and of the ideas they expressed—certain deities begin to stand out.

In the world of southern Europe, men clung fast to the cult of ancestors, to megalithic tombs and to a belief in the power of spirits and of forefathers. In the northern, poly-theistic world the gods emerge as individuals.

The ghost-pictures of Scandinavia do not display the gigantic heads and grimly distorted visages that we see in Spain. Often the northern spirits are slender, elongated and sometimes raise their two hands as in supplication or prayer.

Most of the men represented wear a beast's tail. They may be either priests in their vestments for some cult-ceremony or gods themselves, but the deities have, most of them, animals' heads and hold in their hands their symbol—a Wheel, a Ring, a Hammer, Spear or Bow and Arrows.

It is plain that sacrifices were offered up at these rocks, almost all of which bear depressions, small troughs that were cut at the same time as the oldest drawings. Such runnels are found in all the Mediterranean lands, in France, in the British Isles, in Germany—and in Scandinavia. There is a stone from a huge megalithic tomb near Gunsoh (in the southern Dithmarschen district of Holstein) and this stone is punched with several small pockets or cups, as well as being engraved with a wheel-symbol and human footprints. The custom of hollowing out such 'cups' spread with the tradition of making megalithic monuments and maybe these pockets are connected with sacrifices offered for or to the dead. Probably oblations of foodstuffs, fats, water and beer were laid in these depressions which can often be seen upon isolated stones lying about in the fields. In such places, indeed, they can hardly have served in a cult of the dead, but they may have been used in rites for conciliating the ghosts and the gods and for procuring fertility for the fields.

In central Sweden there are several places (such as Hamarstedt) where, at sunrise and sunset, offerings are still brought to the hollowed-out stones into which fat or oil is poured. These stoops or little basins are called in Swedish *älvkvarnar*—that is, 'elves' mills'. Almgren states distinctly that offerings are laid in these stones when people are sick. The earthly Powers of Nature are helpful to Man not only at the critical seasons of the year but also in the critical moments of a man's life—as when he is ill.

There is a saying in Sweden that elves live under these stones and grind their meal in the cups. Hence the name *älvkvarnar*.

Originally these 'cups' seem to have been symbols of the fructifying of the soil by the Earth Deity. In the logic of sympathetic magic the boring or drilling of the cups was assimilated to the act of copulation.

This explanation is also suggested by a comparison with

121 ENGRAVINGS OF ANIMALS, MEN, SHIPS, SHOE-SOLES AND DAGGERS Himmelstadlund
(Norrköping)

Indian evidence. In the Rigveda, the boring of the holy cups is related to the twirling of the fire-stick and to the symbolism of fertility.[1]

Near Göhren, on the island of Rügen, there is a cupped-stone called *Buskahm*, a name derived from the Slavonic words for 'God Stone'. To this day when a wedding takes place in the neighbourhood, the guests repair to the *Buskahm* and dance a round dance upon it. Some echo of the rocks' old holy power has survived until our days.

In the course of centuries, little depressions have been scratched out from the stones carved into the form of crucifixes or holy images to be seen on the outside of many churches. The powder or 'meal' obtained from the stone is used for medicinal purposes and is particularly efficacious against fevers while fat is rubbed into the holes made in the sculptures. Such practices are carried out to this day at, for instance, the Marienkirche in Greifswald.[2]

The different significations of the 'cups' are, perhaps, combined in the vessels borne upon the heads of female idols of the Greek geometrical epoch—that is, between 1000 and 700 B.C. These figures bear the signs of fertility—zigzag and spiral patterns. Into the hollows of the cups oil was poured: female divinity, fertility symbols and the vessels of sacrifice.

In Scandinavia engravings of human footprints (Fig. 121) are common—especially near the cupped stones. On the Bunsoh stone, indeed, footprints and cups are found together.

[1] The symbolism has survived into modern Hinduism and is represented by the *voni* and the *lingam*, the female and male organs. In every temple and on every hand in India one may see such carvings.

[2] Greifswald, the university town in Mecklenburg, lies opposite the island of Rügen.

175

Representations of footprints occur all over the world. They commemorate gods, saints, evil spirits and celebrated men. We have already seen the footprints in the Mosque of Omar at Jerusalem. All over India may be found footprints of Vishnu or of the Buddha. On Adam's Peak in Ceylon I was shown a footprint of the Buddha. It is called *Phra-Bat*, that is 'Footstep of the Sun'.

At the famed Käppele pilgrimage-church (built by Balthasar Neumann in 1747–1750) on a hill just outside Würzburg one is shown the footprints of the Virgin, while at the pilgrimage-church at Einsiedel and on the Rosenstein in Swabia there were, at one time, what were reputed to be the footprints of Christ. The footprints at the Rosenstein (called popularly the *Herrgottstritte* or 'Lord God's Footsteps') were much frequented by pilgrims until on 14th June, 1740, the stone was blown up by order of the reigning Duke, who disliked the superstitious reverence paid to it.

The footprints of saints are quite common, while, in the Kreuzkirche at Dresden and at Gnesen (Gniezno) in Poland, the Devil has left the impression of his feet. Herodotus tells us (IV. 82) that in his time, on a cliff by the river Dniester in Russia, one could see the footprints of Herakles.

It is an ancient belief that the feet of a divine being bring fruitfulness. We have a reference to this in Psalm 65,[1] and of the Virgin Mary it is said that where she walked sprang up the most lovely flowers on earth. When on the Tirolean heights a streak of lush grass is seen, people say, "Alber, the Spirit of the Alp, has walked this way." In Swabia, all the spots where elves or fairies have walked remain green for fourteen days longer than other less favoured spots, while the fruits of such places are most excellent.

Baudouin tells that at the town-hall of the French village of Solférino (in the department of the Landes) a bronze plaque was set up on which was written that in August 1857 Napoleon III set foot on the soil of the Landes "in order to make it fruitful". On the plaque is the representation of the

[1] 11th verse: "Thou crownest the year with thy goodness and thy paths drop fatness." In the German Bible: "*Du krönest das Jahr mit deinem Gut und deine Fussstapfen triefen von Fett.*" (Translator's Note.)

Emperor's footprint. So the sovereign is sometimes thought of as a fertility-deity.

From feet also arise new beings. One foot of Ymir produced with the other a six-headed son from whom the race of giants is descended. There are, also, tales of girls who trod upon hedgehogs and then, later, bore urchins.

The Devil has horse's or goat's feet. The Spirits of the Forest have often but one foot. Indeed, feet play a most important and significant role in legend. St. Eligius expressly forbade the use of models of feet. In A.D. 573, at the Council of Aix-la-Chapelle, wooden images of men—and of feet—were among the articles forbidden, while in a catalogue of 'heathen superstitions' of the time of Charlemagne, one chapter is headed *de pedibus vel membris ligneis pagano ritu*—that is, "Concerning wooden feet or limbs according to pagan rites". Burchard of Worms (who died in 1024) also denounces the reverence paid to footprints and forbids the magic that it was common to perform in connection with such signs and symbols.

From this mass of custom, legend and superstition, we may gather something to shed light upon the innumerable representations of human footprints that occur in the Bronze Age engravings of Scandinavia. In this art we are, indeed, confronted with exorcism and the conjuring of gods and ghosts from whose manifestations men hope for the blessings of fertility.

Together with the cups and the footprints, the Wheel is one of the commonest of the signs on the Scandinavian Bronze Age rocks. Often the wheels are isolated and stand alone. Often they are associated with figures of the gods. Sometimes the wheels are carried in vehicles. Sometimes they are borne upon long poles. Pictures that show deities near the wheel-signs are to be found at Trättelande near Tanum, and at Litselby in the same neighbourhood, at Ingelstrup oos Herred, Zealand, and at some places in Östergötland.

A solar disk upon wheels can be seen at Disåsen, Backa, Brastad (Fig. 122), at Lilla Gerum near Tanum, at Kalleby nearby this last site and at Lilla Arendal also not far from Tanum. A solar disk upon a pole, or upon poles, is to be

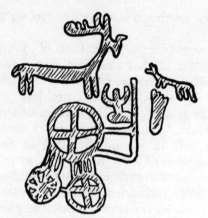

122 STYLIZED REPRESENTATION OF
A WHEELED VEHICLE
Disåsen (Backa, Brastad)

seen very plainly at Ekenberg near Norrköping (Fig. 123),
at Stora Berg, parish of Biskopskula, Uppland, at Skälv
near Norrköping and at Backa near Brastad. Figures pulling
or turning solar disks occur at Hede, parish of Kville,
province of Bohuslän (Plate LXXIX). Wheels are also
represented on ships at Himmelstadlund (Figs. 124–125),
at Leonardsberg, at Ekenberg, at Skälv near Norrköping
and at Egna Hem in the same locality.

123 SHIPS AND MEN
Ekenberg (Norrköping)

124 & 125 SHIPS AND WHEELS Himmelstadlund (Norrköping)

The wheel is one of the most ancient holy symbols of the whole Eastern Mediterranean and of the Near East—especially of Mesopotamia. The wheel also occurs in the rock-pictures of Spain, Brittany and Ireland. The symbol seems to have originated with the Sumerians. They appear to have been the first to have taken the four great planets, then known, as the four boundary-marks of the cosmos and also to divide the year into four seasons, each one of which was identified with a particular planet.

From the Sumerians, this idea—as so many others—passed over to the Babylonians. In texts found at Boghazköi and dating from about 1300 B.C. (and thus to about the time many of the Scandinavian rock-engravings were executed), there is a Babylonian star-catalogue in which the four Lords of the four Corners of the Universe are prominent. They are the four planets, Mars, Jupiter, Saturn and Mercury. These cosmic corner-pillars are also endowed with great power over Man's destiny.[1] In the Gnostic texts the lore of the Four Planetary Lords is also to be found.

In the Old Testament these planetary Powers appear as archangels which themselves are of Babylonian origin.[2]

Among the Babylonians the four planets were identified with gods that had their origin in the sun: Saturn with Ninurta, Mars with Nergal, Mercury with Nabu and Jupiter with Marduk.[3]

From 2300 B.C. at the latest, then, in all the Mesopotamian

[1] In all illnesses the patient must lie so that the planetary influences are favourable: "Samas before me, Sin behind me, Nergal on my right, Ninurta on my left."

[2] An ancient Jewish prayer runs: "To my right stands Michael, to my left Gabriel, before me Uriel, behind me Raphael and over my head the *shekinah*" (i.e. more or less, the 'Glory of the Lord').

[3] Marduk is the full revelation of the sun, Nabu is the evening and autumn sun, Ninurta the midday and summer sun, Nergal the winter and night sun that rises once more at the solstice and in the morning as the Unconquered One.

region, the Wheel and the Cross are the fundamental symbols for the division of the universe into four sections and of the year into four seasons.[1] The symbol appears also to have travelled eastwards from Mesopotamia. In the Far East the swastika form of the wheel and cross is particularly the symbol of Buddhism and may represent the Buddha himself. Cross, quartered wheel and swastika are among the signs on the painted pottery of Susa (first phase) which must be dated not later than 3000 B.C.; that is, almost two thousand years before the Scandinavian rock-pictures that bear the same symbols. These symbols, of course, spread along the eastern trade-route, or Amber Way, from the Mesopotamian lands, through Troy, Hungary and eastern Europe to the Scandinavian peninsula. The same symbols also travelled by the western sea-route and both streams met in the North.

And it is in the North that the original signification of the wheel has been preserved. In northern Europe and also in Germany, France and eastern Europe, the custom existed of celebrating the solstices by setting fire to a wheel which then, by means of a stick, was hurled through the air; or, again, the burning wheel was sent rolling down a mountain-side into the valley beneath.

These customs are very ancient. There is extant a sermon by St. Eligius (who died at Noyon in 659) in which it is declared: "*nullus in festivitate Johannis baptistæ solstitia exerceat*",[2] and even more conclusive documentary proof is afforded by the annals of Lorsch Abbey (in Hesse) for the year 1090. Herein it is related that on 21st March, the abbey was burned down because of the sun-wheels that were hurled through the air and set light to the buildings.[3] For the 12th century we have evidence from France in a work of Johannes Beleth.[4] Johannes Boemus reports in his *Omnium*

[1] The four streams that flowed from the Tree of Life in Paradise have, doubtless, their origin in the same idea of the quartering of the world and year.

[2] *Mon. Germ. scr. Merov.* 4, pp. 634–741: "No one at the festival of John the Baptist may celebrate the solstice."

[3] Quoted in *Zeitschrift für Volkskunde*, 1893, p. 349: "*discus in extremâ marginis hora ut solet accensus, per aera vibratus.*"

[4] "*In festo Johannis baptistæ rota in quibusdam locis volvitur.*" "At the festival of John the Baptist a wheel is rolled about in those several places." In an Anglo-Saxon author of the Middle Ages there occurs this passage: "*dicamus de tripudiis,*"

gentium mores (1520) that, at mid-Lent, youths had rolled a burning wheel down into the valley. The wheel had been wrapped in straw, so that those who had not seen such things before thought the sun or the moon had fallen down from the heaven. Boemus relates further that, on the Night of the Festival of St. John, the courtiers and followers of the Bishop of Würzburg, when they had lighted a fire upon a hill, laid small perforated disks in the middle of the fire and then hurled them, all ablaze, into the air.

Sebastian Frank, in his *Weltbuch* for 1524, mentions that at Eisenach it was the custom, at mid-Lent, to roll a burning wheel down into the valley. The same sort of thing is reported from Treves and also from Basle. In 1566, in the Palatine countship of Leiningen, orders were issued that, at the time of the St. John's fires, no disks should be thrown into the air and neither should other *heydnische, abergläubische Gebräuche* (that is, 'heathen, superstitious practices') be observed.[1]

Even today the 'rolling' of wheels is common in the Eifel district of Germany and also in the Tyrol, in Baden and in Carinthia. As the flaming wheel is cast upwards a formula of blessing is pronounced and each one of those present wishes the others good luck and good health. Often the blazing disk is thrown out over the fields so as to ensure their fertility and fruitfulness. The remains of the disk are worked into the soil so as to keep vermin away. And often enough the solar character of the rite has been remembered, as, for instance, when in Beleth's book it is stated: "*rota involvitur ad significandum, quod sol tunc ascendit ad alciora sui circuli et statim regreditur: inde venit, quod faciunt volvi rota.*"[2]

---

quæ in virgilia (sic) *Sti. Johannis fieri solent, quorum tria genera . . . Tertium de rota quæ faciunt volvi; quoxd. cum immunda cremant, habent ex gentilibus.*" "We mention the ceremonies which are accustomed to be held on the vigil of St. John's Day, of which there are three sorts . . . the third concerns a wheel which they roll about at which time they burn unclean things, a custom they have from the heathen."

[1] In the Church calendar for 1608 Martinus Bohemus forbade the carrying round of wheels in Swabia. In 1779 we have notices of firewheels at Maxberg, near Treves, and at 1816 at Geroldstein: *vide, Handwörterbuch des Deutschen Aberglaubens,* 1935, Vol. 7, p. 467.

[2] "A wheel is twirled about to signify that the sun has then reached the highest point of its course and forthwith begins to turn back, therefore they make a wheel to revolve."

Here, indeed, is expressed the whole complex of thought attaching to the wheel as a solar symbol and to its fertilizing and fructifying powers.

The expression 'Sun-Wheel' has survived to our times and is to be found in fairy-tales, in the *Song of Triturel*, in the Eddas and even in Goethe and Schiller.

The wheel-symbol was also used by the Greeks, the Romans and the Indians. In India was developed the concept of the 'Wheel of the Law', while in Buddhism the Wheel is the essential symbol, comparable with that of the Cross in Christianity, and it is, in the last analysis, nothing else but the emblem of the world, of the cosmos, of the universe.

Since both Cross and Wheel typify the world, the wheel, quite early on, assumes the form of a lucky sign or Wheel of Fortune. The Romans conceived of Luck as hurrying through the world upon a wheel; hence we have the wheel as a symbol of health, of luck, of fertility. Wheels are also placed upon roof-trees so as to protect the house. A wheel may be placed over the entrance-door. Luck-bringing magic is performed when the wheel is rolled at Christmastide through the villages. Instances of the occurrence of solar-wheels, 'lucky' wheels and fire-wheels could be almost endlessly adduced. In these circumstances, therefore, it is not surprising that in pictures of the Bronze Age the image of the Wheel occurs again and again and often borne upon

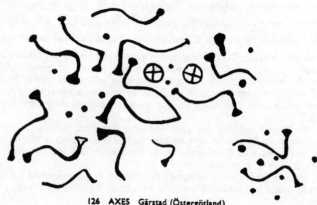

126 AXES Gärstad (Östergötland)

a pole. Thus was the holy emblem carried round in processions. So also we have wheels on ships, wheels near the divine figures and the sun's disk borne upon a cart. An example of this solar symbol is the Sun-Wheel of Trundholm, discovered near that place in 1902 while a field was being ploughed.[1] The object is a vehicle that bears a disk, overlaid with gold on one side, and is drawn by a horse.

The axe (Figs 126–128), too, is very common among the objects represented on the rock-engravings.[2] Reverence for the axe as a symbol of the thunder god spread far and wide with the sale of copper axes (at this time common objects in Asia Minor). The cult-significance of the axe is noticeable in Crete, in Mycenæ, in the Balkans and in the Germanic North. At Skogstorp in western Södermanland (Sweden) were discovered in 1864 two magnificent bronze axes adorned with gold and amber. These are not massive objects but are moulded from thin layers of bronze and overlie a pottery nucleus. They could never have been used for tools, for, at the first blow struck, they would have been shattered. Several similar axes have also been unearthed. They have always blades curved sharply backwards and it is axes of this

[1] Trundholm is near Nykjöbing on the Danish island of Zealand.

[2] The author inserts at this point some considerations of a philological character that it is perhaps best to bring down into a footnote: "Indeed the word *Beil*" (that is, 'axe' in German) "is of Mesopotamian origin. The word 'axe' corresponds to the Greek word *axine* (ἀξίνη), the Latin *ascia*, the Gothic *aquizi*. In Assyrian the word is *chasinu*, in Hebrew *chasin* and in Sumerian *chazi*. The word was exported from Mespotamia and in the Hittite realm, in Egypt and elsewhere, is a foreign term. The word *Beil* (that is, the Greek πέλεκυς) is derived from the Akkadian word *pilakku*. During the period between about 2350 and 2200 B.C. there must have been close communication between the Near East and Europe. Probably at about this period the Indo-European tongues which had, up to then no prepositions, adopted the Akkadian prepositions *in* and *an* (which in later Akkadian were pronounced *ina* and *anu*). The Cappadocian cuneiform inscriptions (especially those of Kültepe) bear witness to a thriving trade in metals between Mesopotamia and Anatolia. The trade brought not only tin and copper to the Near East but also drew along with it many religious ideas from Anatolia to Europe. There is a Sumerian deity who appears in the inscriptions about 2400 B.C. and his symbols are the Triangle and the Axe. Often, also, he is represented by a bull. He is the Lord of Heaven, of the Clouds and the Rain, of the Lightning and the Thunder. He rules the thunder and thus he controls the floods and so in his hands he holds either hunger or plenty. The axe in Crete reached such a degree of significance that (in its form of the double-axe, the Greek *labrys*, that is λάβρυς) it appears all over engravings on stone, over houses and on utensils. It was from this *labrys* that the Greek named Minos' palace the 'Labyrinth'."

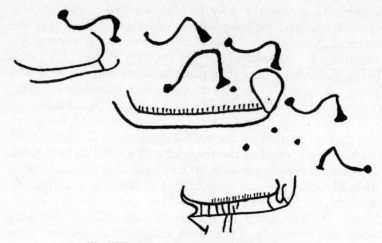

127 SHIPS AND AXES Himmelstadlund (Norrköping)

very type that are depicted upon the wall-slabs of the funeral
chamber in the Kivik tomb.[1] Here, indeed, the axes are
above the representation of a ship as though they were
protecting signs. On a rock-engraving near Simrisland[2] is
a man with a very large penis who is carrying a huge axe
attached to a mighty shaft. In shape this axe is very like that
at Skogstorp. It is clear, then, that in the North (as also in
Crete and elsewhere) the axe played a considerable part in
cult-ceremonies. Great cult-axes were carried around in
solemn procession. Often above the crowd of axe-bearing
men we can make out clearly the figure of the god to whom
the axe was sacred. He is Thor (or Donar).

The axe has retained magical associations right until our
own days. We can find any number of instances of this in
folk legends. On the eve of Thursday in Holy Week, both
in Denmark and in Sweden, axes are flung over the sown
fields. Thor is also a god of fertility. When the sacred axe
is hurled, then follows thunder and beneficent showers of
rain. Prehistoric axes (that in German are often named
Donnerkeile) have been, from time immemorial, objects of
superstitious reverence. As Thor's hammer always returns
to his hand, so the *Donnerkeile*, though they bury themselves

[1] Kivik is in Scania (Skåne) the southernmost province of Sweden.
[2] Simrisland is also in Scania.

184

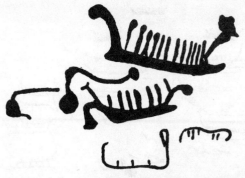

128 SHIPS AND AXES
Skälv (Östergötland)

nine fathoms deep in the earth, push up little by little every year until, in the ninth year, they reappear at the surface. Moreover, the place where the *Donnerkeile* lay will never be struck by lightning. For this reason a *Donnerkeil* is laid under the roof or buried in the house. Who carries a *Donnerkeil* about with him waxes in strength and becomes endowed with magic powers. If the hunter when moulding his bullet drops in a piece of a *Donnerkeil*, then any beast touched or grazed by such a bullet at once falls stricken to the ground. If a cow is sick she must be milked through the hole in a *Donnerkeil* or she must be stroked with the magic object. And as a curse of malediction "*Donnerkeil*" is still in common use.

Many customs indicate that the *Donnerkeil*—or just an ordinary axe—is a harbinger of fertility for man, for beast and for fields. In Hesse, young married couples step over an axe laid upon the threshold of their new home. Similar customs have been preserved in England and America. In The *Thrymskvida* (in the Edda) we read:

> "Then spake Thrym,
> The Thursens King,
> 'Bring the hammer
> To bless the Bride!
> Lay Mjölnir
> On the Maid's knee!
> Bless us together
> With the hand of Vár.'"[1]

[1] Vár (literally 'the Vow') was the goddess of oaths and promises. The phrase translated "with the hand of Vár" (in Icelandic *Várar hendi*) means "as though Vár herself carried out the blessing". (Translator's Note.)

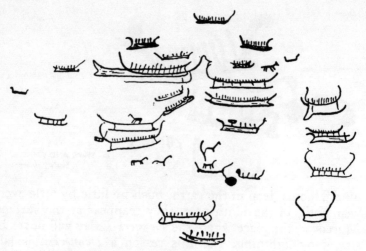

128 SHIPS AND ANIMALS Himmelstadlund (Norrköping)

There is a rock-picture at Hvitlycke (near Tanum) that illustrates these lines. Here we can see a couple in close embrace while over and above them is a figure twice as large as theirs. It is a great phallic creature with a beast's tail and a goat's head. This monster holds an axe over the man and the women. Most probably it is the god Thor thus depicted.

The axes, then, have a meaning cognate to that of the cupped stones, of the footprints and of the wheels. All these symbols will bring luck and blessings which are essentially and primarily those of fertility.

As we have seen already, the most frequently represented objects in the Scandinavian rock-engravings are ships (Figs. 128–132). In itself this occurrence of ships is not surprising among a seafaring people. But the thousands and thousands of engravings of ships do make us think that they are the expression of some special and particular preoccupation. Many of the ships show individual characteristics. There are sun-symbols [1]; other ships convey sacred trees [2]; great axes

[1] As at Backa near Brastad (Bohuslän), Bottna (Bohuslän), Disaosen (near Backa), Brastad (Bohuslän), Tose (Bohuslän), Löckeberg near Foss (Bohuslän) and at Himmelstadlund near Norrköping, all in Sweden.
[2] E.g. at Kalleby near Tanum, Slänge near Vanum, Himmelstadlund near Norrköping and in Valla near Tossen (Bohuslän).

186

figure on many ships[1]; and the presence of these symbols
indicates that we are in the presence of no ordinary ships but
of cult-ships, magic-ships.[2] On many rocks there are men
jumping over the vessels. Sometimes divine figures hold these
ships in their hands.[3]

These cult-ships indicate a mythical journey. This concept can be paralleled from the legends of other peoples.
There is a small silver rowing-boat found in a grave at Ur—
it dates from about 2600 B.C. The Babylonian idea that the
dead reached the after-world upon a ship is found again in
Egypt, where some of the most ancient engravings depict
vessels. For the Greeks also there was the ferryman Charon
who bore away the dead to Hades.

Perhaps the most ancient mention of a cult-ship is made
in an inscription set up by King Gudea of Lagash (about
2600 B.C.). He relates that he has built for the god Nin-
Girsu a precious ship to which he gave the name "The ship
of the Spirit arising from the Pool of the Depths". Nin-
Girsu is a god of fertility, a god of grain and a god who turns
darkness into light.

Arthur Evans published in 1909 a gold seal-ring found

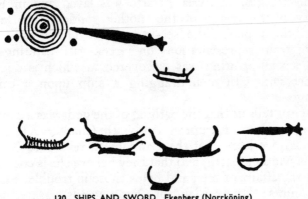

130 SHIPS AND SWORD Ekenberg (Norrköping)

[1] E.g. at Sotorp (Tanum) and Hvitlycke (Tanum).
[2] E.g. at Sotorp near Tanum, at Görlöv near Skee (Bohuslän) and at Bro near
Tanum.
[3] E.g. at Backa near Brastad, at Ryksö near Brastad, at Himmelstadlund near
Norrköping, at Öster-Röd near Kville and at Brandskog site near the church of
Boglösa not far from Enköping, Uppland.

131 SHIP
Hästholmen on Lake Vättern, Sweden

132 SHIP Himmelstadlund

on the island of Mochlos off the Cretan shore. Engraved upon the ring can be seen a ship, and over the ship's cutwater a horse's head. Upon the vessel is a tree and near the tree a female figure (probably that of a divinity) who, as she alights upon the entrance to a temple, makes a sign of greeting with her hands. The tree, emblem of life, here again indicates a fertility symbolism.

Widespread over the earth we find examples of the symbolical bathing, or washing, of deities. The divine images are taken out upon a vehicle to a pool and there immersed. On contact with water the idols renew their fructifying and protecting powers. Images of Shiva are often bathed in India.

Theocritus[1] tells of the bathing and washing of the Adonis images. In Syria Astarte was laved and in Rome each year the image of the mother-goddess Cybele was dipped in a pool. The sea-journey of Dionysus is well known from representations on Greek vase paintings. At Ostia a wall-painting was discovered in which is depicted a procession with men dragging a ship upon a cart or carriage.

Tacitus tells us that the bathing of the gods was a common rite in northern European lands. In Chapter XL of the *Germania* we learn that the Langobardi reverence Nerthus (that is Mother Earth) and that they believe she is concerned about the affairs of men and helps those in trouble. Further he recounts: "In an island of Ocean stands a sacred grove and in it a vehicle that is kept covered with a cloth. Only the priest may touch it. He knows when the goddess is present in her sanctuary and then he attends her and with great reverence as her car is drawn by kine. Then come days of

[1] Theocritus: Idyll XV.

188

rejoicing and merry-making everywhere that the goddess favours with her visit. No one fights, no one bears arms. All iron is locked away. Then, indeed, peace and quiet reign and are valued, until, when she is tired of the society of human beings, the goddess is restored to her sanctuary by the priest. Then the car, the covering cloth—and, if we can believe it, the goddess herself—are washed clean in a secluded lake. This task is performed by slaves who, once their duty is done, are drowned in the lake. Thus mystery breeds terror and dread and a fearful reluctance to ask what that sight may be that can be looked upon only by those about to die."

This passage from Tacitus throws much light upon the mystery of the rock-pictures. We have a sacred car, a goddess who is bathed and washed, a divinity that is the deity of Death or of the Dead.

The name Nerthus, moreover, resembles that of the Swedish divinity Njörth, so often mentioned in the Edda. His home is in that mansion of the heavens known as Noatun, that is, 'Ship's Grove'. He rules the winds and stills both sea and fire. Men call upon him when sailing upon the sea or when they are fishing. Njörth, like Nerthus, is a deity of death and fertility—the two are closely connected—just as is Odin. Moreover, Njördh is associated with ships and seafaring and, also like Nerthus, is bathed in the waters.

Tacitus also tells of a goddess whose emblem is a ship.[1] At Deutz, near Cologne, there was discovered a stone showing a goddess with a ship. A similar engraved stone was discovered on the Dutch island of Walcheren. On these late Roman monuments the deity's name is shown as Nehalennia, that is to say, 'she who protects ships'.[2] What better name can be found for Mother Earth? During the winter she sinks into the dark bosom of the fields and meadows. In the springtime she emerges radiant and decked in a thousand hues.

It is therefore not surprising that a magic ship should figure in the Edda. It was built by dwarfs for the god Freyr. It was called Skidbladnir, that is, 'put together from thin, small planks'. And of this ship it was said that it was the best of all ships known. In the 'Grimnismal'[3] a passage reads: "Ivald's sons in olden times set about making Skidbladnir, that was the best of all ships, for the radiant Freyr, the blessed son of Njördh."

In the 'Gylfaginning'[3] it is said of the ship: "It is so large that all the Asen, together with their weapons and armament, could sail in it. As soon as the sail is hoisted there is always a following wind in whatever direction the course may lie. And when the ship is not being used it can be folded like a cloth and stuffed into a bag, with such cunning art are the many pieces of the vessel put together."

It is, then, a magic ship, a ship of the gods, a ship of the earth deities, of the fertility spirit that returns in the springtime. In another section of the Edda, indeed ('The Sun Chant'), Odin's consort, yearning for love, sails upon the Ship of the Earth.

Here, then, we have a key to the explanation of the rock-engravings. They are magic pictures, representations of the

[1] The passage occurs in *Germania*, IX, and reads thus: "Certain of the Suebi also sacrifice to Isis. I know not the origin or the significance of this foreign cult, but Isis' emblem is in the shape of a light warship and this proves that her worship came from abroad." (Translator's Note.)

[2] *Nehal* is connected with the Latin *navalis*. The same root is present in Njördh's dwelling-place *noatun*. The same root may be preserved in the word Nerthus, so that it may mean the 'diving or disappearing being'. Nehalennia is but another name for the same divinity. On the stones she is depicted bearing in her hands a basket of fruits and a cornucopia. She is a goddess of fertility and of death.

[3] Sections of the Edda.

fertility god or the fertility goddess. The ship signifies re-birth and resurrection in the springtime, means fertility and death, means death, disappearance and reawakening.

The custom of carrying around ships in procession is one that has survived to this day. One of the ancient references to this custom is to be found in the chronicles of a Belgian abbey.[1] The date is 1133. "A peasant of Inden built in a wood near that place a ship that ran upon wheels. Men hauled the ship first of all to Maastricht where mast and sail were added and then it was taken round the countryside, to Tongres, to Looz and to other places. Everywhere the ship was accompanied by a great concourse of people. When the ship arrived in any place then there were outbursts of joy, there was jubilation and men and women danced. The women, filled with joy or desire, were especially glad and happy. Dancing was held around the ship until late into the night. When the coming of the ship was announced, all doors were opened and the ship was hailed and received with festivity. Finally the protestations of the churchmen induced the Count of Louvain to disperse with force the procession of the ship."

There was an official proclamation issued at Ulm in 1531 in which it was expressly forbidden to carry ships and ploughs around the fields in order to make them fertile and fruitful. In the region of the Chiemsee and in many other places in southern Germany it is still usual, in the spring, or on Church festivals, to carry ships around the fields.

Since the ships are symbols of waxing and waning, and of the seasons' shift, so also they are very suitable places for the dead. Queen Ose was buried in the Oseberg ship and great Baldur himself was placed upon a pyre lighted upon a vessel that was then cast out to sea. The belief that the dead journey over the water on a ship is deeply enrooted in men's tradition.

Representations of ships on the Written Rocks are preserved all over Sweden and Norway. There is a picture at Ekenberg near Norrköping[2] of a procession with a ship.

[1] *Gesta abbatum Trudonensium*: Mon. Germ. Hist. Script. X, p. 309.
[2] In Östergötland, Sweden.

Before the vessel are two horses joined by a rope to the ship itself. The pictures of ships with sun-wheels signify nothing less than the sun's course from rising to setting.

From all this we may deduce that the ships in the pictures are no real vessels, but magic and ghostly things, symbols of rising and setting, of the hours of the day, of man's life's span from birth to death. The representations of trees, too, are holy fertility symbols—borne upon ships.[1]

Maypole scenes are to be seen in the rock-engravings at Lilla Gerum near Tanum. Here is a great pole and from it extend lines which represent the thongs that the maypole dancers to this day twine round and round.

Trees, shrubs or branches are fixed upon house or stables as a protection against sickness and evil spirits. Linked with these prophylactic objects are thoughts of fertility, of resurrection and of vegetation's renewal in the spring—and also of the green fir-trees that survive the winter.

The village maypole is the trunk of a tree stripped of its bark and branches. At the top of the pole is fixed a small birch broom or some other ornamental object—this feature may be seen also at Lilla Gerum—and in the Bronze Age, as now, the dancers twisted themselves and their ropes into multicoloured lattices around the pole.

If one travels through Germany, such maypoles can be seen, at certain seasons of the year, in almost every village. They are also known in France, England, Scandinavia, Russia and south-eastern Europe. The ideas of fertility-magic that attach to the maypole are so obvious that it is hardly necessary to stress them, but it is related that in England, in 1585, the sexual licence was so great at the times of hauling home the maypole and of setting it up that everywhere in the woods intercourse took place.

The one dominant preoccupation of the artists who drew the rock-pictures was that of fertility and of the blessing of fruitfulness. This idea is reflected in the resurrection of nature and in intercourse between men and women. The idea is expressed in many different ways, and assumes varied forms which often appear to have little or no connection one

[1] Such fertility symbols live on in the Christmas tree (and in the *Pfingstbaum*, or Whitsuntide tree in Germany) and in the maypole.

with another. However, they all signify the same thing: fertility and water; sun and rain; luck and health. It is in the light of these ideas that we must regard the cupped stones, the footprints, the wheel—and sun-signs, the axes and ships, the sun-signs upon the vessel and the vehicles carrying the sun's disk—even the maypole.

To the same complex of beliefs belong the processions, the carrying of the divine images, of sun-disks upon poles, the dances, the sacrifices and the ritual plough. There belong also to this assemblage of ideas and traditions ritual representations of the year's course, of the appearance of spring-time, of the blossoming of summer, the withering of autumn and the mystery of winter lasting until the resurrection again begins the drama of the seasons.[1]

In the rock-engravings are half-men, creatures who, struck by the gods' axes, lie upon the ground but yet, in another place, rise again. So we can say that, generally speaking, the Scandinavian Bronze Age rock-drawings represent the drama of the year's seasons and, in it, the life of the gods. The gods appear in these pictures and this is a matter of the greatest interest to us, since no literary document takes us so far back into the thought of the Northern peoples.

Two gods stand out and may most easily be recognized. They are the god with the Hammer and the god with the Spear.

The representations of the other deities are more vague and they merge into each other. Indeed, even the two main divine figures are sometimes confused, that is to say their distinctive signs are not always clearly confined to one god only. However, we can, as we look at the pictures, tell the one figure from the other. There is only one other deity, a third one, which is always easy to identify. He bears a bow and arrows. His is a figure that later tradition has hardly

---

[1] The fairy stories of the Sleeping Beauty, of Snow White, of Little Red Riding-hood are illustrated by the rock-engravings. Jakob Grimm said once that our fairy stories reach back into the Stone Age; and he was right. When in the Sleeping Beauty story (as in the *Völsunger Saga*) the maiden is awakened by the kiss of a young man, that is a symbolism of the seasons. The drama of the year's course is also symbolized in Little Red Ridinghood (who is swallowed up but reappears) and in the tale of Snow White who dies and comes to life again.

preserved, but earlier on he was great in power and strength. He is the god the Edda calls Ull.

In the very foreground of all the divine figures stands the god with the Hammer. His is a very clear form and shape. It is the god Thor (or Donar) who, just as he lived on longest in the hearts of the Germanic peoples, so also stands out most distinctly from the rock-pictures of Scandinavia.

His representation occurs again and again. There are variants of it but there are few rock-pictures where he is not to be found. The divine figure with the Hammer, most often with a goat's head and with a wheel on or near the body (Fig. 134, Plate LXXXII). The wheel upon the body is, in itself alone, enough to tell us that we have here no ordinary man but a god. Thor travels sometimes in a vehicle drawn by two goats. Often his girdle is depicted and his gigantic hands stand out, the hands encased in the iron gauntlets in which he clasps his hammer. Often he is represented with a gigantic penis, for he is also a god of fertility (Fig. 135).

All these symbols are mentioned in the Edda and although the Edda was written two thousand years after the Scandinavian pictures were executed, nevertheless in it the portrait of Thor is very distinct.[1]

In one passage of the Edda we have: "Then asked Gangleri: 'What are the names of the other Asen, what have they done, what are their attributes?' Hoch said: 'At their head is Thor, who also is called Asen-Thor or "Thor of the Vehicle". He is the strongest of all gods and men. His realm is called Trundheim and his halls are called Bilskirnor. In his hall are five hundred and forty doors. It is the largest building man has ever heard of.'"

[1] The pictures were drawn between 1500 and 1000 B.C. The Edda was written about A.D. 1220, the time of the Hohenstaufen emperors in Germany, of Walther von der Vogelweide the Minnesinger, of the sculptures in Bamberg Cathedral, of the Strasbourg Cathedral statutes, of King John of England and of Magna Carta. Thus, at a time when our great European Romanesque churches and cathedrals were already built and when Cologne Cathedral was begun in its Gothic form, the Edda was being written in Iceland. But in this remote island (where Christianity, we may remember, was adopted by a vote of the Thing—or parliament—as late as A.D. 1000) the older paganism was preserved and the traditions kept. It is true that the author of the Edda, the prose Edda, who calls himself Snorri Sturlason, was a Christian, but he handed on the old lore of the gods because it seemed to him valuable, important.

134 Representation of a DEITY
Järrestad (Scania)

135 MAN TAKING PART IN A
CEREMONY Simris (Scania)

Thor was master of two goats whose names were Tanngn-jost and Tanngrisnir and since the vehicle wherein he travels is drawn by these goats he is known as 'Thor of the Vehicle'.

"He possesses also other most valuable things and of these the first is Mjölnir ('The Crusher') his hammer . . . another precious treasure is his girdle of power. When he puts it on then is his strength doubled. The third of his treasures is the pair of iron gauntlets, and these he must wear when he wields his hammer . . . and no man is so cunning that he may know all of Thor's deeds."

This passage from the Edda describes Thor just as he appears upon the rocks, with his goat's head, the wheel, the hammer, the girdle with its pendent tail, the huge gaunt-leted hands bearing the hammer.[1] He rules over rain, storms, sunshine and wind. Adam of Bremen (who died in 1085) has left us the most ancient account we have of the Northern lands. He says of Thor: "He rules in the air, he brings

---

[1] Cf. this passage from the medieval German *Frauenlob*:

> "*Der smit uz Oberlande*
> *warf sinen hamer in mine schoz*
> *und worhte siben heiligkeit.*"

("The smith from the upland
Threw his hammer into my breast
And gave sevenfold blessing.")

195

thunder and lightning, wind and rain, sunshine and fruits ... Dudo reports that human sacrifice is offered up to him and that people invoke him to obtain lucky sea passages. If he lets his voice be heard, then the storms arise. When men go forth to war they imitate his voice ... everywhere his figure may be seen...." Adam of Bremen relates that Thor's image at Uppsala stood in a temple between the statues of Odin and Freyr, adorned with gold and silver. He bore a hammer in his hand.

At Möre near Trondhjem there was a seated figure of the god made of gold and silver. It was upon a carriage with two wheels. Harnessed to the vehicle were two goats carved out of wood and around the goats' horns were wound silver chains—the goats, the wheel and the hammer again.

There is in existence a small bronze statuette that was found in Denmark, though at what exact site is not known. The figure wears a helmet with horns and originally bore a hammer in the right hand, but the hammer was broken off and lost after the discovery of the piece. A girdle or belt is bound round the waist—the god's Girdle of Power. This object is the most ancient plastic representation of Thor that we know of and may be contemporary with the rock-pictures.

In 1942, on Broens Moor near Viksoe in Denmark, were discovered two horned helmets of bronze. They are in form and shape exactly like that on the statuette and may have been dedicated to Thor.

Thor's association with goats has lived on until this day in popular German speech.[1] In the year A.D. 600 Pope Gregory the Great complained that the Lombards offered up goats as sacrifice to the Devil (that is, Thor) and that the ceremony was accompanied by singing and dancing.

When Christianity came and the gods lost their power, they turned into idols, devils, and thus it comes about that our Devil has goat's horns, a beast's tail. The god Thor lived on, indeed, as an idol and was sometimes depicted in the sculpture of our Romanesque churches. He figures as the Power that has been overcome. At Hirsau in Swabia

[1] As, for instance, in such phrases as *Bockshorn jagen*, that is, 'intimidate', or *einen Bock schiessen*, to 'make a blunder'.

there is a church dedicated to SS. Peter and Paul. It was built from 1082 to 1091. On all four of its outer walls is Thor displayed. On the north side he can be identified by the goat, the wheel and the girdle, the same emblems as he shows in the Scandinavian rock-paintings.

At Belsen, not far from Tübingen, is a church known as the *Heidenkirchkein* (that is the 'Heathens' Chapel'). Here Thor's form is shown on the exterior of the building and above the image are two goats' heads, but over the heads again is the Cross that exorcises the god's power. The church was built during the second half of the 11th century. At Oberröblingen am See, near Halle an der Saale, we can again see Thor outside the church and over the door. Again he is recognizable from the goats' heads. On the Johannis-kirche at Gmünd, at Kastel Abbey, at Worms Cathedral, on a font at Freudenstadt, and on the Abbey Church at Alpirs-bach, on all these monuments we may behold the god Thor. He has become the Foul Fiend, the Devil himself, but he lived on into Christian times and his Hammer has been preserved in the folklore until this day.

Thor's name is common to nearly all the Indo-European languages. In India the word is *tanayitu* that is 'thundering', in Latin *tonans*, in Anglo-Saxon *thunian*, in Old Norse *Thor*, in Old High German *Donar*, in Celtic *Tanaros*. Thor is, in fact, primarily the God of Thunder.[1]

Baltzer's copies of Scandinavian rock-pictures have been repeatedly reproduced and in these copies it is not easy to make out the heads of the divine figures wearing goats' horns. But I have studied the engravings on the spot and they are, as a matter of fact, much clearer than they appear in Balt-zer's reproductions. In the open air and on the stones themselves it is quite easy to make out the wheels, the animals' tails and the goats' heads for human heads.

None of the early northern European deities is so regu-larly represented as is Thor. His emblems are always the same and whether we seek him upon Scandinavian rocks or

---

[1] If, therefore, the word is common to all the Indo-European languages, it must date from the time when these languages were one, that is to say, from about 3000 B.C. The god and his name are ancient. A pottery ram, discovered at Jordan-smühl in Silesia, and datable to about 1800 B.C., may be an indication that the Thunder god and his images have been revered from very early times in Europe.

upon Romanesque churches he is always accompanied by the same signs.

The other divine figure that very frequently occurs in the Scandinavian rock-engravings is that of the god with the Lance, Spear or Javelin. Typical examples are those at Tanum (Plate LXXXI) and near Leonardsberg, Norrköping (Fig. 136). In each case a ring is shown before the figure. In both drawings the god raises a spear aloft and his form surpasses in size all others at the site. The picture at Tanum, indeed, is nearly 10 feet tall. In other representations, also at Tanum, the god's hands are in the form of horses. The deity to whom these emblems belong is Odin (Wotan or Odin).

In the song called 'The Infatuation of Gylfis' (in the Edda) occurs this passage: "From the cold of Nebelheim and from a stream of heated air arose a human form, that was the giant Ymir. One of his legs engendered a son upon the other leg and thus arose the race of Giants. And as the hoar frost fell it produced a cow called Audhumla from whose udder ran four streams of milk that nourished Ymir. The cow then licked the salty hoar frost stone and upon the first day when it so licked, at eve, a man's hair could be seen, on the second day a man's head and on the third day a whole man stood there. He was called Buri and he begat a son called Borr, who took to wife Bestla, the daughter of the giant Bölthor, and they had three sons, Odin, Vili and Ve. These three were the lords of Heaven and Earth. Odin's

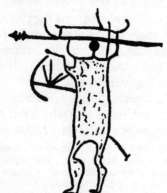

136 FIGURE WITH A SPEAR
Leonardsberg (Norrköping)

wife was Frigg, the daughter of Fjörgwin, and from them came the race of men called Asen that lived in old Asgard and its territories, a race descended from the gods."

However, there seems some confusion about Odin's origin. In one passage of the Edda he is called a *Saxagod*, a 'god of the Saxons'. In another passage he is said to have come to the North through Denmark. Adam of Bremen tells us that in the Uppsala temple Odin stood between Thor and Freyr. Since, however, the Odin (or Wotan) cult does not seem to have struck very deep roots among the Northern peoples, it may be that Odin did come from the South, and that once he was established in the North, Odin took the place of an earlier deity called Tyr.

The rune for Tyr is the spear and it is thus probable that the pictures on the Scandinavian rocks are not of Odin at all but of his predecessor Tyr. Jan de Fries has, however, recently, sought to prove that Odin is a very ancient divinity. But for an understanding of the rock-pictures it is not really important whether the figure is that of Odin or of Tyr.

In the Edda, anyway, Odin is the All-Father, the Chief of all the Gods. His eight-legged horse is called Sleipnir. Other emblems found upon the rocks are also mentioned in the Edda; thus the spear Gungnir that can never be deflected from its target. It was fashioned by dwarfs who are known as Iwaldi's sons. The dwarf Brokk made Odin's third emblem, the ring Draupnir, from which, each ninth night, eight rings drop off each as heavy as the original ring. On the great rock-picture of Tanum (Plate LXXXI) we can see a huge ring (incorrectly given by Baltzer as a semicircle) before the god. The rings that drop off may symbolize the division by the old Germanic tribes of the month, into three weeks of nine nights and the 'little week' of three nights.[1]

[1] At Borkendorf, Deutsch-Krone district, in what was formerly West Prussia, was found a ring-shaped Bronze Age calendar (phase V; that is, about 900 to 750 B.C.); it is preserved in the Danzig Museum. About a wheel-shaped centre are arranged three times nine spirals and double-spirals. The fourth week (that of the three nights only) is represented by three spirals. The priest seems to have worn this calendar on two loops wound round his neck. This calendar may explain the significance of Odin's ring. It is the symbol of the year's course.

Odin is the knower of the seasons, of the runes of wizardry. He is the healer and the oldest document in German speech, the Merseberg magic sayings, refers to him as a Lord of Magic.

Odin's animal, the horse, was accounted especially holy. It was offered up in sacrifice and its flesh eaten at cult-festivals. In the year A.D. 600 Pope Gregory the Great expressly forbade the eating of horse-flesh. Ever and again the ban has been renewed by the Church. It may be that the widely spread aversion to the eating of horse-flesh in Germany is due to this ancient tabu. Horses' heads were placed upon roof-ridges so as to protect the house.

Even more significant is the other emblem of Odin, the Spear or Lance. It is the emblem of kings and emperors who descend from the Father of the Gods. The lily in the blazon of France was most probably a spear-head or lance-head. The Holy Lance was a very precious object in the Imperial Treasure. In 939 the Emperor Otto I prayed before the Royal Lance. In 955 he carried it with him in his campaign against the Hungarians. The Emperor Henry I assigned a whole city to the Holy Lance, symbol of dominion. In 983, also, Otto I hurled his javelin over territory as a sign that he had taken possession of it.

When in 587 the Burgundian King Gontran recognized Childebert II as his heir he gave the Frankish sovereign a lance, while he said: "This is the sign that I make over to thee my whole realm." Thus Gregory of Tours. Again, Paulus Diaconus (or Warnefridi or Casinensis, about 720 to 800, the historian of the Lombards) relates of the election of Hildeprand as king of the Lombards (in 735) that, when the newly recognized and acclaimed monarch was enthroned, a spear, as a symbol of his dignity, was given into his hand. So also at the election of the Emperor Henry II in 1002 a lance or spear was delivered into his hand.

Of course, in those days, no one was thinking much about Odin—especially as his figure was merged into that of Christ: the great Lance of the Scandinavian god and the Holy Lance that pierced the side of Christ had become as one.

On disks dating from the time of the great Migration of

Peoples (that is to say, in this case, about A.D. 700) which have been found in several places (as, for instance, at Oberesslingen in Wurtemberg, at Bräunlingen in Baden and at Kleinberg, near Riedhof in Switzerland) we can see a rider bearing a lance—the figure may be that of either Odin or Christ, for at that time Christ was often represented as a rider. On the disk from Bräunlingen, however, the Ring of Odin is plainly visible. On a Christian gravestone at Niederdollendorf near Bonn is a figure clearly recognizable as that of Christ, since it is shown with a nimbus, but there is a spear in one hand, a ring upon the breast and the image is represented standing upon a snake—the mythical Snake of the World.

In the small and isolated Kunigunde chapel near Burgerroth in Franconia can be seen a corbel-figure which, in its hands, bears two emblems, a lily (originally a spearhead) and a ring. The lily is repeated upon the figure's head.[1]

The Scandinavian rock-engravings show that already by the middle of the second millennium B.C. the peoples of the North had clearly defined ideas of their gods. At that time, also, there existed a fairly coherent mythology. It is true that occasionally symbols are interchanged, exchanged or confused, but, generally speaking, they are kept distinct. From all of which we may conclude that there was some logic in, and coordination of, religious ideas. The divine figures must have taken shape long before this time.

Since we now have palæolithic pit-houses with niches containing female statues[2] it is reasonable to think that the Northern gods represent religious ideas which are linked with those of the Ice Age. And the rock-pictures lend support to this supposition. They are derived from the stylized forms of earlier times, which again are connected with the naturalistic art of the Ice Age.

The æsthetic value of these stylized Scandinavian rock-engravings lies in their firm, well-thought-out composition

[1] The figure is near one of the windows of a belfry where, by the chime of bells, infernal powers are exorcized and kept in subjection. The old Father of the Gods lives on in Christian times but as a devil.

[2] The author adds here: "from which we may conclude that as early as the Ice Age a primitive monotheism had been established". (Translator's Note.)

of forms. The pictures have no depth, no spatial quality, no plasticity. The artist-sorcerers, or priests, who engraved these drawings did not desire, it would seem, to represent a real ship or a real animal and certainly not a 'real' god, that is, one having the form and shape of a man. What was desired was the symbolical, the imaginary, the mythical—things dreamt of, but never seen.

There is no appearance of logical grouping. Here is a wheel and there an axe, there a ship and here a divine figure. Throughout the centuries the rock-pictures have been places of pilgrimage, and throughout the centuries the sorcerers, wizards and priests have, again and again, engraved some sign during the cult-ceremonies. In this way have fertility and blessing been brought upon the fields. The dead were buried and then the holy pictures were visited. Nordén says that, during his study of the Written Rocks, he found traces of funeral pyres at ten different sites in Öster-götland—the remains were composed of clumps of charcoal, charred wood and weathered, calcined stone, in some places a layer of debris, a stratum of charcoal, nearly five inches' thick covered the rocks. At one of the sites and among the rubbish he found a bronze knob of a sort rather common during phase IV of the Bronze Age—that is, between 1000 and 900 B.C.

Men repaired to the rock-pictures; there they brought their sacrifices, there they burned their fires. No bones have been found near the engravings. The Written Rocks are not burial places, they are cult-places hallowed to the seasons of the year. Here the solstice festivals would be held, here would the fires burn bright that spread benediction far and wide upon the land.

We must imagine an atmosphere such as this if we would understand the drawings. Æsthetic considerations take an altogether secondary place. Content, meaning, symbolism are the dominant aims and objects of the artist.

The more ancient drawings are deeply engraved, the more recent are drawn with a lighter stroke. The patinated surface of the rock covers also the grooves and furrows of the pictures. Generally the whole interior area of the drawings is hammered or pecked out, more rarely only the outline is

202

worked. Still, all sorts of techniques occur and, even now, it is possible to identify the hammer-blows, the points where the instrument of percussion was applied and the places where pieces have been detached from the rock-surface. There is no painting at all in this late Bronze Age Scandinavian art-complex.

We may form a fairly clear idea of the economic circumstances in which these artists and their fellows lived. There was, first of all, pastoralism, then a little agriculture. The plough appears and cattle that draw the ploughs. Then we have ploughmen who follow the plough. The ships, of course, indicate sea traffic. They are of several sorts but no more hollowed-out logs; these vessels are clinker-built, they have fore and aft posts and, in addition to a sort of ram, what looks like double posts on either side.

In 1921 there was a ship dug out of Hjortsprinkobbel bog on the Danish island of Alsen. The vessel may be dated to about 400 B.C. and is built just like the ships represented upon the Scandinavian rock-engravings. It is over 40 feet long and almost 7 feet wide. The material is lime-wood. Fore and aft there is a double ram. No sails were used. The benches for the oarsmen have been well preserved. Bow and stern are exactly alike so that the ship could move either backwards or forwards without being brought about. The rudders are so loosely attached that they must be regarded rather as paddles than rudders.

It is interesting to compare with this Alsen ship the most ancient description of a German ship that we possess. Tacitus[1] wrote in Chapter XLIV of his *Germania*: " . . . the states of the Suiones, that lie along the Ocean's shores, possess, in addition to warriors and weapons, strong fleets. The shape of their ships differs from that usual with us, in so much that they have a prow at both ends which is always ready to be put in to shore. They do not use sails or fasten their oars in banks at the sides. Their oarage is loose (as in some river-craft) and can be moved, as and when required, from side to side. . . ."

This description is well suited to the boat unearthed on the island of Alsen. Another ship (dating, this time, from about

[1] In about A.D. 98.

203

the fifth century of our era) was recovered from the Nydamer bog in Schleswig. The bog-water had so well preserved the oak that the whole vessel could be easily reconstructed. The body consists of eleven mighty planks and there is one post at the bow and another at the stern. The length is about 75 feet and the width nearly 10 feet. The hull was well caulked with hair and wool and some fatty substance. Sails were not used. This ship was, apparently, a sacred vessel, since it was sacrificed in a bog together with a great quantity of weapons, ornaments and coins.

From such craft as these were developed the Vikings' ships in which the Norsemen sailed through all Europe and of which the Oseberg (Norway) and the Sutton Hoo (England) ships are examples. Another Viking vessel (that of Gokstad) is 80 feet long and about $16\frac{1}{2}$ feet broad. It was discovered near the Norwegian town of Sandefjord.[1]

In 1893, and for the World Exposition at Chicago, there was made a copy of the Gokstad ship. The new vessel was built just as the original and had a feather-like elasticity. The Viking ships had sails (they were the first Northern vessels to be fitted with canvas) and this second Gokstad ship was sailed across the Atlantic and up the St. Lawrence River and through the Great Lakes to Chicago. Captain Hornberg, who took the ship across, reported: "She behaved beautifully in every way, was easy to steer, skimmed along like a sea-bird and, with a favourable wind, shot forward like a racing-yacht. She often made 9–10 knots, sometimes more, and once, indeed, 11 knots—an astonishing speed for so small a vessel with so little sail. The hull yielded a good deal under strong pressure but remained entirely water-tight. Fine lines and great suppleness were her characteristics. After Viking times such well-designed and swift sailing vessels were not made until the 19th century."

Shipbuilding technique was highly developed in the North; apparently it was a specifically Northern art and had evolved through the millennia from dugouts to these splendid Viking vessels.

The rock-engravings tell us also of the domesticated

[1] The discovery was made in 1880. Sandefjord is near Larvik in southern Norway. (Translator's Note.)

animals, of cattle, sheep and swine. We get then, a picture of an economy dominated by stock-raising but which also comprised a primitive sort of agriculture in which ploughs were used. There was active traffic by sea and times and seasons were reckoned by the moon.

The religious and spiritual world into which these engravings allow us to peer is quite another one from that of Spain, although the arts of the two countries are, in their stylization, very similar. In Spain rules the *Magna Mater*, the female deity associated with symbols of the earth, of water, of the moon, of the serpent and the bull. It is a complex bound up with the worship of ancestors, with the existence of spirits, with the influence of the moon, the waxing and the waning star, the rebirth of men and gods. Hence we have the megalithic monuments that are inspired by the thought of enduring life, of the eternal existence, of the divine powers, and of the spirit of Man.

The world of the North is quite otherwise. A world of pastoralists and not of agriculturalists. Fertility is conveyed by the male strength and potency of animals. Here is no *Magna Mater*, nor are there any symbols of moon and serpent, bulls and horns. The symbols of the Northern world are male figures, male gods, the spear, the axe, the sun, the wheel, the wreath. Here then, also, we may get an idea as to why this Northern world eventually received with alacrity and cherished deeply the concept of the Man-God. Christianity stems from the Jewish world that had also its foundation laid in pastoralism.[1] We have also here some explanation of why the Madonna-complex of the southern European lands never really flourished in the North. Luther himself, in the Apology of the Augsburg Confession, styles the Virgin Mary *dignissima amplissimis honoribus*,[2] but still northern Europe was swayed to a cult without the Madonna.

From prehistoric times until our own days, in northern Europe, thoughts seem to have been directed towards

---

[1] The great task, and the successfully performed task, of the Old Testament prophets was to keep alive faith in Yahweh, the one god, as opposed to Astarte (Ashtoreh) and the golden bull-calf.

[2] "Most worthy of the greatest honours."

masculine deities who cause lightning and rain, thunder and the change of seasons. In this North, Christ assumes some of the attributes of Odin. In the South, the Madonna is invested with some of the characteristics of Ishtar, Isis, Demeter, Proserpine, Venus and Diana. They all stand upon the moon's crescent or wear it in their hair. All are associated with the serpent. Odin, however, and in early times, Christ, are adorned with crowns and carry spears, the decisive emblems of masculine lordship.

In fact, these Scandinavian rock-pictures are of incalculable worth for an understanding of the ancient history of the northern European peoples. The Written Rocks show us northern Europe as it was in 2000 B.C.

THE ROCK-PICTURES OF RUSSIA

THE Russian rock-pictures are nearly related to the stylized engravings of Scandinavia. In Russia we have the same sort of reproductions of ships. There are the same divinities and the same symbols. It is worthy of note, however, that—in contradistinction to what we find elsewhere—often we see, superposed upon the Russian engravings of ships, relatively large, naturalistically executed figures of elks.

The Russian rock-pictures are to be found, for the most part, along the eastern shores of Lake Onega and the western shores of the White Sea. Comparable rock-engravings have been found in the Altai, along the course of the Yenissei, in Kazakhstan and in other parts of Asia, notably Mongolia and Afghanistan. In the early forties of this century Bahder reported further discoveries of Written Rocks, this time near Melitopol on the Sea of Azov in the south of European Russia.

The pictures in the Lake Onega region were recognized in 1848. The first report on the engravings at Besovnos and Perinos was made by P. Schwed in a book with reproductions of the designs but also with a highly imaginative text. A more reliable and scientific account is that of C. Grewingk which followed some years later. As far as international scientific literature is concerned, the first study of the Russian engravings was made by Brögger who, in his book *Den arktiske Stenalder i Norge*,[1] described them as 'neolithic'. He compared the Onega and White Sea pictures with the Scandinavian and Siberian rock-engravings and explained them as connected with hunting-magic.

Hoernes mentioned the Russian rock-engravings very briefly and seems to have set no great store by them. In 1914 a local amateur, one A. Sidlovsky, published at Petrozavodsk (on Lake Onega) a book about the pictures, but it is of no value.

[1] That is, *The Arctic Stone Age in Norway* (1909).

207

In this same year, 1914, Burkitt and Hallström visited the pictures and Burkitt in his book *Prehistory* (1920) not only included some remarks about the Onega rock-engravings but he devoted several plates to them. A good series of reproductions was published in 1925 by Linevsky (*Sur les Pétroglyphes de Carélie*), but these related to only a few of the rocks. In 1928 Brusov discovered more engravings and near them excavations were undertaken.

However, it was not until 1934–35 that the first really exhaustive study was made. The work was carried out, on official orders, by Raudonikas. All the known rock-pictures were carefully surveyed, measured, photographed and published in an important book called *Les Gravures rupestres des bords du Lac Onéga et de la Mer Blanche* (Moscow, 1936–38). Most of the White Sea pictures were, indeed, discovered during Raudonikas's researches.

For the dating of these pictures we can rely first of all upon the style and technique and then, secondly, upon a series of objects excavated near, or at the foot of, the engraved rocks.

The style indicates, obviously, that we have to deal with an imaginative art similar to that of the Scandinavian Bronze Age. From most points of view, the two groups are identical. Both represent a world of ships and gods. In Russia we have the same symbols and signs' as in Scandinavia. However, in Russia, there are, also, semi-schematic pictures of beasts, pictures that are fairly close in style to the naturalistic Scandinavian art of the second and third groups. The Russian pictures form, then, a sort of link between the two main types of Scandinavian prehistoric art, the sensorial and the imaginative, which, however, as we have seen, are in Scandinavia itself articulated, as it were, one with the other. In fact the styles merge into one another.

Still, the first phase of Scandinavia is lacking in Russia, where what we get is solely pictures of the second phase, pictures half-schematic and executed in the pecking technique. The Russian engravings also display examples of the third technique, that is to say a light pecking or pitting of the whole surface of the figure. None of the Russian engravings shows a clear outline formed by a deep incision or groove, but, in every case, the whole figure is slightly concave or excavated.

The style, then, indicates that these pictures belong to the latest phases of the Bronze Age, that, indeed, the Russian engravings constitute a continuation of the Scandinavian Bronze Age art and that they cannot be explained without reference to that art. The latest Bronze Age pictures in Scandinavia fall into phase V, that is from about 750 to 500 B.C. To the same epoch, or rather to a somewhat later (let us say to round about 500 B.C.), I would assign the Russian pictures, even if among them there are semi-schematic animal figures resembling those of Scandinavia, which, however, are, no doubt, earlier in date than the similar Russian rock-engravings.

From the point of view of the chronology it is important to note that at Zalavruga the animal figures are superposed upon the representations of ships. We must conclude from this evidence that a semi-naturalistic art lingered on for long in the Russian area, and, if we bear this fact in mind, the phenomenon of 'Scythian' art both in Russia and in Siberia becomes more understandable. Scythian art is always half-naturalistic in its bronze and gold figures of animals. We can set a beginning for this art at some time during the centuries between 1000 and 500 B.C. Scythian art is, indeed, the last and remote flowering of Ice Age art, right out in the East, in the regions of vast forests and huge lakes, where the chase remained of vital importance for Man's subsistence and where Man's ways of life had, indeed, hardly changed from Ice Age times.

The objects excavated near the Russian rock-engravings quite confirm the dating we propose. At Besovnos, at Perinos and at Kladovets in the Lake Onega region, stone implements and remains of pottery were found, most of which must be assigned to phase III of the Bronze Age and only a few to the transition period from phase II to phase III.

Everywhere near the White Sea rock-pictures portions of pottery have been found, as, for instance, in several places near Besovy Sledki and on Yerpin island. Here, again, most of the objects which were recovered belong to phase III (with the characteristic comb-ceramic) of the Bronze Age, although some must be assigned to phase II.

The Finnish prehistorian J. Ailio has devoted much study to working out a chronology for this ceramic—which also occurs in Finland. His conclusions are that the first type of comb-ceramic can be dated to 2400–1500 B.C., the second to 1500–1000 and the third to 1000–500 B.C. Since most of the White Sea finds belong to the third phase we may date them to some time between 1000 and 500 B.C.

These remote northern parts of Europe were still living in a neolithic economy when in the rest of Europe Bronze Age or Iron Age (Hallstatt or La Tène) conditions prevailed.

We can, then, with some certainty, call the Russian rock-paintings neolithic if we bear in mind that what was neolithic in northern Russia was Bronze or Iron Age elsewhere. In any case, the excavations give the same indications as the style-analysis. The Russian rock-engravings date to some time between 1000 and 500 B.C.

The Russian prehistoric rock pictures, like those in other parts of Europe, owe their origin to religion. Indeed the numinous, or sacred, character of these engravings has survived. The names of some of the sites indicate this. Besovnos is opposite the islet of Besika—that is, 'the female demon''[1] The pictures have always, it seems, been known as those of devils or shamans. The sites with prehistoric engravings are regarded with awe. Nearly everywhere legends show the religious character of the images.

When, in the 14th and 15th centuries, monks from Novgorod settled in this land and preached Christianity, they founded, some sixteen miles south of Besovnos, a cloister they called Murom. At the time of the monks' settlement the power of the pictures must have been so great (and perhaps indeed cult-ceremonies were still performed near the Written Rocks) that the holy men felt constrained to exorcise the engravings. If the sign of the Cross be made in the Devil's presence his power and strength fail him; so, upon the great quasi-human figures of Besovnos an Orthodox

[1] *bes* in Russian means a 'demon'. (Translator's Note.)

137 SWAN: WITH SUPERPOSED CROSS
Besovnos, Lake Onega

cross was set (Plate LXXXV). Over the cross was placed the monogram of Christ and above the whole a circle with a dot, the magic circle for the spirits.

At other sites, too, there are similar crosses. One of the Besovnos engravings (Fig. 137) shows an Orthodox cross with three cross-pieces, the lowest of which is inclined, cutting across the representation of a swan. We may judge, then, that the swan had some magic or religious meaning.[1]

Even if we had not this evidence we must conclude that there is some such significance in these engravings. It is true that we are no longer in a world of hunting-magic, although thoughts of such sorcery are here and there clear—even if not obtrusive. What, however, we are faced with is a world of gods, of symbols, of abstract ideas and of belief in personal and active divinities. In fact, just as the pictures show a mixture of art-styles—the imaginative 'agricultural' and the sensorial 'Huntsmen's'—so the ghostly content, the spiritual significance, is compounded of magic and animism.

There are representations of hunting-magic, such as, for instance, the shaman wearing a beast's mask that can be seen on the sixth promontory of Perinos (Fig. 138). The man stands with bent legs. Upon his head is a mask of some horned animal—maybe an elk. In his hand he holds some object not easy to identify, perhaps it is a drum such as the Siberian shamans use to this day in cult-dances. Raudonikas, however, reads the sign as a moon-symbol. He may well be right since, in the age when the engravings were executed, men's minds were much turned towards the heavenly

---

[1] Possibly the swan's significance lay—as we may judge by Babylonian and Greek pictures—in the idea that as water is the symbol of fertility, so waterfowl, and especially swans, are the bearers of fertilizing and preservative powers.

138 SORCERER
Perinos, Lake Onega

bodies—and sun and moon symbols are everywhere common enough.

One of the pictures at Karetskinos is a wizard. He too wears the mask of a horned animal. He too stretches forth his hands as though he were dancing.

A magician on the sixth promontory is depicted in the movements of the dance (Fig. 141). The legs are wide apart. The arms raised. On his head he wears a pair of tall antlers. Another shaman, at the same site, is also dancing. His mask is not easy to distinguish clearly but it seems to be that of some horned animal. There is still a third wizard dancing and wearing great horns.

One of the most interesting of all the enchanters' figures is one on the northern promontory of Besovnos (Plate LXXXIII). Here stands a figure of a man wearing an animal mask, and animal's tail and snow-shoes upon his feet. In his hands he bears the symbols of the sun and of the moon —a crescent and a disk joined together by lines. Before the shaman is a stag. Hunting magic. Hunting magic, however, that is reinforced by the power from the heavenly bodies, a strength that is derived from an agricultural way of life and thought.

The great central frieze at Zalavruga (Fig. 139) offers an especially large and significant representation of hunting-

139 HUNTER AND REINDEER   Zalavruga, on the Shores of the White Sea

140 WIZARDS   Zalavruga, on the Shores of the White Sea

magic. There is a whole herd of big and of little reindeer.
They press forward from all sides, a herd of some twenty
beasts. Behind them stands the magician on snow-shoes. He
wears an animal-mask and an animal's tail. With his bow and
arrow he is shooting into the herd. The arm that holds the
arrow is connected by a line with the last of the great beasts.
The scene reminds one not a little of the vast picture-rock
of Tiut in North Africa, where there are also magic hunting-
pictures.

At Tiut, as at Zalavruga, there is a man with bow and
arrows shooting at beasts, while a line links him with a
woman standing some way away and raising her arms in
prayer. There is no female figure at Zalavruga but at both
sites there are lines by which are transmitted the power and
force that the magic generates.

On the median frieze (Fig. 140) at Zalavruga there are
many shamans. Almost all wear beasts' tails and beast-
masks. Very often these magicians hold bows and arrows.
Also at Zalavruga is a scene of rather a different sort. A
magician wearing an animal's tail and snowshoes is hunting
game. There is a similar scene in the northern group of
engravings at Besovy Sledki. Here we have a hunter aiming
his magic arrow against a beast before him. In this same
group of pictures is a tall man with huge feet, upraised
hands and an enormous penis. He seems unmasked, though

213

apparently he wears some sort of ornament in his hair. He might be a fertility-spirit. The representation of the magician merges into that of the god. It is for us today almost impossible to decide whether we are looking at the representation of a shaman or of a god. In the picture of the unmasked figure that wears no animal-tail, a picture in which are stressed the three seats of power, the head, the foot and the penis, it is probable that we are face to face rather with a god than a magician.

In any case, it is almost certain that we have a deity depicted upon the great frieze of Zalavruga (Fig. 140). From an anthropomorphic figure, on all sides, jagged lines of lightning flash forth. From the head is one stroke (or maybe an arrow), the bow emits two strokes. From the rest of the body emerge six more flashes, while at some distance are several more flashes that have already been emitted.

This spirit of the lightning which is again represented upon the same frieze (this time with a beast's tail and huge lance, spear or javelin held by an arm that is itself zigzagged) may be the lightning god of the Slavs, of the ancient Prussians and of other peoples in eastern Europe,

141 SORCERER
Perinos, Lake Onega

142 MAN ON SNOW-SHOES
Besovisledki, Southern Group, White Sea

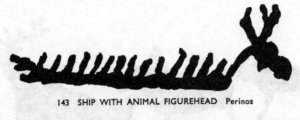

143 SHIP WITH ANIMAL FIGUREHEAD Perinos

named Perkunas or Perkun.[1] The image of the god with the long lance appears often on Yerpin Island (northern group) and at Zalavruga (central and northern groups).

Fertility magic is also indicated in scenes of human beings copulating, as, for instance, on the western promontory of Besovnos and on the third promontory of Perinos. The central group at Zalavruga contains the representation of a birth.

Signs and symbols are very numerous. That of the sun occurs everywhere and, as in Scandinavia and in Italy, is often furnished with a pole, so that a solar disk must have been carried in cult-ceremonies. The symbol would not be represented so often had it not been frequently used. There are also moon-symbols, crescents—also on poles. Footprints are common—signs, we may remember of divine presence—and with these are, ever and again, waterfowl and snakes, creatures of fertility and creatures that disappear into the earth and reappear out of the earth.

The pictures, then, reveal a world of religion anchored in an agricultural complex in which, however, many legacies of hunting times are preserved. The general picture is not one of a transition between the two economies but the dominant art is an imaginative one of stylized forms that present all the classical characteristics of an agricultural way of life. The star symbols, the figures of the gods, the signs of holy ships and footprints, these do not belong to a hunting culture-complex but are the expression of a way of thought that is more abstract, that is linked with the shift of the seasons,

[1] He is hailed when it thunders, sword dances are held in his honour and during a storm a flitch of bacon may be offered up to him. Men swear by him and curse by him. The oath *Schagrew Perunie* is still used in eastern German lands (cf. *Donnerwetter* or *Donnerkeil*, common as an expletive throughout Germany).

144 ANIMALS   Zalavruga, on the Shores of the White Sea

with the fruitfulness of the fields and with the idea of passing away and then of rising again.

However, together with all these things we can discern traces of the spiritual world of the chase that has survived in these northern regions until our day. As at the present time, the Yakut and Chukchi shamans in Siberia represent the cultural elements both of hunting and of pastoralism, so also the wizards of the Russian Written Rocks served two cults.

These angular pictures of an imaginative art convey their meaning more by content than by outward appearance. Now and again, however, some half-schematic animal figures stand out and display a certain charm.

The rock-engravings tell us of a people that knew ships (Plate LXXXIV), that sailed the sea, that practised agriculture, that in winter glided along on snow-shoes (Plate LXXXIX) and that hunted reindeer and elk. As in Scandinavia, the herds were rounded up, they were enchanted by pictures and were driven into a river or over a precipice into a lake below or into the sea.

We have, then, an image of what men's life was like in these remote regions at a time when Greek art was flourishing, and when the peak-periods of Mesopotamian and Egyptian cultures had been left behind.

THE SENSE AND MEANING OF THE ROCK-PICTURES

Wʜᴀᴛ Man thought, what were the main preoccupations of his being, were, in the long centuries before writing, confided to the rocks and in the form of pictures. These rock-drawings and paintings are, therefore, of the highest importance for us if we would learn something of the evolution of human thought, of the development of spiritual movements and of the beginning of Man's knowledge of the world around him. The rock-pictures show us Man's dialogue with his circumstances, with reality and with dreams.

As in this conversation there are two parties, Man and the World, so there are some periods when what is received dominates and others, which are dominated by the receiver. In other words, at one time the World occupies the centre of Man's thoughts and at other times it is Man himself.

Goethe once spoke of subjective epochs and of objective ones, and he meant, no doubt, by that statement that there are periods dominated by dreams, by what is thought, imagined and contrived by Man, times of new ideas, of creation. And there are other times when men live in reality and have no feeling for the Beyond, for imagination, for dreams.

Both of these two poles, or extremes, are represented in the prehistoric pictures of Europe. The first pole, that of thought for the Here and Now, is represented by the Ice Age art. The pictures of the times after about 2000 ʙ.ᴄ. are directed away from reality. They represent the preoccupations of men whose faces are averted from reality and directed towards dreams, towards an imaginary world, a world of cults, and animism, a world of spirits and gods.

The pictures of the period between about 10,000 ʙ.ᴄ. and, say, 2000 ʙ.ᴄ. represent the transition from one

217

extreme, from one pole to the other. In this transition can be recognized all the stages and phases, all the modifications that lead from the naturalistic to the highly stylized, from the sensorial to the most imaginative.

After the peak of imaginative art is reached, then Man's spirit begins to veer round once again towards reality. In southern Europe—in Crete—the change had occurred by 1600 B.C. But this evolution, this artistic transformation, was linked with adaptation to town life and to the use of script and money. It was, therefore, a development which could not take place, so early on, in northern Europe. The North had no cities, script or coin and therefore none of the economic, administrative and governmental organization dependent upon them. Most parts of Europe, indeed, lived on in their old pastoral and agricultural economies.

The cultural currents that flowed forth from Crete (and after about 1400 B.C. from Mycenæ) are easily enough recognizable. They are marked by the appearance of the spiral-motif (right up to northern Europe), by the emblem of the axe and by the domination of a female divinity which reached Ireland. However, the realistic art of the eastern Mediterranean was not borne along upon these cultural currents. In other parts of Europe than the Mediterranean basin conditions did not exist for the growth of ideas—and consequently of an art—reflecting the 'reality' of the visible world.

It is true that after the collapse of Cretan power traces of Cretan civilization survived in continental Europe until about 1200 B.C., but these gradually faded away, leaving only a few legends to indicate the former importance of the island's culture.

It was not until after 500 B.C. that the Greeks revealed to the world the wonder of naturalistic forms. The Greeks' influence was incalculable. It can be seen in India, in Hither India and in China, in southern Italy and *Magna Græcia*, in Etruria, in Iberian Spain and even in Celtish Gaul. But there were regions where the Greek influence did not penetrate, for once again the spiritual was bound up with economic structure.

The Greek world depended upon the same three factors

which had dominated in Crete—the City, Writing and Money. All three were lacking in central and northern Europe; only in Gaul could the beginnings of these things be seen. In central and northern Europe thought and its expression did not change. Even when Roman troops reached the Rhine and the Elbe, when the Romans founded cities in southern Germany, the fashions of thought and the economic structure of most of the rest of Europe remained what they had been for ages. It is true that Roman coins, statuettes and glassware are found throughout Germany (and as far to the east as East Prussia and Russia) and are discovered in Denmark and in Scandinavia, but these objects are not the indications of a general change of ideas. The decisive factors that would have made for such a change—cities, writing, money—had not yet appeared.

Until about this period of Roman domination, rock-pictures were still being engraved in the North. It is true that after 500 B.C. or so they lose much of their significance, but still these engravings were executed until around the year A.D. 500. Indeed, these later pictures are much the same as the earlier ones, except that the former are more lightly engraved, more carelessly executed and less sure in outline. The Spanish rock-pictures come to an end earlier, however —about 500 B.C.

In connection with the art of the Written Rocks there are two main problems which must be faced. How did the pictures originate and why did they disappear?

The beginnings of rupestral art lie in the Ice Age. Often, in this book, I have mentioned that all later rock-pictures are derived from those of the Ice Age. If we look over the whole complex of this art we shall see that there are two centres in which rock-pictures flourished especially—Spain and Scandinavia. In these two regions we may witness comparable phases of art-development. In Spain it is the Levantine art that links the Ice Age with later periods. In Scandinavia there is a sensorial, naturalistic art that is also in the Ice Age tradition.

As the ice melted, as the glaciers rolled back, the hunter of the Ice Age followed the beasts retreating northwards and, thus, in Scandinavia, a new centre of art was created. The men who migrated from Ice Age France, for instance, took their magic with them, took with them their ideas rooted in a hunting way of life. So, in the North, in a region of huntsmen, the art of the Ice Age could last longest and hold most firmly.

In both regions occurs an evolution into a stylized, imaginative art. The transformation was accomplished after 3000 B.C. in southern Europe and after 2000 B.C. in northern Europe. It is true that in their fundamental characteristics these two arts are much alike but they are, nevertheless, differentiated from one another by a host of peculiarities.

The Spanish pictures are dominated by the presence of a female divinity which owes much to the figure of Astarte as a prototype.

At the peak-period of Scandinavian rock-art two male divinities—Thor and Odin—are the most prominent figures.

The differences in content as between the Spanish and the Scandinavian pictures are differences which reflect on the one hand an agricultural and on the other a pastoral way of life.

The agriculturalist lays the seed in the earth. It is, then, natural for him to think of the earth as female and as fertilized by the liquid of rain. So the plough may become the symbol of the act of fertilization.

The pastoralist conceives of fertilizing power as inherent in the male animal, bull, he-goat or stallion. So the pastoralist makes male gods and the agriculturalist female. Thus the ancient divinities of the Mediterranean region are female. Female were the deities of the mystery cults. At the beginning of the Bible we have Eve and the Serpent. The representations of female divinities in Crete have snakes around their arms. Snakes, water, earth, woman, moon, all express the preoccupations of Eastern Mediterranean agriculturalists and the symbols of these things are scattered along the Tin Road, the Gold Way that led up to Ireland.

These are the signs and symbols that also found their way through Hungary and eastern Europe to Scandinavia, though in this latter region the specifically feminine symbols are not reproduced.

In southern Europe and where agriculture dominated, we have the female divinity, the symbol of the Earth. In northern Europe, where pastoralism dominates, we have the male gods with Hammer and Spear. Both regions were penetrated by influences from Asia and these influences were accepted differently and worked out in one way in the North and in another way in the South.

So we must regard the origin of the rock-pictures. The art arises during the Ice Age. With the decadence of the chase, the pictures stiffen into stylized forms. The transformation takes place slowly, almost imperceptibly, until we reach a peak-period of extreme stylization.

The other question is that of why the pictures faded away. Why did not men go on making them?

The answer is not the same for the North as for the South. In the South, in Spain, instead of pictures upon the rocks we get Iberian art, bronze objects, drawings upon pottery vessels. The apogee of Iberian art is reached between 500 and 133 B.C.—the latter date being that of Scipio's reduction of Numantia. Iberian art is dominated by Greek models and penetrated with Greek influences. The Italian rock-engravings cease at about the beginning of our era, for the last pictures bear inscriptions in Latin letters of Imperial times. The great stream of æsthetic significance, the mighty force of illumination that issued from Greece, signified the end of the rock-art.

The end for much of Europe, though in the North the art lived on longer—in outlying districts until well into our era and in Russia until about the 6th century A.D. The reason for this late-lingering Northern rock-art is to be sought in the interruption of the quickening influences from the South. About the year 500 B.C. the Celts so extended their realm that they lay like a ruler diagonally across central Europe. From the line of the Rhine they conquered France and Spain to the west and then followed the Danube valley to the Black Sea and even into Asia Minor. The Celts cut the old trade-routes. These happenings are reflected in the extinction of the Bronze Age cultures. The North is cut off from the South that gave not only metals but a host of ideas. The North got poorer and poorer until it came to present the picture that Tacitus gives of it in his *Germania*, a poverty-stricken region where nothing happened.

Thus, then, we have our explanations for the ending of the rock-pictures. In the South, the spread of Greek influence and, in the North, the development of Celtish influence and the consequent interruption of communications with the South. The Greeks had no more amber, but they no longer worked it and they did not want it, though at Mycenæ Baltic amber has been found, for the trade was a far-reaching one. After the Celtic domination of central Europe, the Amber Way is cut. The North is left to its own devices.

When, then, we regard the evolution of European rock-art we may enquire whether an analogous movement from the naturalistic to the stylized can also be discerned in the rupestral art of other continents. Only if we could note such tendencies would it be legitimate to speak of a general 'law' corresponding to some working of the human spirit. However, we can detect such an evolution.

The rock-art of the South African Bushmen is, in its essence, akin to the European rock-pictures of the post-glacial epoch. The 'Bushman'[1] drawings are, indeed, often so like the pictures of Levantine Spain that even experts can hardly tell some South African pictures from those of Levantine Spain. The Bushmen live—or lived until recently —in economic conditions very like those of the men of the European Palæolithic and Mesolithic. They were hunters and gatherers and their world was encompassed by magic.

The rock-pictures executed by pastoralist and agriculturalist peoples are, in all parts of the world, similar to those paintings and engravings made by Europeans in the same stages of culture; that is to say the art is an imaginative one.

There exist, for instance, a number of excellent works dealing with the pre-Columbian rock-art of South America and, notably, relating to the pictures in the Argentine. These, in style, are very like those dating, in Europe, from about 2000 B.C. Here we have once again the same sign for water, the spirals, the zigzags, similar symbols for the clouds

---

[1] I put the word Bushman in inverted commas since, although it is a useful generic term, it is by no means certain that even the majority of the South African rupestral art was the work of Bushmen. (Translator's Note.)

from which rain drops, the wheel again. In South America we have the same unrealistic delineations of animals. There are, of course, differences, but we have clearly the reflection of a world similar to that of Europe four millennia ago. There are rupestral pictures in the Near East which have the same character. There are rock-pictures in India. They are all the stylized art of agriculturalists or pastoralists.[1]

So I am inclined to think that we are justified in speaking of a 'law' that reflects something in Man's very essence and is not peculiar to any one nation or culture but is common to all humanity.

In his book *Die Götter Griechenlands*, W. F. Otto wrote: "Cultures that are young and intact know nothing of any religion that is not indissolubly intertwined with the whole existence of Man. Then all experience, thought and action find ... their glory in the concept of divinity." Here, then, Otto expresses what is the main argument and conclusion of this book.

All the rock-art is founded on religion, that is to say, is rooted in Man's attitude to the Eternal. Goethe sensed this truth. In a conversation with Riemer in 1814 he said: "The inventions of antiquity were all dictated by belief." In this terse aphorism Goethe expressed the essential about pre-historic art.

Attempts to explain the pictures from any standpoint but from that which we may call the numinous have been un-successful. There was a time when it was fashionable to ignore the might of religious ideas, therefore all sorts of odd explanations were offered to account for the rock-pictures. Men painted caves "to make them pretty". A rather foolish statement. And even the most able were led astray. For instance, so great a prehistorian and specialist in pre-historic art as Hoernes of Vienna was unable to realize the meaning of this most ancient art. Thus, his important work, though of great value, entirely ignores the essence of the rock-pictures.

[1] It should, perhaps, be stressed, that the author is not suggesting contempo-raneity but merely similarity of technique and content. The Indian rock-pictures (e.g. those of the Mahadeo Hills), for instance, are not prehistoric and the com-parisons that have been made between them and the Spanish Levantine paintings are not convincing. (Translator's Note.)

There is another passage from Goethe that I should like to quote. It is this: "Art reposes upon a sort of religious feeling ... for this reason is art so readily united with religion. ..."

The art of all periods has been bound up with religion— the art of Crete, of the Greeks, of the Middle Ages, of the Renaissance. It is only in our times, or, at least, within comparatively recent years, that art has cut the link with religion. Still, even today art is to some extent bound up with religion, since art is always the expression of the inexpressible.

When, in the Ice Age, Man painted beasts, when he represented a sorcerer, when he sought out caverns and remote and dark recesses, he was moved by what we must call religious urges. Magic is, indeed, the exercise of a religion. There is evidence to indicate that the content of the most ancient religions was a monotheism, a thought of a one God, an All-Father, a Great Spirit.

If, about 3000 B.C. in the Eastern Mediterranean and from about 2000 B.C. in the Western Mediterranean and in other parts of Europe, Man turned over to the use of symbols, if he painted ghosts and spirits, emblems and gods, then he was engaged in a religious activity. The epochs imagined during the 19th century, epochs ruled by totemism, animism or magic without any concept of a god, seem never to have existed. The study of the most ancient rock-art has changed our ideas.

Researches into the beginnings of religion were, until not so long ago, either pure and gratuitous supposition, or conducted by means of analogy with the practices of the so-called 'Nature Peoples'. But only prehistory and prehistoric art can show us what was the real course of the development of religion.

There are times when religion is derived from reality and these are the times represented by the most ancient Ice Age naturalistic paintings and engravings. There are times when religion is centred in the symbol. These are times such as are reflected in the stylized art of about 2000 B.C.

Goethe also expressed this when he wrote: "Symbolism

transforms Appearance into Idea ... so that the Idea is eternally effective while remaining unattainable. ..."

There remains one very important consideration. It is that of a parallelism between the phases of most ancient art and the art-phases of our own times. Impressionism, Expressionism and Cubism follow one another in prehistoric times and in our own days. Have we here some tendency that is inherent in Man's being? The problems raised by this question are too new, too unfamiliar for answers easily to be found.

I think that the parallelism we can trace does indicate something that lies in the fundamental nature of Man whose being is torn between the Here and the There, between the Present and the Eternal. There are epochs when the present is in the forefront of all men's preoccupations. There are epochs when the eternal is regarded as the only reality. We are, at the present day, experiencing a change in our modes of thought and our ways of envisaging life. And the change is reflected in our art.

Until about 1900, Positivism, Realism, Neo-Kantianism dominated. After 1900 we had the appearance of a philosophy of phenomenology represented by Husserl and Scheler in Germany, Bergson in France; then the re-emergence of Vitalism with Driesch and of Existentialism with Jaspers and Heidegger in Germany and Sartre in France.

It is hardly too much to say that the rock-pictures of pre-historic times open our eyes to the problems of our own time. Goethe had never seen any rock-pictures, but in a little-known essay with the title *Simple Imitation of Nature, Mannerism, Style*, he contrasts three art-groups which, indeed, correspond to the art-styles both of prehistoric times and of today.

The art phase he calls 'the imitation of nature' is, he says, solely devoted to natural objects and he adds: "If we reflect carefully upon these conditions, we must perceive that in this manner can be treated ... only a limited number of objects." Then follows a definition of Mannerism and finally a very illuminating passage in which he clearly defines the non-naturalistic art he calls 'Style': "Style is the expression of a deep knowledge of the essence of things—in so far as we may be able to recognize this in comprehensible form."[1]

The development and evolution of art-styles are surprisingly constant. The artist who stands in the forefront of his epoch is, indeed, in advance of his age; he senses, feels, experiences what other men will perceive later on. He records what later generations will understand. And what shall we say if the art-movement that today seems so revolutionary, so incomprehensible, so inconceivable even, is to be observed right back in the early stages of Man's æsthetic history?

We are living in an epoch of change, so, at the end of this essay upon the evolution of styles in prehistoric art, I would like to quote a profound piece of poetry in which Goethe expresses the thought that has been with me while I have been writing this book:

> *"Was kann der Mensch im Leben mehr gewinnnen,*
> *Als dass sich Gott-Natur ihm offenbare,*
> *Wie sie das Feste lässt zu Geist verrinnen,*
> *Wie sie das Geisterzeugte fest bewahre."*[2]

[1] The passage occurs in the *Nachlass*, Vol. XLVII of the *Sophien-Ausgabe*, published at Weimar, 1896.

[2] "What higher thing can Man in life obtain
Than that the God-Nature should reveal itself to him,
And let the material merge into the spiritual,
As it holds fast what is begotten of the spirit?"

INDEX

The following Index comprises the most important place and proper names. The latter are in italics.

DATE DUE